OPEN
TALENT

Leveraging the Global Workforce
to Solve Your Biggest Challenges

OPEN
TALENT

JOHN WINSOR & JIN H. PAIK

HARVARD BUSINESS REVIEW PRESS
BOSTON, MASSACHUSETTS

Library of Congress Cataloging-in-Publication Data

Names: Winsor, John, 1959– author. | Paik, Jin H., author.
Title: Open talent : leveraging the global workforce to solve your biggest
    challenges / John Winsor & Jin H. Paik.
Description: Boston, Massachusetts : Harvard Business Review Press, [2024] |
    Includes index.
Identifiers: LCCN 2023028121 (print) | LCCN 2023028122 (ebook) |
    ISBN 9781647823887 (hardcover) | ISBN 9781647823894 (epub)
Subjects: LCSH: Business networks. | Ability. | Business logistics—
    Contracting out. | Information storage and retrieval systems—
    Personnel management. | Labor and globalization.
Classification: LCC HD69.S8 W57 2024 (print) | LCC HD69.S8 (ebook) |
    DDC 650.1/3—dc23/eng/20230908
LC record available at https://lccn.loc.gov/2023028121
LC ebook record available at https://lccn.loc.gov/2023028122

ISBN: 978-1-64782-388-7
eISBN: 978-1-64782-389-4

The paper used in this publication meets the requirements of the American National Standard for Permanence of Paper for Publications and Documents in Libraries and Archives Z39.48-1992.

*To the Six: Emily, Harry, Charlie, Baker, and Alice for the love,
support, and guidance.*
—John

*To my wife, Amber, and my wonderful kids, Elle, Amelia,
Ainsleigh, and Asher*
—Jin

Contents

PART THREE

Developing Operations and Leadership for Open Talent

Foreword

The dawn of the 2020s has ushered in two pivotal events that are set to fundamentally transform both business and society for the foreseeable future.

First, the Covid-19 pandemic necessitated an abrupt transition to remote work. Despite—or because of—the imposed lockdowns, numerous organizations discovered that their employees could foster collaboration and innovation effectively from the comfort of their own homes. This unexpected "remote work revolution" has effectively shattered antiquated beliefs that physical colocation in an office was a prerequisite for productivity. The era of flexible work methodologies has arrived.

Second, the introduction of sophisticated generative AI (artificial intelligence) tools, such as ChatGPT, promises to supercharge human talent. Similar to how the advent of the web browser reduced information costs and heralded the internet era, the AI advancements are reducing the cognitive cost of tasks. These tools are set to augment the abilities of workers across all skill levels.

These transformative events directly influence talent and business models. The pandemic has led to a demand for greater flexibility in work arrangements. Generative AI will empower skilled workers to accomplish more in less time, providing a competitive advantage to those who can effectively leverage these tools.

While we are still unraveling the long-term impacts of the remote-work transformation and the growth of AI tools, the immediate opportunity is evident. We can adapt talent strategies to attract and empower this increasingly dynamic and autonomous workforce.

This timely book provides pragmatic guidance for organizations seeking to navigate these changes. It presents the concept of open talent, that is, the leveraging of abilities from a globally distributed, digitally connected workforce. Companies can now access specialized talent from platforms on demand, as opposed to employing all abilities full-time.

In my research on digital transformation and communities, I have had the honor of partnering with large-scale organizations through our lab, the Laboratory for Innovation Science at Harvard (LISH). Jin Paik, as the founding general manager, played a critical role in our journey to scale LISH, creating avenues for government partners and corporate organizations to tap into open talent and open innovation ecosystems. Through our collaboration, we have experienced the enormous potential of open talent in driving innovation and solving intricate challenges. By harnessing global talent, organizations can access diverse perspectives, expertise, and creativity at an unprecedented scale. This experience has shaped our mutual belief in the transformative power of open talent, and this book serves as an indispensable resource for leaders navigating this new frontier. Jin has been a pivotal pioneer in framing an operational groundwork and fostering the cultural shift required.

Open Talent: Leveraging the Global Workforce to Solve Your Biggest Challenges introduces the concept of the networked organization—an innovative framework that transcends traditional boundaries and harnesses the global talent pool. By nurturing a culture of openness, collaboration, and continuous innovation, organizations can tap into the collective intelligence of a global workforce and address challenges with unmatched agility and effectiveness. By embracing open talent, enterprises can connect with a vast network of people and organizations, generating innovative solutions.

Open talent, while offering immense opportunities, also presents unique challenges. Having witnessed many of these benefits and challenges firsthand with John Winsor at Victors & Spoils and Havas, I can attest to John's advocacy for understanding and mitigating these risks. The stories shared here serve as both a cautionary tale and an opportunity to plan for all aspects of open talent, including potential obstacles and, ultimately, adoption.

At the core of *Open Talent* is the vision of a connected world, where organizations can break free from traditional confines and foster a culture of collaboration and innovation. This mindset positions leaders for success and contributes to the growth and prosperity of the global economy. Drawing on real-world examples and providing practical guidance on building open talent centers, Jin and John offer a road map for organizations to embrace change, harness the power of the global workforce, and address the complex challenges of our time.

This book represents a significant milestone in the evolving landscape of business and leadership, redefining how we perceive talent, innovation, and problem-solving in the AI era. As we embark on this transformative journey, *Open Talent* equips us with knowledge, insights, and experiences gained from collaborations with governments and corporate organizations.

The authors provide compelling examples, and they outline steps to build open talent capabilities, including ways to reshape mindsets, culture, strategy, and processes. The book charts the journey from initial experimentation to eventual integration of open talent across business operations.

If you are a leader navigating an environment of constant change, this guide equips you with the ability to source and empower talent. The principles contained herein can help you shape your organization to adapt swiftly to digital transformations. This agility will be indispensable as AI and other disruptive technologies continue to redefine work.

As we chart a course through this unexplored terrain, one certainty emerges: the organizations that engage talent the most creatively will lead the pack. This book provides a road map to that high ground. It arrives at a crucial juncture as businesses strive to reboot themselves and to reimagine the future of work.

Karim R. Lakhani
Cambridge, Massachusetts, 2023

Preface

Years before the Covid-19 pandemic, the digital wave had already been lapping at the walls of organizational boundaries. But few large companies had changed much. Bureaucracies chugged steadily along. Then the lockdowns began, and as organizations struggled to right themselves, freelance and gig work exploded. Around the world, workforces gained an appetite for deciding where, how, and when their work gets done. When it came time to open corporate doors again, leaders were left wondering where their employees had gone.

Just like that, the war for talent was over—and talent had won.

It isn't that suddenly there were plenty of skilled workers to go around. It's that the whole value proposition had transformed: talent was no longer buying what organizations were selling.

Thus the future of work quietly reorganized around talent: programmers, code writers, content providers, financial wizards, project managers, visionary innovators, and the like. The freelance economy skyrocketed and a little-used but powerful solution—open talent platforms—began to rise like a phoenix, helping organizations reinvent their operating models and rejoin the global economy. All aspects of organizations are being digitally transformed. The same is happening in talent. Open talent, which taps into a globally distributed workforce via digital connections and platforms, is one key step in accelerating this digital transformation. By leveraging digital technology to crowdsource talent powerfully and effectively, open talent has quietly turned many organizations into problem-solving, innovation-driving machines.

Like most technology-fueled disruptions, the open talent revolution began at the fringes of the business world, with hackers, startups, and a few smaller companies. One of us, John Winsor, was among them. His open talent journey began in 1989, when he took out a second mortgage on his house and purchased a bankrupt magazine, *Women's Sports & Fitness*. The magazine's previous owners had kept a large staff of writers, photographers, and editors. Cash poor at the time, John took a leap of faith and invited the magazine's readers to cocreate its contents instead. This meant tapping into a crowd of customers for ideas—essentially crowdsourcing before Jeff Howe coined the term in a 2006 issue of *Wired* magazine.[1]

The experiment succeeded beyond his wildest dreams, helping to usher in the women's sports revolution. Eventually, John sold the magazine to Condé Nast in 2000. The new paradigm of cocreation allowed Condé Nast to flip its internal fixed-talent costs to variable external talent costs, gaining diversity and creativity in the process.

Soon after, in 2001, John launched Radar Communications, which took cocreation to the next level, using crowds of customers to help brands like Levi's, Nike, Intel, and Hewlett-Packard solve marketing and product design challenges. Along the way, John's three books—*Beyond the Brand*, *Flipped*, and *Spark*—created a framework and documented how organizations could adopt those methods. That same year, Topcoder was launched—the first crowdsourcing platform inspired by the open-source software movement. Around that time, two online marketplaces for freelancers—oDesk and Elance—were also getting started and eventually merged to become Upwork.

In 2007, John merged Radar Communications with Crispin Porter + Bogusky (CP+B) and became its senior vice president of strategy and innovation. Like *Women's Sports and Fitness*, CP+B was too small at the time for people to work on specific accounts. Everyone worked on everything, essentially building an internal creative crowd at its core. Although unintentional, the strategy worked well, and CP+B won account after account.

With such a growing portfolio of clients, however, hiring the right talent soon became a massive strain. In 2007, the problem became abundantly clear one day when John and Alex Bogusky, the chief creative officer, were making plans for their latest client, Brammo, maker of electric motorcycles. Though Brammo was tiny, it was a potential paradigm shifter, and John and Bogusky knew they could put it on the map. But they had no creatives to assign to the account. So John thought about what had worked at *Women's Sports & Fitness* and suggested sourcing creative ideas for the campaign externally, from online crowds. Bogusky loved the audacity of the idea, so they put a brief up on Crowdspring, a popular crowdsourcing platform at the time, offering $1,000 for the best campaign for Brammo.

The industry was scandalized. "Crispin Porter + Bogusky Crowdsourcing Experiment Backfires" was how *Fast Company* put it.[2] But those media pundits hadn't seen the responses CP+B received. Within the first week, the agency was flooded with twenty-five hundred proposals, some from the very best creative talent in the industry. It was as if CP+B had run an open casting call and a bunch of bona fide movie stars had shown up.

The lesson couldn't have been clearer: if the best creatives in the world were willing to participate in an open brief on a digital platform, then the rules of the industry had changed. In fact, in 2009 CP+B was named Global Creative Agency of the decade after winning eighteen pitches in a row for such big accounts as Microsoft, Domino's, Volkswagen, and American Express.[3]

That same year, John launched his own ad agency, Victors & Spoils, built strategically on crowdsourcing and freelancing (which we now think of as open talent). The *New York Times* took notice and profiled V&S on launch day. That morning, the partners were sitting in John's garage with no employees and no clients. By the end of the day, three thousand people had signed up to work for the company, and Ira Bahr, the chief marketing officer of DISH Network, had given V&S his advertising budget, becoming its first client.[4]

Fast-forward to 2011. Coauthor Jin Paik didn't have the faintest idea about open talent and crowdsourcing when Karim Lakhani hired him at the Laboratory for Innovation Science at Harvard (LISH, previously known as the Harvard-NASA Tournament Lab and Crowd Innovation Lab) as the founding general manager. After completing his graduate studies at Harvard, he had spent a few years looking at human services and health-care program efficiency. Suddenly, Jin was at the center of the LISH collaboration with National Aeronautics and Space Administration (NASA) and the rest of the federal government. After two weeks on the job and getting a crash course in open talent solutions with Karim, he flew to Houston to tell the people at the Johnson Space Center about using tools such as contests to innovate at a whole new level. "Together," Jin told them, "we can solve the energy output problem on the space station, figure out how to improve Robonaut's vision algorithms, and detect asteroids in space more efficiently." (Robonaut 2 is a humanoid robot on the International Space Station that helps astronauts with tasks.) It felt a bit like the movie *Armageddon*, he said later, except Bruce Willis was nowhere in sight.

As NASA's capabilities grew over the next ten years, solving problems not only for NASA but for all US agencies, LISH went on its own journey to partner with other elite institutions, including the Harvard Medical School and the Boston biotechnology hub. It was hard to believe how effective crowdsourcing was. When Karim and Jin would ask their senior scientists to validate the solutions that LISH was getting, the scientists were as surprised as they were. By 2017, under Jin's leadership, LISH had solved more than 750 discrete innovation projects, including 40 large-scale data science competitions in medicine, computational biology, and space technology, to name a few, with project success rate exceeding 95 percent.

In 2018, Karim and Jin launched the Crowd Academy, a global meeting that brought academics, corporate leaders, and platform creators together to explore how to adopt new talent models such as crowdsourcing, open innovation, and freelancing. There, John decided to form a consultancy, Open Assembly, with Jin as adviser. Grounded in thinking about how to use open talent strategically, the company would help organizations adopt those approaches. Additionally, in late 2020, Jin drew on his expertise in leading data science teams and organizing talent to cofound a technology development platform with Robert Maguire. Altruistic assesses, maps, and matches skills of data professionals to organizations using proprietary artificial intelligence (AI). Around this same time, Jin and Maguire also acquired Maguire's previous company, Mathesia, which had been founded on open principles of accessing talent, and its community of four thousand data scientists working to solve complex analytics and AI-based problems.

Meanwhile, NASA's Steve Rader played an integral role in building out both Open Assembly's conceptual framework and its community, which is now four thousand strong. Other principal architects of the company are Deloitte's Balaji Bondili and Dyan Finkhousen, who formerly ran General Electric's GeniusLink.

The world has changed, and there's no going back. When a few people with an internet connection can compete with big ad agencies or even manufacturers, traditional organizations have no choice but to change their cultures, processes, talent policies, resources, and even their business and revenue models to keep up. Our goal in writing *Open Talent: Leveraging the Global Workforce to Solve Your Biggest Challenges* is to provide a framework, insights, and guidance to help organizations make needed changes to overcome the tough talent challenges we're facing today.

We've been there. And we know what lies ahead. Read on.

OPEN TALENT

The Digital Transformation of Talent

In early fall of 2021, the software company SEI held an all-hands video meeting with a thousand engineers. Ryan Hicke, executive vice president of technology, dove right into the meeting's main agenda—touting the benefits of returning to the company's state-of-the-art campus in the Philadelphia suburbs. It had stood mostly empty since the end of March 2020 and the beginning of the Covid-19 lockdowns. When Hicke finished his remarks, the dead silence that followed spoke volumes. No one was scrambling to return to the office.

What might persuade his people to come back? Hicke sent out a digital survey asking for input and giving employees twenty-four hours to respond. He got back only twenty surveys, and less than 15 percent of SEI's forty-nine hundred employees had agreed to return. Then, just when he thought things couldn't get worse, one of his best software engineers gave his two weeks' notice. The engineer had loved his time at SEI, but a New York financial services startup had offered him the same job for $225,000—almost triple what he had been making. And the job would be fully remote.

Hicke was starting to understand why keeping talent had gotten so hard so fast. Employees had just enjoyed eighteen months to rethink the way they worked, and now they were reluctant to return to the status quo. He couldn't get over the irony. The beautiful campus that SEI had built to attract and retain talent had become a liability. He was competing for talent with startups built in a virtual world; they could afford to put most of their money into people, while SEI was stuck paying for the upkeep of a physical plant where no one wanted to work. Meanwhile, with his engineers going AWOL, Hicke wondered how SEI would keep up with the skyrocketing demand for its software.*

It was a perfect storm that was wreaking havoc everywhere, not just at SEI. A survey of 30,000 people from thirty-one countries showed that by March 2021, nearly 41 percent of the global workforce reported they were considering leaving their jobs.[1] Then in April 2021, as US companies got ready to resume business as usual, 4 million workers quit instead, kicking off what would become known as the Great Resignation. An additional 4.3 million left their jobs in August 2021—nearly 3 percent of the US workforce.[2]

Suddenly, large organizations, which had held all the power regarding talent for decades, helplessly stood by as remote work became the norm among their ranks. Or, as was often the case, the ranks were leaving the company altogether.

A New Era for Talent

Let's be clear: people like Hicke's software engineers may have been leaving their jobs—but they were *not* leaving the workforce. Instead, former employees everywhere morphed into self-empowered nomads as they figured out new ways to work. Today you'll find them freelancing for multiple companies or starting single proprietorships and small businesses of their own, as talent everywhere enjoys a new level of

---

* Hicke ultimately adopted an open talent strategy at SEI to address these challenges. His adoption of this strategy would be one reason he was appointed the company's CEO in 2022.

power, literally at their fingertips. Using platforms such as Freelancer
.com, Fiverr, and Upwork to negotiate new jobs for themselves, workers are taking back control from corporate, setting their own terms for
work: what, where, how, when, how much, and at what price.

The result? The democratization of talent is spurred on by digital
transformation. Catalyzed and accelerated by the pandemic's massive
reset, the world of work was beamed ten years into the future, obliter-
ating organizational boundaries and taking talent with it.

Consider Jan, a bookkeeper for a midsize accounting firm in Port-
land, Oregon, who made $42,000 per year. Soon after the Covid-19 pan-
demic began, she was laid off—a tough situation for a single mother
with two daughters. Then she got a serious case of Covid-19 and had to
go on public assistance. Things looked bleak until Jan started learning
about talent platforms like Upwork, Fiverr, and Freelancer.com. She
signed up with all of them and started selling her services, charging
companies $800 each for their monthly bookkeeping. After three
months, she'd acquired thirty-two companies as clients. Today she
makes $300,000 per year doing the same thing she'd done at her
pre-pandemic job. No way is Jan going back to work in that accounting firm.[3]

But Jan's experience is not merely a Covid-19 story, and these dynam-
ics have only increased. Stories like hers represent the biggest headache global businesses are feeling today, not to mention their most
considerable cost: securing talent. No matter how big you are or how
strong your brand is, your organization is experiencing or will soon
experience a severe talent crisis. Today's talent has choices. And the
best talent doesn't want to work for you—not when they can work for
themselves.

With serious talent shortages and more control in the pockets of
workers, the problem isn't going away anytime soon. In 2021, there were
10 million new tech jobs globally. This number rose by another 25 million in 2022 and is forecasted to reach 150 million by 2025.[4] With this
immense surge in demand, it's estimated that by 2030, more than
85 million jobs could go unfilled, resulting in an $8.5 trillion talent

shortage.[5] In the meantime, the specter of a recession has slowed down full-time hiring—and driven up demand for freelance and contingent workers as companies seek more flexibility amid the uncertainty.

Companies no longer *own* talent but instead must find ways to access and convince people to work with them. Applying our old solutions to this new crisis simply doesn't compute. Even recent solutions such as crowdsourcing, at least as we've known it, are leapfrogging to a whole new level. What's required, and what is in fact taking place, is a new mindset and a new model. It's called *open talent*. Open talent is the shakeup in consciousness that will open a new landscape of attracting, acquiring, and utilizing the best talent for the job at hand, at any given moment.

OPEN TALENT refers to the accelerated digital transformation of talent through a globally distributed workforce, accessible to companies on demand via digital connections and platforms. Members of these platforms can be either internal to companies or external. Open talent represents the rise of micro-entrepreneurs who look at work as a thing to do, fitting it into their lives, instead of a place to go or a definition of who they are. The term *open talent* was inspired by *open source*, a driving force in software development for years. (Open-source software licenses leverage the power of crowds by allowing users to improve them.) In practical terms, with this technology-enabled approach to work, companies simply rent the skills and knowledge of working professionals as opposed to hiring them. Platforms like Upwork match companies with programmers, engineers, data scientists, creatives, project managers, and even chief financial officers when they are needed to solve a problem, develop an initiative, or simply fill a temporary skills gap.

Up to now, the concept of open talent and the phrase itself have lived mostly in the niche world of technology workers. But here we're talking about expanding open talent, moving beyond crowdsourcing and gig work to a new level that reflects this great reshaping moment in which we've landed. Open talent is nothing less than the reinvention of work.

Note that gig work and open talent are not synonyms. While gig work is certainly related to open talent, it is more focused on business-to-consumer transactions, such as drivers and passengers, and restaurants and takeout customers. The rise of the gig economy through platforms such as Uber, TaskRabbit, and Grubhub has surfaced many pressing issues, including exploitative wages and a lack of basic workers' rights. Open talent workers, in contrast, are highly skilled providers of professional services and domain expertise. They interact directly with companies and have significant negotiating leverage.

Although the pandemic brought the underlying issues of hiring and talent into stark relief, organizations struggled to find the best talent even before the pandemic. It might have seemed as if they could secure the talent they needed, given their resources. Large companies especially were all about owning talent. But even in pre-pandemic days, the biggest organizations were unable to find the talent they needed to consistently accomplish the "big three" of success simultaneously: doing things cheaper, faster, and better. Giant bureaucracies prevented companies from doing that. This state of affairs was confirmed for Jin by NASA engineers, who told him of the difficulties they'd had scaling programs, even before Covid hit.[6]

As this book will show, using an open talent approach is the answer to resolving those issues that have always been hiding out in organizations. With open talent, everything gets more efficient because costs are cut from organizational bureaucracy, while speed and quality increase.

What makes us so sure that open talent is the answer? We know it is, because it's already succeeding, as we'll show in several examples, such as those from NASA and Deloitte. Our model reflects two key mind

A NETWORKED ORGANIZATION has not only adopted an open talent strategy but also made open talent its operating model. Such organizations tap into a global workforce of both internal and external talent. Networked organizations take a holistic approach to talent by creating platforms to tap into full-time internal employees, outsourced external workers, contingent labor, and freelance work. The goal is to pursue both individual and collective organizational goals by ensuring that all participants can work where, how, and when they want to.

shifts that have already begun to happen: First, talent is now the center of companies, emerging as a more distributed idea of organizations that revolve around people and individual projects—not around divisions and offices. And second, talent is now being culled from both inside and outside the organization. Ultimately, these shifts together redefine business structures into *networked organizations*.

The trouble is that the elements of the open talent economy, including freelancing and some crowdsourcing, have grown independently of one another. Currently, we have cataloged more than eight hundred platforms. Like other industries that have emerged quickly—cloud computing, for example—they lack the common language and process that allows all the players to agree on a common course. Each platform has its own way of describing its work and process to help organizations hire people from open talent platforms.

With this book, we try to create—for the first time—a unifying framework for the burgeoning open talent economy. We see this framework as a guide for leaders in large organizations to pivot more intentionally toward practices that some managers in their companies have already long relied on, hiring freelancers to help them meet deadlines, for example. But the principles in this book will also serve small and midsize enterprises and digitally native companies, which will find that open talent helps leverage global workforces, especially when they need to move in an agile way. These small and midsize groups need to develop products and processes faster and do not always have the luxury of waiting for resources to become available.

The remainder of this introduction will detail where business has come from in terms of workforce hiring and what it will take to recenter themselves on talent and projects. We'll end the introduction with a summary of the book's organization and how these chapters can serve as a waymark to the future of work and organizations themselves.

But first, let's go back in time to when a seed of today's open talent solution was planted—around a decidedly low-tech business: motorcycles.

Back to the Future: The Case of Harley-Davidson

In 2011, John's ad agency, Victors & Spoils (V&S), was a small startup in Boulder, Colorado, when he heard the news that, after thirty-one years, Harley-Davidson had split with its advertising agency. Over cups of coffee, John and his chief creative officer, Evan Fry, cooked up a plan. Instead of waiting to be invited to make a pitch, they posted a brief on the V&S platform, inviting *their* ten thousand community members to create a campaign for Harley. Then they tweeted to Mark-Hans Richer, Harley's chief marketing officer: "Hey, Mark-Hans, we're working on Harley-Davidson."

The tweet created quite a stir. "V&S Sends Unsolicited Brief to Harley" read the headline in *AdWeek*.[7] Soon after the initial post, Richer tweeted back: "@Victorsnspoils, while we don't need another 20th century agency, your approach is worth a look so go for it. MHR."

Two weeks later, John and Fry flew to Milwaukee to make the pitch. Afterward, Harley released this statement: "We saw more great ideas in one meeting with V&S than we might see in an entire year under a conventional agency model." V&S won the account in just two weeks and at a cost to themselves of only $25,000—while traditional agencies spend hundreds of thousands of dollars over weeks and months on a pitch for a company of Harley's size.

The icing on the disruptive cake of the Harley example? The person who came up with Harley's winning no-cages theme—which was still the company's brand anthem two years later—was Whit Hiller, a no-name outsider with zero experience in advertising. Now he had come up with a slogan for one of the world's most iconic brands and made $150,000 doing it. Hiller's win reflected the story of V&S itself. It had gone head-to-head with the biggest ad agencies in the world to win Harley, using an amalgam of freelancers and crowdsourcing.

While startups like Victors & Spoils proved that an open talent concept can work at the fringes, other organizations—including NASA and Deloitte, as we'll show in later chapters—have illustrated that it can be scaled to work even in very large organizations. What V&S did out of necessity NASA and Deloitte did intentionally and strategically.

Now to return to our more recent story: 2021 and the Great Resignation—and the surprisingly good news this shift represents for both talent and organizations today.

The Good News

When we last saw Ryan Hicke, his software engineers were setting out on their own after a mass exodus from SEI. How did they find work? They signed up with digital platforms that both allowed them to pick and choose the jobs they wanted and provided them with feedback, coaching, and access to online learning they needed in order to advance.

All well and good for talent. For organizations that found themselves set adrift from their workforces, however—in the midst of a pandemic, no less—things seemed bleak. But look closely, and the silver lining for business emerges. There, nested in the apparent disaster created by those same talent-stealing platforms, lies the solution. Crowdsourcing and all the various other ways to tap into freelancing are growing into a profusion of platforms that function on a higher and broader level than before. And it turns out the whole is greater than the sum of its parts, with all those solutions coming together under the umbrella of open talent.

Companies can no longer presume to own workers' skills, but they can still rent the skills. And companies save money in the process because digital technology has taken friction out of matching the job to the person. In the same way that Amazon, Google, and Kayak swiftly and efficiently removed the intermediary between consumers and the services and products the consumers sought, platforms like Upwork inject talent straight into where it's needed. Previously, brands like Deloitte could charge five times their employee's salary to a client that wanted to match with the right talent. Now the scale is tipping toward digital platforms that can make those matches more accurately and, by taking companies like Deloitte out of the middle, charge a fraction of what traditional agencies charge and enable talent to make more money.

There is another piece of good news from the open talent economy: the ways it improves diversity, equity, and inclusion in the global workforce. Open talent does more than simply give work opportunities to folks who, because of location, time, and other circumstances have been forgotten and left out of the workforce. From a corporate perspective, open talent models also allow organizations to diversify their workforce with less friction by creating a variety of roles that people can play in companies, maximizing their strengths and minimizing the traditional barriers to working and getting hired.

As vice president at Kelly Discover, Kathy Hardy ran one of the most interesting diversity programs we've seen. She focused on finding ways to connect neurodiverse people with companies so they can use their skills without enduring the social hurdles they might encounter in a traditional work environment. For example, open talent creates opportunities for someone who may be brilliant at solving hard technical problems but may have a difficult time with the give-and-take of office politics.

The big question that critics have about open talent, of course, regards equity and fairness. Some ask, Isn't this just a new way to exploit workers? Of course, some companies will use open talent as a way to shift more costs onto workers while giving them less in return. That approach is not only morally wrong but also functionally unsustainable.

At its best and as it's intended to be used, open talent is about getting the highest-quality and fastest solutions available by mining the often-unused talents of the people inside and outside your firm. And you can pay them well for their work because you're saving costs elsewhere.

Think of open talent as a lean, clean way of bypassing traditional bureaucracy and getting better results. For example, we know of a travel agent named Jo, who lives in Cambridge, England, and is bringing up her young daughter. But Jo also earns an extra £3,000 to £5,000 per month answering customer inquiries for Microsoft on the Limitless platform. What she loves most about the open talent economy is that she can make a little money at 3 a.m., an hour when her daughter frequently wakes her up. That's a win for Jo and for Microsoft.

When the Digital Revolution Overlooks Talent Acquisition

Historically, larger firms especially had approached talent with a touch of arrogance, thinking that their brands were powerful enough that job candidates would always be lining up to apply. It wasn't until Covid-19 that those organizations lifted up their heads from their analog talent processes to realize they didn't work. It was a wake-up call, with many organizations forced to adapt to a new reality and become more agile and flexible almost overnight. In addition, the lockdowns and shift to remote work highlighted the need to keep company employees digitally connected and productive from afar.

While many companies had spent a lot of time and money digitally transforming every other aspect of the organization, the way they dealt with talent and hiring was stuck in a bygone era. Few businesses realized then—or realize now—that they also need to change their approaches to hiring and to work itself.

This isn't anything new in the sense that open talent platforms began to emerge when the internet became popular in the late 1990s. People began to organize themselves differently, and the effects of that shift spawned companies like Topcoder. Jack Hughes, former chair and cofounder of this global crowdsourcing company, noted how swiftly the change took place:

> It's pretty obvious now, but back in 2000, the internet was still new—at least to how business would be conducted. Having managed many developers working on enterprise applications (much of it centered on new internet business models), I felt that developers, due to the digital nature of their work, would start to migrate online. I was actually surprised by how quickly this happened. Topcoder was quickly matriculating members from all over the world, something that was just not possible in any traditional sense. Topcoder had over one million members by the time I left.[8]

That same shift is happening now, but even faster. Today, we need to think of open talent as the catalyst for the digital transformation of outsourcing, contingent work, and community-based problem-solving. What's more, open talent connects internal workforces more efficiently, using the right talent for the right tasks.

All of this reinforces the fact that even before the pandemic, large organizations (for all their hubris, believing talent was flocking to their gates) weren't always able to find the best people when they needed them. To meet deadlines on budget, division managers would quietly skirt bureaucratic hiring processes to use contractors and freelancers from platforms.

In that sense, you could say that open talent has already been operating under the noses of many organizations but as an expedient rather than a strategic solution. You've heard the stories, told in hushed voices, of the mid-level marketing manager who developed a breakthrough strategy but who couldn't get the graphic design department to create a presentation deck because the team needed six weeks of lead time and a battery of approvals. In desperation, the manager registered with Upwork, found an available graphic designer, and had a finished deck in hand the next morning. From then on, the manager used freelance graphic designers to create all the team's decks.

The client profiles of various platforms tell a similar story. For example, Upwork's revenue was $618 million in 2022, but an organization would have only had to spend $1.5 million to become one of its top twenty clients.[9] Correlate those numbers with Freelancer.com's clients, and a pattern emerges. While Freelancer.com has signed up only a few dozen *Fortune* 500 companies as enterprise clients, it has users at four hundred of them. These company executives use freelancers to get around their companies' established ways of doing things so that they can get more work done.

"It's been a bottom-up movement," says Hayden Brown, Upwork's CEO. Brown told us that some of her biggest users don't want Upwork to use their names, especially when the company is talking to people in their own organizations. Those managers regard Upwork as a career accelerator. "I'm always surprised by the number of our clients that see Upwork as their superpower or secret sauce," she says.

To summarize, more people at large organizations are using open talent than you might realize, but they are mostly doing so to solve discrete problems or to get through a crunch. They're failing to grasp that open talent is not the same thing as contingent work or outsourcing and that open talent platforms are not just digital temp agencies.

Meanwhile, according to our research at Open Assembly, the more than eight hundred open talent platforms available today have an estimated half billion community members who are connected, vetted, and ready to work. Yet so far only a few brave companies have figured out how to use open talent as part of their explicit strategy. Why isn't every company rushing to embrace open talent solutions? Most people are aware of what 20th Century Fox's Darryl Zanuck said about the threat of TV in 1946: "People will soon get tired of staring at a ply-wood box [in their living rooms] every night."[10] As with any paradigm shift, incumbents pay more attention to their would-be disrupters' weaknesses and mistakes than they pay to the strengths. That's natural, especially when people have invested as much as they have in the old models.

Of course, startups, small companies, and even some midsize companies have always been known for their ability to adapt quickly to changing market trends and new technologies to stay competitive. Many were built on digital transformation. They don't have the money or the time for bureaucracies. Hence, they are more likely to embrace digital platforms and global connectivity to reduce obstruction and to work with talent to create results that are better, faster, and cheaper.

For example, small companies were quick to realize the potential of digital advertising and social media marketing, since they could not afford working with agencies doing traditional marketing. Small businesses could experiment with different digital marketing techniques and leverage their success to gain a competitive advantage. Today, digital marketing has become a more mainstream practice and is now fully embraced by large enterprises. Another example of the digital advantage is the rise of cloud computing. Small companies were some of the first to recognize the benefits of cloud-based services, which offered greater flexibility and lower costs than those afforded by traditional on-site software. As a result, these companies quickly adopted cloud solutions for everything, including data storage and customer relationship management.

Companies that were born digitally intuitively understand the digital advantage. Most have developed global ecosystems of talent—full-time and contingent, remote and in-person, skilled and unskilled—that give them massive strategic advantages. Amazon was already used to working with platforms; that was why it was able to onboard a staggering half a million new workers in a matter of months in 2020, as it scaled to meet the pandemic-fueled surge in demand.

Clearly, traditional enterprises have some catching up to do. So far, traditional incumbent organizations are having a harder time adapting because, even as their work is increasingly digitized, how they're organized to do that work remains linear, top-down, and firmly rooted in the past.

The Big Disruptor

To be sure, many view the prospect of open talent as disruptive—and it is disruptive. But it also isn't going away. This is what the new world of work looks like. As with cloud computing capacity—which most companies rent—rather than buying talent, businesses should expect to lease from platforms the skills they need or create platforms of their own.

As one CEO we know told us, "If we can't figure out how to work with open platforms that tap into a global ecosystem of talent, then we won't be in business in five years."

For organizations, open talent is an idea whose time has come and, we'd say, an idea that is overdue. This book provides a model for businesses to adopt. The hardest part will be persuading managers to try something they've never done before, getting them to identify tasks that could be better accomplished by freelancers, and then taking the leap.

How can companies begin their journey into this new world of open talent? For starters, they must change the siloed approaches to talent acquisition in which human resources (HR) works with employees and contingent workers, procurement handles outsourcing partners, and innovation offices work with external partners. All of that needs to shift into organizations in which all talent is viewed through a single lens as a global network that can be tapped as needed.

Our colleagues Professor Zoe Szajnfarber (George Washington University) and Professor Hila Lifshitz-Assaf (Warwick Business School) have conducted some extensive research on the value of task-based thinking, which can be adapted to on-tap talent. For example, they illustrate a lesson from the game of golf.[11] Golfers excel at the game by mastering different components of how they play, but no one golfer can master everything. Each golfer has unique strengths, such as hitting long drives or sinking putts, and the capitalization of those strengths often leads to victory. Similarly, businesses can benefit from an open talent strategy that sources the right talent for the right task at the right time, maximizing outputs and streamlining processes.

Just as golfers choose the appropriate club for driving off the tee, businesses must be able to identify and engage the ideal candidate for each specific task. In addition, businesses can achieve better results by tapping into a wider network of specialized individuals passionate about, and experienced in, their respective areas. By engaging freelance professionals skilled in areas such as programming, graphic design, or writing, companies can improve their reach, expand their talent pool, and reduce their overhead costs.

In golf, players practice and attempt various approaches to achieve the best possible green placement with the fewest strokes. Similarly, businesses can benefit from a more strategic and agile approach to talent management. By breaking down larger projects into smaller, achievable steps and assigning the most suitable person for each component, companies can ensure the highest level of productivity and efficiency. What's more, unlike golf, you can have your best putter sub in or have an expert dig you out of the rough.

Ultimately, transforming into fully networked organizations is something we believe today's organizations must do and can do. They can learn and evolve. Two centuries ago, in the early days of the first industrial revolution, factory managers learned to break the work of skilled artisans down into sequences of regimented tasks that could be mechanized and scaled. Today, twenty years into the fourth industrial revolution, even highly skilled and creative work is being similarly broken down into tasks and scaled.[12]

About This Book

Consider *Open Talent: Leveraging the Global Workforce to Solve Your Biggest Challenges* as a guidebook to digitally transform your talent practices. You will find here in-depth examples and case studies for leaders at every level, from innovation teams to the C-suite, and in organizations from startups to multinational corporations. Middle managers will come to appreciate open talent hiring as the search-engine approach—a way to quickly tap into a wide range of verified talent from many platforms, all in one place. For CEOs who are thinking about digitally remaking their companies, this book offers a comprehensive answer to the question of why—and how—organizations should embrace open talent.

We address everything from building an adoption system that takes security and compliance into account to the frustrations that startups face when they lack access to data scientists. Most important, we show you step-by-step how to deploy an open talent strategy. For leaders and managers alike, it all begins at the very basic human level: examining and changing your own mindset. Only then can you hope to start shifting the organizational culture, your strategy, and, finally, your business operations and processes toward a networked organization.

The book unfolds in three parts. Let's look at them next.

Part 1: Moving toward open talent

Chapter 1 explores the predominant mindset of leaders, workers, and organizations across history. By improving our understanding of how we learned to lead the way we do, we see why we're now facing a talent scarcity, among other issues. We also look at some precursors of the open talent movement.

Chapter 2 outlines the next step toward open talent systems, which entail shifting the organizational culture. The networked organization is decentralized and harnesses a web of connections, accelerating a new business architecture as companies shift to a hybrid and remote work environment. Meanwhile, the passionate innovators underlying the open talent economy are embracing its promise to create new opportunities for collaboration, creativity, and growth. Tapping into this passion, companies can develop healthy relationships with talent as they collectively aim toward a more equitable, successful, and productive world.

Part 2: Integrating open talent strategies in organizations

Chapter 3 describes how pioneer companies have built centers of excellence in which a dedicated person or team, working with senior management, educates and evangelizes others about open talent approaches in the culture. The center assesses the organization's needs and experiments with small-scale initiatives. Then it builds and scales the organizational elements needed to deploy agile practices using platforms. The ultimate goal, which only a few digitally nonnative enterprises have achieved, is transformation into a fully networked organization.

Chapter 4 pivots toward the new architecture of work that emerges when you assess your organization's capabilities and learn and experiment directly with different platforms. We share our assessment model that companies can use to evaluate their risk tolerance and identify where open talent can help. Then we dive into how to structure experiments with external, open innovation, and internal pilots.

Part 3: Developing operations and leadership
for open talent

Chapter 5 describes how to build an external talent cloud for your organization. Solving talent crises quickly will mean tapping into outside talent—the cloud of half a billion people globally working on platforms and ready to work for you immediately. Essentially, the organization rents talent via platforms, tapping into talent that's full-time or contingent, remote or in-person, skilled or unskilled, for massive strategic advantages.

Chapter 6 examines how open innovation addresses the cold-start problem by challenging the traditional notions of top-down, in-house ideation, and it looks at ways of generating rapid solutions. You frame the problems in a certain way so that you can use crowds to innovate faster, at a reduced cost, and for better results. We explore how companies can generate breakthrough thinking by tapping into the networks of subject matter experts who can bring adjacent knowledge and fresh thinking to your toughest problems.

In chapter 7, we look at the details of building a talent marketplace in-house. Sometimes, the organization's structure allows for more momentum through an internal talent marketplace rather than external hiring. Digitally transforming your internal workforce can help you redeploy skills and return the power of career trajectories back to your talent, enabling them to follow their passions without leaving the organization for another job. Moreover, an internal market boosts the organization's diversity, equity, and inclusion efforts by giving workers more latitude to address any inequities they identify.

In chapter 8, you complete your company's initial makeover, embracing open talent processes and scaling them internally and externally. Here you scale your new organization to take full advantage of the digital transformation possibilities of an open talent strategy. This crucial step allows you to diffuse your open strategy into your organizations with limited friction.

Chapter 9 describes the internal shifts that leaders must make to embrace a new way of organizing work. It then shows you how to accelerate your organization's adoption of open talent. Helping yourself and your company to adopt open talent solutions (a task especially challenging in legacy digitally nonnative organizations) involves breaking through entrenched silos of linear, top-down work systems. Careful attention is given to the effects of AI on the changing landscape of talent.

In the book's conclusion, we look ahead at digital's rapid evolution as we stand at the edge of radical technological changes, including generative AI. We also take a hard look at how practice, policy, and perception influence the way open talent and your center of excellence transform your organization.

. . .

Open talent might seem like a radical idea that changes the building blocks of work. Yet, if you were in the newspaper business in the 1960s, you could have never imagined a world where readers would tap into such platforms as Facebook, TikTok, and Google to get their news. No matter how much we'd like innovation to occur in a linear progression, it almost always comes from somewhere out of line, at the edges of what's possible. Whether we embrace it or resist it, the world of work is no longer what it was. Emerging communities of practitioners are testing and refining different approaches. We await their discoveries with interest; the open talent movement must, above all, remain a community of learners.

Think of *Open Talent* as your playbook for that new future of talent writ large. Far from being a sidenote, open talent is the digital transformation of the total talent business. Historically, much of the talent tech has been built on the backs of analog mindsets and strategies. This book represents a sea change. Welcome to the modern world of talent, one in which companies will use platforms to tap into a global workforce ecosystem.

Let's get started with chapter 1, where we look at how we got here and explore some precursors of the open talent movement—all to get a handle on why companies are managed as they are and what's required for change.

PART ONE

Moving toward Open Talent

Chapter 1

How We Got Here

You wouldn't imagine that a company approaching 180 years old and supporting a 400,000-plus global workforce would become an early adopter of open talent. But that's what Deloitte, the world's largest professional services firm managed to do, thanks to some forward thinking from Balaji Bondili, who is currently managing director of new product and asset innovations, strategy, and analytics at Deloitte.

This is a story of one man's shift in mindset. And fortunately for Deloitte and the rest of us, it is an example of how other leaders can do the same. Bondili had spent years running Deloitte, consulting in life sciences and health-care projects the same old way, by charging clients for his team's time and increasing his team's size and hours as needed, depending on the job, and increasing revenue. Then in 2014, he hit a wall. He saw a growing need to find the best resources that enabled things like rapid market insight, mock-ups, prototyping, and analytics, but those insights were taking too long to develop within the firm. Deloitte was having trouble finding the right talent at the right time to work on the projects the firm was getting. The old way of hiring and training full-time talent wasn't working, and this shortcoming was affecting the growth of the organization.

Suspecting that some clients were already farming out work using talent platforms, Bondili wondered if that approach might work for a big organization like Deloitte. In late 2014, he made some calculations that projected the potential value of the overall global open talent market at $6.5 billion, with an annual growth rate of 46 percent.

To help Deloitte and his clients capture as much of that market as possible, Bondili set up a dedicated center within the company. This center, called Deloitte Pixel, would ultimately "taskify" clunky old strategy processes by breaking down projects into manageable tasks. The team would then solicit crowds for ideation and project execution, using platforms such as Topcoder and Freelancer.com. Deloitte Pixel started as an innovation project and got an amazing amount of momentum, especially with progressive partners. They became convinced that getting more work done for clients might decrease the hourly revenue in the short term but would produce more work and more revenue in the long term.

Later in the book, we will show how Bondili moved from changing his own thinking and that of a few progressive partners to changing the minds of some serious naysayers and an entire organization. But for now, we'll describe how leaders like Bondili make the crucial leap in imagination that leads to success. As we see it, people fall into one of two camps: those who operate from a fixed mindset, believing that talent is innate and basically immutable beyond basic skills training, and those who believe that people's talents can be developed (through effort, coaching, and continuous learning), which is a growth mindset. Bondili was firmly in the growth mindset camp, and so are we.

At this post-pandemic time in history, when the digitization of everything has fundamentally altered how people need to lead, we firmly believe that humans can grow and change on a deep level, for their own and others' good. A focus on one's individual work of imagination is a key first step on the journey toward the open talent economy of the future, which helps change to ripple outward. Just as Bondili had to change his mind about what was possible regarding how to complete client work, this is necessary before work processes and cultures align with open talent to create networked organizations.

This chapter explores what has historically been the predominant mindset of leaders, workers, and organizations. By detailing how we learned to lead the way we do, it will help us understand why we're facing a talent crisis today, among other issues. We also look at how the pandemic and the state of the world are snapping all of us out of our complacency. The era of predictability around work has passed. But the promise of open talent awaits, bringing with it an increased sense of agency and equity for the workforce—and flexibility and agility for organizations.

Why You Lead the Way You Do

It's neither your fault nor the fault of organizations, that so many of us are wedded to old ways of thinking about leadership, work, and place. Leaders have come by their ideas honestly, schooled by systems that once functioned quite well but that we've ultimately outgrown—again and again—as time, innovation, and world events continue to alter the fabric of how we do business.

While most of the work we do is digital, the way we organize people is still firmly rooted in the industrial age—it's rooted in the operational capabilities of the factory. Briefly, the first industrial revolution, two centuries ago, was driven by mechanization and the use of steam and waterpower. At that time, factory managers learned to break the work of skilled artisans down into sequences of regimented tasks that could be mechanized and scaled. The mental model and business structure was top-down and well suited to transporting goods, supplies, and services over a long distance. The system was complex and needed exceptional top-down control.

The landscape of labor and industry has seen significant shifts with every subsequent industrial revolution. The second industrial revolution, characterized by mass production and the advent of electricity, allowed pioneers like Henry Ford to revolutionize the manufacturing process through the implementation of assembly line systems, enabling faster and more efficient production of automobiles like the Model T. It was during this era that the top-down corporate structure was solidified. As we moved forward into the third industrial revolution, electronic IT systems and automation led to the boom of Web 1.0 and Web 2.0, laying the groundwork for the tech-centric world we know today. As we stand on the cusp of the fourth industrial revolution, which is being driven by cyber-physical systems that emphasize communication and connectivity, we must find new ways of working that better suit this modern era. To journey through these significant changes in how we work, companies must not only adapt to new technological advancements but also maintain forward-thinking approaches to the work that enables them.

Similarly, the command-and-control tools that managers relied on a century ago are not appropriate for software development, finance, or any of a host of other postindustrial products and services. The rise of networks, platforms, and hyperconnectivity demands new management and governance structures as well. Users want to control their own data, identity, and destiny. Technologies emerging with Web 3.0 (or Web3) allow for better user-centric experiences. Machines can learn from data and experience and can adapt to different environments without human guidance. In the Web3 world, people can access and use AI technology like OpenAI's ChatGPT to create content in video, audio, text, and computer codes with a few simple prompts. Other good examples are the experimentation with the holacracy organizational structure (which embraces the humanity, autonomy, and creative problem-solving abilities of individuals) and the emergence of decentralized autonomous organizations, or DAOs, where there is no CEO but rather a blockchain infrastructure to which groups must authorize access.

But most of the time, we cannot fully understand the technological changes when we're in the midst of them, and they're changing at an accelerated pace. We are the proverbial frogs in the pot whose temperature is slowly raised so that we hardly feel the effects until it is too late. Today, the fundamentals of work and talent management have shifted so quickly that we still lack a firm grasp on what lies ahead. Like the example of SEI in the introduction, most organizations thought they would have a long time to figure things out. But as Ernest Hemingway famously wrote about bankruptcy, the talent crisis happened gradually, then suddenly. Everyone has been pushed into a new arena to compete, and most are woefully unprepared.

We don't have to be frogs in boiling water. A shift toward the mindset of open talent presents a chance for today's leaders and managers to see more clearly what's happening and where we're headed. Notably, Covid didn't create the talent crisis; it pushed the crisis past the tipping point.

Here we'd do well to learn from history and apply some of its lessons. The great flu pandemic of 1918 spread with such ferocity that by the time it ended in 1920, it had killed fifty million people worldwide. Between March 1918 and April 1920, businesses, already stretched thin by the mobilization for World War I, suffered dire labor shortages. People stayed home more and spent less at restaurants, in stores, and on entertainment. Total, world goods trade volume dropped 12.9 percent during the Covid-19 pandemic, and the world's gross domestic product slid by 3.4 percent.[1]

The flu pandemic destabilized lives, societies, and economies at such scale that it compelled people to question how they could fortify their communities for the future. This introspection led courageous and forward-thinking people to embark on major redesigns that massively improved lives. The following changes are good examples:

- Social norms, wherever possible, evolved so that more significance was placed on preventive care. People began coughing into handkerchiefs, washing hands, and opening windows for fresh air.

- Public health officials in the United States recognized that the stack-and-pack approach to urban housing contributed to the spread of disease. By the 1930s, apartments were required to have main hallways that were at least three feet wide, separate bathrooms, and fire escapes.

- Health-care leaders realized populations couldn't thrive when individuals were blamed for getting sick and left to heal on their own. In the 1920s, a few European countries began offering free health care to their citizens.

Similarly, we see today's post-pandemic era as a once-in-a-lifetime opportunity for leaders to be more forward-looking. It's a chance to redesign around today's business challenges, honoring the demands of the workforce and safeguarding your organization for the future.

The Game Changer

A disruption opens up space for innovation. Incumbent companies built on traditional talent practices are experiencing an existential crisis that is likely to get worse. The talent crisis was already in full swing before the pandemic hit. For example, in data science, the backbone of many digital jobs, a 2018 McKinsey & Company report projected shortfall of 250,000 data scientists in the United States alone by 2024.[2] Moreover, when Covid-19 effectively shone a blinding light on all the ways that companies and their leaders were failing to meet their employees' changing needs, the challenges were impossible to deny any longer. The digitization of work and the changing workforce demographics have altered the global economy. For example, in the United States, baby boomers are retiring from the workforce, and the replacements— millennials and Gen Zers—have different motivations not only for the type of work but also about when and how they do it.[3]

That's why we think the onset of Covid-19 was such a game changer. It was the rare bird, the archetypal black swan about which the second-century Roman poet Juvenal wrote. In 2007 Nassim Nicholas Taleb brought the term new salience with his bestselling book *The Black Swan: The Impact of the Highly Improbable.* Part of the reason it struck such a chord was because shortly after the book was published, the world was recovering from one of the biggest black swan events in memory. The crash of the subprime mortgage market in 2008 had erased trillions of dollars of wealth and nearly melted down the world's financial system.

The post-Covid era has been an even bigger black swan, one that calls into question all our assumptions about how the world is supposed to work. According to Taleb, black swan events contain three elements:

- The element of surprise, which catches everyone off guard

- Impacts and outcomes that are substantial, with potentially global repercussions

- The appearance of inevitability after the fact, given all the relevant signals and data

Predicting the timing of a worldwide pandemic is nearly impossible, but in hindsight it seems incredible that the world could have been caught as flat-footed by Covid's onset as it was. After all, the disease's predecessors like the health crisis involving SARS (severe acute respiratory syndrome) in 2002, the swine flu outbreak in 2009, and the Ebola scare of 2014 had repercussions felt throughout the global economy.

The Grand Redesign

The changes you can make in this moment could be so spectacularly positive that instead of echoing the common description of this recent era as the Great Disruption, you could think of it as the Grand Redesign. To grasp this idea of redesign, leaders must make a big mental shift and recognize that companies are no longer in the driver's seat. Skilled talent has the real power, and these people are using that power to work however and wherever they want, whether you like it or not. Digitization and globalization create formerly unimaginable economies of scale.

Although networks, platforms, and hyperconnectivity have been increasing for some time, recent advances in technology coupled with the black swan event have accelerated the need for companies to structure themselves in new ways. Gone are the command-and-control tools managers leaned on to get work done. Organizations must finally innovate their organizational structure with advancements to remote work, AI, and platforms. With the ever-increasing reliance on transformative technologies like 5G cellular networks and generative AI, companies that do not remake themselves from the bottom up may not survive.

Without the cost and logistics of the physical movement of matter, the digital platform economy has removed massive amounts of friction and can now be structured around the ability of firms to think about digital tools and processes. The platform economy has long been in development with the rise of first-generation platforms like Amazon and Facebook. These new businesses have become an existential threat to their competitors because they provide the infrastructure for other companies to build their businesses on.

Marco Iansiti and Karim Lakhani's *Competing in the Age of AI* discusses how these new opportunities force companies to create new value for consumers and capture that value based on new markets. These platforms radically not only shift the reality of market conditions but also affect how we work and how talent engages in the work itself. Multisided platforms shape how different participants interact with each other, including mediating work and providing services. New operating models must consider how to reframe work and tasks.

Platforms such as Uber, Airbnb, and TaskRabbit—which redefine who can be producers in today's world and how they interact with consumers—have already changed the landscape. Digital platforms challenge traditional industries while bringing structure and formality to less organized or previously nonglobal work. Today, a baker in Paris can have a global customer base.

Likewise, the increasing speed and complexity of the internet have drastically reduced the cost of collaboration in every industry. Talent is no different. People can now set up their own networks of collaboration, becoming micro-entrepreneurs and doing work that would have taken dozens of people in the analog age.

The media industry is a perfect example to illustrate the increasing number of challenges to the traditional model. After decades of producing blockbuster films and pop music, the traditional media industry thought it had the model figured out, producing big-budget, perfectly finished productions and pushing them out to passive audiences. Even though much of the media industry has elements of open talent, the aggregation of talent around projects has been disrupted by the democratization of the media business. Most traditional media companies failed to see the rise of social media platforms like Facebook, Snapchat, and Instagram as a competitive threat. They had a limited view of these platforms—as a place for amateur, user-generated content that could never compete with their highly researched, curated, and created content. As long as the traditional media industry stayed within its linear paradigm, it was impossible for them to conceive that people wanted anything else.

It turned out what people really wanted was not just to consume beautifully finished products created by professionals. They also wanted to connect with each other, sharing and creating their own context and content. This shift in sensibility spawned a whole new value proposition that moved from creating content to simply connecting people for sharing and making content on the long tail. Long-tail content offers harder-to-find material aimed at a narrower audience.

This shift applies not only to the media industry but also to every other industry, including retail, energy, and even government. Everything that is touched by technology is deeply affected. On a fundamental level, connectivity has changed people's expectations of how they interact with things. We're moving from an ownership paradigm to an access age.

As Mike Morris, CEO of network company Torc, said at a recent Staffing Industry Analysts meeting where John was leading the panel, "We're not talking about swapping a freelance software engineer with an on-staff engineer to write the same 100 lines of code in a day for a little less money. What's emerging is the freelance software developer that has learned AI tools that allow him to produce a million lines of code." Such an exponential shift in productivity, of course, means that companies need to be organized in a new way, starting at the top.

How to Change Your Mind

Leaders can change their minds by facing certain facts, such as the major trends that have begun reshaping work since the turn of the millennium. Here are five trends that we consider key:

There is a tech talent gap that will only get worse. The world needs an immense amount of tech talent, and it needs it quickly. As mentioned in the introduction, a 2021 Korn Ferry report predicted that the global tech talent shortage will have reached 85 million by 2030, costing the world as much as $8.5 trillion in unrealized revenues.[4] Microsoft predicts that there could be an even bigger shortfall, with 149 million new tech roles that will need to be filled by 2025.[5]

Remote work is here to stay. "You have about 30% who often want remote-only work," says Tsedal Neeley, Harvard professor and author of *Remote Work Revolution: Succeeding from Anywhere*, "and this is typically aligned with certain demographic groups, but remote-only and remote-first is the manner that they want to move forward with. And then you have all the rest who want hybrid work, which is kind of the mix between the in-person and the remote."[6]

Every organization has realized it needs to be digital-first. Even nondigital service industries like food and beverage have had to adapt digital tools to take and deliver orders. While some organizations are simply switching from paper contracts to electronic ones and sending their press releases electronically instead of by mail, others are using digital processes to capture new data and enable better decision-making.

Companies will push more costs, including talent, from fixed to variable. The corporation was invented four hundred years ago to meld talent and capital to create products and profits over time.[7] But now corporations are beginning to shrink, thanks to two factors: automation and outsourcing. Commoditized functions are being outsourced to partners that can do them more efficiently. Many companies are comfortable contracting even core functions, like innovation. Most companies are reasonably reluctant to add back fixed costs of any kind, especially when it comes to recruiting talent. Variable costs include job postings, marketing, and other logistics of finding the talent, which are parts of the recruiting process that companies can outsource to staffing companies.

Predictive technology will help companies map talent pools. With the acceleration of AI in general, CEOs and managers must learn how to combine new and existing talent to the organization's best advantage. Skill specializations are quickly changing, with new paradigms emerging along with these advances. An example of an evolving specialization is *prompt engineering*, the ability to structure effective prompts to elicit better results from AI. Robert Maguire, CEO of Altruistic, was inspired by the approaches used in talent identification in sports to think about how organizations should map their talent pools. Talent mapping enables leaders to visualize their talent in real time, identifying key strengths and weaknesses and highlighting potential areas for improvement. Maguire says, "By gaining a deeper understanding of their employee's skills and capabilities, businesses can make more informed decisions about allocating resources while investing in training and development."[8] As with sports, companies are leveraging the power of data to analyze performance in real time, spot gaps, and predict what they need for the future.

As we emerge from a collective global tragedy, people and businesses naturally revert to a survival mode of thinking. While such a fixed mindset may show short-term success, leaders of networked organizations can benefit tremendously from developing and nurturing a growth mindset. A growth mindset in a VUCA (volatile, uncertain, complex, and ambiguous) world helps you recognize that change can come through chaos and that organizational discomfort is often a precursor to successful innovation.*

The pandemic didn't create uncertainty; it just stirred the pot. Go down the rabbit hole of Industry 4.0 or the emergence of blockchain and crypto technologies, and you'll start to realize how much things have changed—and how much more change is ahead of us. The fact of continuing change is a critical point of reference for success in the future. Leaders (and their organizations) that avoid this truth will suffer the pain of cognitive dissonance as the brain struggles to interpret information that doesn't confirm with their existing beliefs. That dissonance soon spirals into a kind of psychic entropy that manifests itself as disorganization, reduced effectiveness, and an inability to pay attention. In the end, leaders who deny change tend to disengage and withdraw, taking refuge in their most important relationships and processes. That's not a bad thing per se—Covid gave many of us the opportunity to rethink our priorities and reengage with our loved ones. But withdrawal is a terrible approach in business; it leaves you vulnerable to competitors that know how to seize the new and different opportunities that volatile environments provide. And one of the biggest opportunities is open talent.

---

* First coined by Warren Bennis and Burt Nanus at the US Army War College in 1987, the term VUCA is today employed by organizations as a checklist for mapping the kinds of disruptions happening to or in their way of working.

Leaders who want to change their own minds may want to consider an important reframing of recent events. The millions of dissatisfied employees who are joining the Great Resignation aren't rejecting work. They are rejecting jobs that pay them less than they feel they are worth and that constrain their creativity and stifle their potential. They are looking for ways to do more while doing better for themselves. The organizations that have been experimenting with open talent strategies and outside-in innovation are capturing them and, as a result, continuing to push forward and succeed.

For that kind of change to occur in their companies, leaders must first imagine the seemingly impossible. What follows are five guiding principles for open talent approaches:

- **Access supersedes ownership.** People can choose where, when, and how they want to work. Companies can no longer presume to own them or all their output. Talent has the upper hand.

- **Focus on tasks over talent.** Firms will focus less on the management of people and more on the management of demand generation and task definition.

- **Embrace platform-based processes.** The best and fastest way to access talent is through digital platforms, which vet workers, match them to tasks, pay them, and provide them with much-needed training and opportunities for development.

- **Foster both internal and external talent.** Early in the development of open talent, companies believed they would have to choose between internal and external talent. But that belief has proven to be a false dichotomy. Platforms exist to remove friction and to foster collaboration, whether that is within or without existing workforces or some combination of both. Incumbent companies struggle to grasp that the jobs that full-time employees do are changing as well. Going forward, these workers will likely play a more entrepreneurial and strategic role, setting goals and curating the talent needed to meet these goals.

- **Leverage the power of technology.** As the open talent industry becomes more salient, workers will embrace the power of generative AI to enhance their skills and increase efficiency. By utilizing its predictive capabilities, professionals are streamlining their workflows, automating repetitive tasks, and generating personalized content at an unprecedented speed. Integrating generative AI into daily operations promotes collaboration and innovation, enabling workers to tap into their creative potential while they provide valuable insights and solutions for their clients' needs.

Together, these principles encompass the leaps of imagination that leaders must make to guide traditional companies into the future. But to become networked organizations, organizations must also change their culture—toward a decentralized web of connections as companies shift to a hybrid and remote work environment.

KEY IDEAS

The revolution is upon us. Are you ready? No matter who you are, you've been affected by the tech talent crisis. Digital transformation is no longer a nice-to-have driven by the chief technology officer. Now, it's imperative for companies of every kind and size.

Why you lead the way you do. We are all inherently rooted in mindsets that make change difficult. The world has changed digitally, but work is still three steps behind without making adjustments from the industrial age. We need to clearly see what's ahead and map out what needs to be done.

The game changer. Many organizations were caught flat-footed by the black swan event. They must rapidly adjust to a new normal that includes a talent gap, remote work preference, a digital-first mentality, and moving fixed costs to variable ones. However, with any great disruption to legacy systems, you need to remember that the world was never really steady or stable.

The grand redesign. Reframing can help us adjust to the shock. Engaging open talent requires a couple of fundamental shifts in mindset. First, we must pivot from the idea of talent ownership to one of talent access. We must also stop thinking of open or freelance talent as just a short-term workaround and consider it part of a long-term strategy. The open talent landscape features both generalist and nuanced platforms with many people across different focus areas. At the general level, however, they all exist to enable a lighter, faster alternative or supplement classic role-based jobs and hierarchy.

How to change your mind. Disruption offers new opportunities for grand change, especially since the supply of talent has already made the shift. Companies must begin to adapt to talent because talent is no longer adapting to corporations. Platforms fundamentally change how workers engage with their employers and vice versa, shifting the power structure so that talent has the edge. By removing the idea of a physical workspace, open talent is no longer hampered by office politics and can thrive, focused on the things that motivate people the most.

Chapter 2

How Culture Matters in an Open Talent World

The Colorado Backcountry Discovery Route begins in the Four Corners region, where Colorado, Arizona, New Mexico, and Utah intersect, and winds its way north through the Rocky Mountains. It crosses several 12,000-foot passes and even a few streams before it ends at the Wyoming border. In all, the route strings together six hundred miles of dirt roads to create a spectacular scenic drive for motorcyclists.

With a route that extensive, you might think it was mapped out by highly trained cartographers who were also gifted backwoods cyclists. But you would be wrong. The route was created by an informal collaboration of local riders, town officials, and a nonprofit organization. Thanks to that homegrown culture of crowdsourced efforts, more than a thousand motorcyclists make the trek annually, providing an economic lifeline for formerly inaccessible Colorado mining towns like Pitkin and Tin Cup. In this way, maps also benefit the ecosystems they describe. While the backcountry route was mapped out with motorcycles in mind, these trails are also used by hikers, cyclists, and explorers.

Much like the volunteers who strung together the Colorado Backcountry Discovery Route, the handful of entrepreneurs who first set out to plot a path toward open talent solutions improvised, took chances, and deciphered the rules along the way. Today our work is about mapping out a system for the future of open talent—a system that benefits the entire global network economy, from organizations to microenterprises in developing countries to the thousands of people leaving companies to pursue their passions. (Later in this chapter, we'll look at what's been called the passion economy, and throughout the book, we'll meet some of its pioneers.)

But for all its promise, open talent confronts its early adopters with a host of challenges, especially for organizations wanting to harness the benefits of diversifying their talent pool and fostering innovation. For one thing, no common standards exist across platforms, and quality assurance and security vary widely. For another open talent strategies in organizations have primarily been used in a very fragmented way, driven not by the culture but by individuals or teams on an ad hoc basis.

For open talent to reach its full potential, however, companies must make the transition toward a companywide strategic approach. This will mean a comprehensive shift in organizational culture toward encouraging collaboration and knowledge sharing, as well as implementing robust operational changes that promote flexibility and responsiveness. Think mapping the Colorado Backcountry Discovery Route minus the dusty roads and roaring motorcycles.

Our experience with executives trying to transform their organizations toward open talent fall into one of two categories. The first are the super users of platforms we discussed earlier. These people want to use open talent for themselves because they see it as a secret sauce or superpower that can advance their careers. A senior executive at Google was quite frank about this: the open talent practice he was quietly building, he told us, gives him an edge over his colleagues. He has no interest in scaling it to the whole organization so that everyone else can benefit from it too.

The second category comprises people who have approached John and Jin for help after they've tried and failed to work with open platforms on their own. As described in the preface, Jin's work at NASA offers a case in point. When he started working with the space admin-istration's Human Health and Performance Directorate, it had already completed some successful initial pilots with the help of Karim Lakhani, running contests and a technology search through open platforms and executing twenty problems in total. But the organization soon needed to shift strategy because it had begun having trouble getting traction on other projects. A top-down mandate was not enough to get past the pilot experiments. The directorate met with serious resistance within NASA's infrastructure and cultural mindset—including internal stone-walling from some administration scientists themselves. Fortunately, NASA was later able to make the kind of organizational change that led to a core culture shift that embraces open talent platforms. We discuss this in more detail in chapter 6.

As critical as it is for managers and other leaders to take the leap of imagination required to embrace open talent, it doesn't serve them or their organizations well to keep those solutions to themselves. While using open talent as the secret sauce can help the career of one or two managers, this sort of restricted use doesn't help organizations tap into potential opportunities to scale. Any maps that company leaders build through the use of open talent platforms must be expanded and shared throughout the organization. Such an expansion will build a workforce of internal and external talent that is continually iterating on tasks and projects together, ultimately creating a perceptible shift in the com-pany's work culture to one that is open and fluid. In this age of eco-nomic disruption, not to mention how Covid-19 triggered a sudden acceleration of remote work, companies need to think less about build-ing bureaucratic support mechanisms and more about tapping into the best, most passionate people from a diversity of locations.

This chapter looks at how leaders can start building such a map to the organizational culture of the future. If you're a small to midsize company or even a large company that's been using open talent on a tac-tical level, now is the time to start thinking about turning your home-grown process into an open talent strategy that helps you transform your company's culture into a networked organization.

But first, let's look back in time to some early key culture shifts and the important lessons those shifts contain for today's organizations.

From the Horse to the Automobile in Just Over a Decade

The post-pandemic digital revolution we're experiencing today requires businesses to adapt their structures and cultures in almost mind-bending ways. But it's not the first time in history, of course, that culture has had to adapt, in the name of progress, to integrate technological innovation.

When the world was first making the transition from the agricultural to the industrial age, inefficiencies arose as businesses tried to apply historical structures that had become successful when the world was dominated by agricultural production. As new technologies proliferated, two things had to be solved: (1) the cultural adoption of the new technology and (2) the business model that allowed for the rapid growth of production if that adoption occurred.

Cultural disruption is nothing new. When the world moved from an agrarian culture to an industrial culture everything changed, including how cities were built and run. A famous photograph taken in 1900 shows Fifth Avenue in New York City jammed with riders, horses, and buggies (figure 2-1). If you look closely, you can see one early car. Thirteen years later, in 1913, a photo was taken in the same place. In that photo, the intersection was jammed full of cars.

Although the transition seemed to happen fast, there were many things that had to happen to make the shift. Mainly, *the culture at large* needed to accept that these new things called cars would actually work and be safe. For a while, no one wanted these newfangled automobiles. They were in a transition period, much like many technologies are today.

Similarly, a century or so after the automobile, the use of agile methods in software development was a huge cultural shift for organizations

FIGURE 2-1

New York City, 1900 and 1913

(top) Fifth Avenue, New York City, Easter morning, 1900. Spot the automobile.
(bottom) Fifth Avenue, New York City, Easter morning, 1913. Not a horse in sight.

Source: (top) Courtesy National Archives, photo no. 30-N-18827; (bottom) Library of Congress, Prints & Photographs Division, George Grantham Bain Collection, LC-B2-2529-9.

to make when it began to pick up steam in 2001 with the publication of "Manifesto for Agile Software Development."[1] Before agile processes came about, most development teams used the waterfall approach, a methodology that follows a set path dictated by leadership's top-down strategy. Agile is a much more flexible approach that delivers results iteratively, changing its path as needed. You can certainly carry out agile processes using open talent, but the methodology is agnostic about talent per se. When we apply it to open talent, we use the term *light and fast* instead of *agile*, since light and fast is essentially the goal of agile. Yet, the term *light and fast* is inextricably linked to software development, not the digital transformation of talent. Light and fast projects begin with broad objectives and then home in on specific targets as they develop; collaboration and the atomization of problems are the keys to success.

No matter what you call those approaches, however, they are accelerating the shift from hierarchical, role-based views of jobs and functions to a focus on problem definitions and solution management instead.

A New Architecture for Work

To create the kind of dynamic culture that can support open talent solutions, we'll have to take some leaps of imagination and experimentation. Whether such experiments can be scaled into a larger business opportunity often comes down to whether the organization is haunted by the not-invented-here syndrome. Pride and business norms can compel us to shoot down perfectly good ideas simply because we didn't think of them ourselves. The ability to get out of our own way and embrace innovation no matter where it comes from is the difference between an organization that thrives on disruption and one that succumbs to it.

Accordingly, we've adapted a framework for open talent that parallels earlier thinking about various types of innovation—radical, incremental, modular, and architectural innovations—and applied it directly to our view of work and talent. Thus, our open talent model builds on work by innovation mapmakers such as Rebecca Henderson, Kim Clark, and the legendary Clay Christensen, who proposed the theory of disruptive innovation.[2]

Those earlier works describe the developmental stages that ideas and products follow: radical innovation, incremental innovation, modular innovation, and architectural innovation. Radical innovations are fundamentally new—like the first steam and internal combustion engines. Incremental innovations are improvements on existing technologies, like a more powerful steam engine or a longer-lasting nickel-cadmium battery. Modular innovations add new components to existing systems (like the apps you can buy for an iPhone), while architectural innovations pull together a set of existing components in such a way that the combination creates altogether new products or business models, like the iPhone itself. Of the four, architectural innovation is the most difficult to analyze because the components from others are borrowed to create this new effort. Henderson and Clark note that a fundamental shift in architecture can occur but is often difficult to recognize.

The development of talent followed a similar trajectory. The division of labor that enabled factories to become so productive at the dawn of the industrial revolution was a radical talent innovation that could be summarized this way: new roles created for new industries. Manufacturing companies became skilled at generating tasks for unskilled labor and trades workers in their factories. Companies are now getting better at breaking down tasks to digitally assign to workers in the higher-skill markets such as accounting, finance, creative services, and technology. Specialization in managing in industry as previously described is limited in the digital age because, unlike processes in the industrial age, digitization provides increasingly greater numbers of skills. It's a multiplier effect. Most companies attempt to address this shift by making incremental improvements to their hiring procedures, which may cause managers to feel, "I think I've hired the right talent, but it might not work out." In this case, they have based their hiring solely on who appears to fit a particular role—a strategy distinctly lacking the kind of agility that's crucial today.

Next came modular talent innovation, including outsourcing. Using modular improvements, companies began to outsource according to their specific needs and pre-identified resources. Managers in a modular system might say, "I think I can find the right talent, but it's usually the same people I know." By outsourcing the work to the same partners over time, firms limit the pool of potential new labor markets with the skills to innovate.

Finally, there is architectural innovation for talent. Companies use digital platforms to access both internal and external talent to carry out full projects or to solve specific problems. Architectural talent innovation has created a new paradigm for work. This talent system is not controlled by one party but rather is used to organically sow and cultivate new talent. Architectural systems might be summarized as follows "Talent is always on tap and easily accessed on platforms." This shift allows organizations to scale together across industries without the divide of the talent war.

Architectural knowledge—what your firm knows is possible—changes with open talent, while it stays the same in incremental or modular systems. Because this idea is quite subtle, it challenges firms to think critically about existing components. New changes use components differently, including ways to find the right talent but through means far more agile than those used with outsourcing. The architectural shift not only relieves managers of fruitless searches for talent but also enables them to find capable workers through an open talent network (figure 2-2).

Global talent platforms allow companies to plug and play pieces of work as needed, sparing in-house specialists from having to move into domains where they are not comfortable. As Bill Joy, the founder of Sun Microsystems, put it, "No matter who you are, most of the smartest people work for someone else."[3] Paraphrasing Joy, *Fortune* writer Rich Karlgaard says that the founder considered it better "to create an *ecology* that gets all the world's smartest people toiling in your garden for

FIGURE 2-2

An architectural innovation

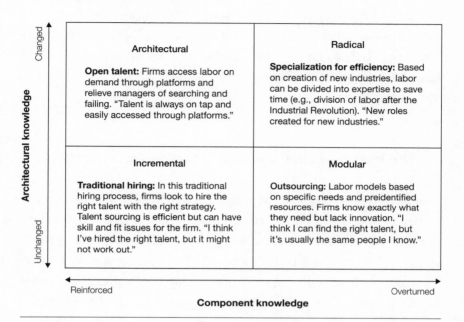

	Architectural	Radical
Changed	**Open talent:** Firms access labor on demand through platforms and relieve managers of searching and failing. "Talent is always on tap and easily accessed through platforms."	**Specialization for efficiency:** Based on creation of new industries, labor can be divided into expertise to save time (e.g., division of labor after the Industrial Revolution). "New roles created for new industries."

Where the vertical axis reads *Architectural knowledge* (Changed / Unchanged), the horizontal axis reads *Component knowledge* (Reinforced → Overturned):

	Architectural	Radical
	Open talent: Firms access labor on demand through platforms and relieve managers of searching and failing. "Talent is always on tap and easily accessed through platforms."	**Specialization for efficiency:** Based on creation of new industries, labor can be divided into expertise to save time (e.g., division of labor after the Industrial Revolution). "New roles created for new industries."
	Incremental	Modular
	Traditional hiring: In this traditional hiring process, firms look to hire the right talent with the right strategy. Talent sourcing is efficient but can have skill and fit issues for the firm. "I think I've hired the right talent, but it might not work out."	**Outsourcing:** Labor models based on specific needs and preidentified resources. Firms know exactly what they need but lack innovation. "I think I can find the right talent, but it's usually the same people I know."

your goals. If you rely solely on your own employees, you'll never solve all your customers' needs."[4]

The services that platforms provide for organizational users tend to be narrow and commoditized; the emphasis is on utility, speed, and cost savings. But the services that platforms provide for their freelance workers allow these people to invest in their own development. For example, when workers finish projects, the person who hired them offers feedback on their performance and suggests online courses and certificates to fill their knowledge gaps. Once the workers have completed the courses and received a certification, their employers are notified that they have upskilled themselves and are ready for another project. This arrangement not only helps the open talent workers create momentum for their careers but also helps companies get better work.

We will explore the specifics of these platforms in later chapters, but for now keep in mind that there are more than eight hundred platforms for open talent, covering every industry. Digital platforms are revolutionizing this architecture by connecting remote, contingent talent—not just full-time talent—directly to companies on a per-task basis. The talent pool is now so diverse that it can spread across multiple industries, especially as the demand for digital tasks grows. Leaders and business cultures that master how to use those platforms can be truly innovative.

The Passion Economy That Drives These Platforms

To engage with open talent, organizations first need to understand why workers are turning to platforms in the first place. In the year before the Covid-19 pandemic turned the globe upside down, two thought leaders separately landed on a term for a development they saw growing in the world of work: the passion economy. One was Li Jin, founder of Atelier Ventures. The other, Adam Davidson, creator of NPR's *Planet Money* podcast, published a book in January 2020 titled *The Passion Economy: The New Rules for Thriving in the Twenty-First Century*. The book describes a still-emerging paradigm in which workers are using the digital revolution to create new rules for themselves, combining their careers with other aspects of life, including their individual passions.

As the term *passion economy* implies, the sea change happening in today's workforce is about more than people simply turning away from the office. It's about people moving *toward* something more compelling and fulfilling than what they're finding in the average organizational workday. People are also flocking to platforms because they are looking for different things to do that aren't limited to their jobs. For people who can swing it financially—and even for some who can't, necessarily—passion sometimes trumps the regular, predictable salary found at organizations.

Jin tells a story about one of LISH's most memorable projects, carried out on behalf of the Broad Institute of MIT and Harvard in 2016.

It illustrates the very human longing for the intrinsic rewards found in doing something compelling. The project involved a critical computational problem in biology. Up to that point, labs used a piece of computer code, called Burrows-Wheeler Alignment (BWA), which had been developed by Heng Li and revolutionized the performance of genomic sequence alignment. LISH decided to try something else.

LISH worked with Li to crowdsource an algorithm that aligned DNA sequences faster and more accurately than BWA could. When the Polish engineer who won the Google Code Jam in 2005 saw that LISH was sponsoring this work, he decided to give it a shot. After he spent a few weeks programming, his algorithm was fourteen times faster than BWA, and it reduced the time to align ten million read pairs from two hours to eight *minutes*.[5] This result was beyond anyone's wildest imagining, and money clearly wasn't the only object, though he did win the top prize of $10,000. The engineer had no prior knowledge in the domain and simply wanted to test his skills in machine learning.

This story has two fascinating points. First, someone who had never worked in the field saw that he could contribute and wanted to. We call this having adjacent knowledge or being close enough to the field that they can see more possibilities in reframing how things should work. It's important to develop a culture that includes these types of open talent workers. They have more exposure than the average expert can ever get. Second, it turns out that many problem solvers simply want to work on important problems. Not only was this engineer new to genetics, but he also wanted to have autonomy in what he worked on, to improve his mastery of algorithm development, and to fulfill his sense of purpose by making an impact. As Steve Rader from NASA likes to say, "The smartest minds in the world like to participate in projects for glory, guts and gold."[6] They're drawn by the intrinsic rewards of fun, learning, self-improvement, proving themselves to their peers, and accomplishing something of lasting importance.

Remote workers are finding so many more benefits away from the office than simply saved commuting time and expense. Whether the motivation is flexibility or the ability to pursue personal passions along with work or *as* work—or a combination of those—it's driving the best people to leave organizations and hang out their shingles on platforms. Doing so promises the kind of balance and quality of life that self-governance offers—control over where, how, when, and how much you work. The desire for freedom is a compelling force. Organizations will need to get better at acknowledging that desire, at working with their employees, and at accessing people on external platforms if they hope to migrate into a future that is already upon us.

Innovators and early adopters of open talent are brimming with passion. Those are the players sitting at the front of the passion diffusion curve, where ecosystems of entrepreneurs and small companies often make up for their lack of other resources with passion for what their idea or business is all about (figure 2-3).

But as companies grow, they become passion deserts. They are more bureaucratic and filled with systems that slow down processes and squeeze out passion. In their effort to create consistency, these companies move from the passion economy to becoming a passion desert.

FIGURE 2-3

The passion diffusion curve

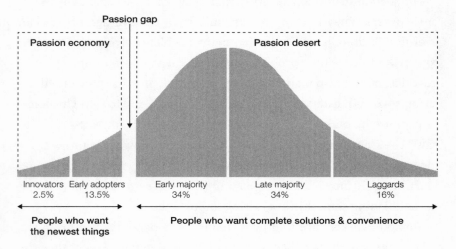

Source: Adapted from Everett Rogers, *Diffusion of Innovations* (New York: Free Press, 1962).

Then, as they begin to scale into larger organizations, they often lose the very sense of passion that led to their success in the first place.

One example is a company like Amazon. Although it was built around innovation and exploring possibilities, the company's explosive growth forced it to put in place more systems and bureaucracy, especially in its warehouses, to make the system run. This change in focus has extracted passion and variability out of the system. Such growing companies switch from exploring new opportunities to exploiting existing processes with top-down management. As they do so, many become passion deserts, places where the only things that keep employees from exploring different paths are the benefits of health insurance and retirement matching (even as those benefits decrease more and more as the company grows). Then the bureaucracy of the HR industrial complex kicks in, crushing out the last vestiges of the passions that their founders used to start the company but that aren't aligned with corporate goals.

In today's global post-pandemic economy, it is more important than ever to keep passion alive in organizations. Platforms do that by helping companies find the best, most passionate people, wherever they might be on the planet. That is why Kelly, the global staffing company, has had to shift the way it works. "Historically," says Tim Proehm, Kelly's vice president of innovation, "we had become incredibly good at operating in a world of scarcity and understanding how to drive value where we could use a push strategy of guiding our clients and talent where we think they should be. Now, after the acceleration of this latest disruption, we have to learn how to operate in a world of abundance and employ a pull strategy of attracting the best clients and talent. It's a fundamental shift."[7]

Case Study from the Front Line of Today's Platform Culture

Let's look at someone who has been working in the passion economy for some time now. Jimmy Chin turned his passions for mountain climbing, photography, and storytelling into art, fame, and a substantial business. Among other things, he is the director, producer, and costar of the Academy Award–winning documentary *Free Solo*. His path to growing his personal brand holds lessons for organizations learning the art of using open talent platforms to find people like Chin, whether it's for a day-long project or a months-long gig to solve a single problem.

Chin's journey began when he was a freelance photographer living out of his Subaru in Yosemite. He was also what's known as a *dirtbag climber*, a term coined by Patagonia founder Yvon Chouinard to describe someone so dedicated to climbing that they're willing to sleep in the dirt to pursue it. After Chin sold some photographs to *National Geographic*, the publication took him on as a staff photographer. When his photos began to appear regularly on *National Geographic*'s Instagram page in the early 2010s, its 148 million followers took notice. Soon Chin leveraged the power of his social media celebrity to create a small media company of his own.

The change for Chin was quite dramatic. In the early days, he would have sent a pitch to a magazine like *Outside* when he was putting together one of his adventures. If the publisher was interested, it would send a team of writers and photographers to cover the trip; if the magazine was *really* interested, it might even front him money for expenses. Afterward, it would spend a few months editing and laying out the photos and the article while selling ad space for $150,000 a page. Six months later, the publisher would distribute the magazine to its 650,000 subscribers and newsstand buyers and release it on Instagram for its 800,000 followers. Chin would have the benefit of the exposure but little else.

Today, Chin has 3.4 million Instagram followers and gets a piece of the action and much more control over his work. Before, when a commercial brand wanted to be associated with him, it would have to either sponsor one of his adventures or pay *Outside* or some other publication to run an ad next to an article about him. Now the brand can call him directly and negotiate a product placement. If Chin agrees to do it, he charges up to $50,000 for each Instagram post that features the product. Instead of waiting months for the article to appear, the brand enjoys a lot more reach, almost instantly and for a fraction of the price. None of this would have been possible without the power of a platform. Think about it: Instagram, TikTok, and a host of business-to-consumer platforms have managed to create a whole new class of creative entrepreneurs like Chin. Business-to-business platforms where open talent lives (e.g., Upwork and Graphite Solutions) are doing the same thing.

Chin has removed a lot of friction for brands, and he has cut out most of the intermediaries. There's a downside, of course: all of that disintermediation affects people's jobs. The print media employed hundreds of people to create the content, produce the magazine, send it to print, and distribute it. Now, it's just Chin and his Instagram account.

But how does an organization use a platform to find a Jimmy Chin? Better yet, what if the company only needs him for a day or two, to work on one problem? Open talent platforms match the right talent to the right need.

If companies are going to survive, they'll have to get much better at tapping into such platforms, thereby migrating talent from a fixed cost to a variable cost. In other words, they will need to become networked organizations.

A Networked Culture

The term *networked organization* was coined more than a decade ago to describe decentralized organizations that rely on webs of connection rather than pyramidal hierarchies. Traditional hierarchical organizations (and even traditional networked ones) are closed systems built on the economics of scarcity. They accept high overhead costs to ensure high levels of productivity. But digital technologies can now capture more of your workforce's cognitive surplus while harnessing the efforts of part-timers, amateurs, retirees, and enthusiasts—and for a far lower cost than was previously thought possible.

Networked strategies recognize that disruption is not cyclical. It's constant. Companies that can move quickly enough to profit from change don't bog themselves down with a ton of bureaucracy when they set out to innovate. They don't micromanage the process from the top down, and they don't insist on owning all the means they employ to succeed. Their teams are light on their feet, have a sense of ownership over outcomes, and are empowered to make their own decisions and recruit all the help they need.

But how and where does the shift to creating a networked culture begin? It starts with a growth-minded leader or leaders who ensure that open talent gets a solid footing in the organization. Establishing credibility for open talent strategies is all about getting the people around you onboard for change.

At the core of a networked culture is curiosity, that is, the impulse to view the world from the lens of "what if." Curious people question fundamental business assumptions and, in doing so, can create something new—like new market value. That kind of curiosity is an impulse with several benefits for organizations that embrace it—everything from making better decisions to doing more with fewer resources.

All of this amounts to what we call creating a *curiosity culture*. That means encouraging your teams—and, to the extent possible, the entire organizational culture—to develop the capacity for, and a fluidity of, rapid, continuous learning that happens through experience, experimentation, and knowledge sharing across roles and beyond traditional boundaries.

There is no one-size-fits-all approach to networked management. However, one way to ensure safety and security in your organizational culture is with flexibility. Here are some guiding questions for leaders who want to foster an environment that leads to a networked organization:

- **Is the organization mindful of psychological safety?** Chief among the twentieth-century psychologist Abraham Maslow's "hierarchy of needs" is safety and security. Be attentive to your people's needs while recognizing that many of them are focused on building a portfolio career: they're likely to stay in their current positions for only a short time before moving on. Create an environment that actively encourages and recognizes curiosity, creativity, and courage, even in the face of failure.

- **Does it foster emotional resilience?** The shift from traditional organizational structures to networks has been described as the most consequential change in workplaces since the first industrial revolution. It is as hard, if not harder, on workers than it is on their managers. Leaders need to model calmness and optimism.

- **Does it recognize the need for flexibility?** Participate in frank, open conversations with the critics on your teams and in your organizations so you can understand and address their concerns.

- **Is it open to learning?** Network with your peers, visit companies in other industries, and read journals and blogs to stay up-to-date. Networked leaders must have a clear vision of what a successful networked organization looks like so they can clearly communicate it to others.

- **Is it digitally connected?** Establish information technology as an enabler of agility; create digital frameworks with common elements that support connected yet autonomous teams. Develop systems that allow application programming interface (API) capability and ways to verify and validate credentials easily. When you build from the ground up, you can start to think about how these technologies can benefit what will eventually become your open talent center of excellence (more on these centers in later chapters).

- **Does it promote conviction?** Provide incentives to your allies and ambassadors financially and with praise, recognition, and mentorship. Develop younger leaders who are digital natives and thus have a better understanding of the next generation.

Effective networked workplaces balance the tension between humility and boldness to encourage the spirit of inquiry among leaders and teams. (For more on encouraging a curiosity mindset in organizations, see the sidebar "Instilling a Curiosity Culture: Tips for Leaders.")

The goal for deploying open talent is to transform our hierarchical organizations into networks—and then develop and deploy networked

INSTILLING A CURIOSITY CULTURE: TIPS FOR LEADERS

Motivate. Lead by example to help employees get curious about their work and buy into the larger mission of a networked organization.

Reframe. Introduce open talent as a model that helps the organization achieve the mission faster through systems thinking.

Celebrate. Highlight innovators who adopt a solution-seeking and continuous-learning mindset.

Unlearn. Teach employees to unlearn old operating methods by focusing on knowledge sharing. Offer meaningful, constructive feedback on their progress.

Provide incentives. Reward open talent solutions advocates with promotion, financial compensation, and recognition from managers and peers.

Reimagine. The total talent ecosystem—not just the skills and talents of your office colleagues, is your capability.

strategies. Organizations must unburden themselves of their past thinking and culture. This recommendation applies not only to leaders trying to create a networked organization that can tap into an open talent ecosystem but also to anyone trying to digitally transform their organizations. Born out of the open-source software movement—where everyone works to improve code, whether they're inside or outside an organization—the networked organization is the end state of digitally transforming an organization's talent process.

Quick Wins to Establish Cultural Credibility

It's important to dip your toe in lightly at first. Aim for hitting singles and doubles at first, not home runs. Resistance is inevitable, but open talent methodologies can supplement and supercharge your existing processes and projects. In that way, open talent can be supplemental, not an outright replacement of your existing workforce. Gaining trust within the wider culture is easier when you take a supplemental approach. Your internal workforce is still very much necessary, and open platforms simply extend the power of your organization. Making sure your team understands this fact helps reduce people's threatened feelings and increase their trust.

For example, in his early days working to source open talent, Jin used just one or two platforms in his projects at LISH. Although they got results, some partners wanted to experiment with different crowds, while others wanted to formulate their own questions. Some wanted to start broader and then home in on a problem. Others wanted to see if there was a match in the market for a technology. In other words, pilots and experiments may work well with one crowd, while a proper buildout may be required by another. The only way to manage is by building strong relationships with a variety of platform vendors.

Later, when NASA began to work with LISH to scale its own center of excellence (which we will describe in a later chapter), managers started asking to work with more platforms. That's when Jin started vetting platforms himself to know what to recommend. He learned about the nuances of working with each of them, such as which platform was more effective at facilitating ideation prototypes or products, which was better at solution-generating ones, and which excelled at particular kinds of relationships.

For example, many-to-many relationships have lots of people looking for answers from a distributed crowd. These are similar to a wiki-type community. One-to-one relationships refer to the best possible match: a single company or manager is looking for a specific resource. Most gig platforms succeed as one-to-one relationships. And many-to-one mechanisms are generally crowdsourcing activities through which a single entity looks for and finds solutions from a cohort of people.

Jin came to understand that not every platform excels at all three types of relationship matches. This realization ultimately saved him and NASA time and money.

A Growth Mindset

To get better at connecting through platforms, companies need to build and support a culture that crosses the passion gap and engages an external workforce alongside their internal employees. That is how companies become networked organizations, by *cocreating solutions with the most passionate freelancers and customers.*

At the core of networked organizations lie the kinds of passion attributes that Jimmy Chin's story illustrated. So how do leaders and organizations learn to think like Chin? They rethink the way they solve problems, and they draw on the skills of free agents who, like Chin, want to work on a project basis.

To rethink how their culture solves problems, leaders need to understand that old scarcity mindsets won't work. They must embrace networked mindsets to help internal employees shift their identities from problem solvers to solution seekers. Let's look at two ways to make this shift.

Ditch scarcity mindsets

Think about it: in the world of open talent, the universe is full of abundant resources of people and skills. A fixed, limited, or scarcity mindset simply can't survive in today's organizational cultures. Instead, leaders who adopt a growth mindset can help their organizations overcome the kind of thinking that kills many companies. In companies with scarcity mindsets, "what's worked before" becomes the default and competitiveness seeps into every corner of the company. Such organizations often end up with a perverse incentive culture, where professionals value themselves and their peers solely for their ability to solve problems. Likewise, when managers value only their internal teams' ability to execute solutions, the company culture is inherently limiting and engenders unhealthy competition. Under such conditions, it's no wonder that some employees might develop a crisis of confidence when the organization introduces an open talent strategy, making them wonder, If outsiders on a platform are creating the firm's value, what is our purpose?

Contrast that response with companies that are built on a networked mindset of abundance and growth. These companies access as a matter of course the wide-ranging expertise of open talent platforms. Their leaders recognize that change can come through chaos and that their own discomfort and that of the organization are often what herald successful innovation. In other words, leaders must be the ones who shift the frame so that their organizations can change too. We would go so far as to say that, sometimes, shifting the frame *is* leadership.

Help employees become solution seekers

When diving into any project, employees need to feel empowered to ask, "Where can we find the next Jimmy Chin on these platforms, and how can we work with them?" Just as social platforms have done a good job linking interests between people, networked organizations must similarly align company interests with the passion of potential workers found on open talent platforms.

But remember, alignment goes both ways. While your employees need to find the right platforms and the right people to work with, the people working on platforms also want to be sure they find the right fit with the companies they work with. What we are talking about, in simple terms, is *attraction*.

This is where brands play a powerfully transformative role. We saw how social media platforms allowed a talent like Chin to grow his personal brand, turning his passions for mountain climbing, photography, and storytelling into a substantial business. Today a wide range of organizations seek out Chin to work on projects. Likewise, networked organizations must use their brands to attract the Chins of the open talent world. A strong brand is a much-needed competitive advantage to attract external talent.

Branding is a tool of marketing, of course, but it can be much more. According to Kirstin Hammerberg of Tangible, a brand says, "This is who we are, this is why we're here, this is who we serve, this is how we're different, and this is the value we create."[8] For open talent, branding is a way to encourage companies and platform workers to align and connect around a larger purpose.

Part of the power of brands is how they can focus a diversity of cultures, experiences, perspectives, and cognitive styles on one goal. That brings us to one final point about brands and the benefits that both organizations and external workers see from the open talent culture: a much wider range of human beings working on solutions to organizations' problems—and those of the world.

. . .

So far, we've talked about why open talent is here to stay. It represents an extension of the digital transformation wave that every company must ride now, as this transformation drives the digitization of the talent industry. We've also touched on the new mindset and cultural changes that leaders must initiate to take advantage of the open talent opportunity, much as a gardener must prepare the soil to have a successful crop.

Now, it's time to plant, starting with strategy. In part 2, we get into the dirt, using the tools we've built at LISH and other organizations with which we've worked. The rest of the book provides the kind of practical guidance that will help you digitally transform your talent practices to offer better solutions to your problems, reinvigorate your culture with more passion, and give you more flexibility to be successful.

KEY IDEAS

It's time to start shaping the future of your organizational culture by laying the foundations for a strategic approach to open talent. Don't just think about how open talent is used on a tactical level, but build a map that looks toward the priorities of your long-term goals as a company, including the effects on culture. Technology can transform your workplace faster in a collaborative, networked organization. The digital age has given birth to a powerful trend: the rise of the micro-entrepreneur and the ownership economy. Our ever-more-digitized world has opened new opportunities for work that aligns better with life's realities. This means that individuals and companies using open talent platforms have been cultivating an uncharted culture fit for today's workforce. Most companies lack an understanding of this new territory and are struggling to find ways to expand their reach onto these platforms.

From the horse to the automobile in just over a decade. We're not dealing with the kinds of inefficiencies that businesses faced during the transition from the agricultural age to the industrial age. Rather, today's emerging technologies are exponentially accelerating connectivity while organizations aren't adapting quickly enough to how work is being performed. We can take some lessons from agile software development and apply them generally across all principles of organizing work.

A new architecture for work. Companies can now use digital platforms to access and foster relationships with both internal and external talent. This shift in architectural talent innovation provides companies with a new framework for organizing talent. These platforms supply the fuel that businesses need to carry out full projects or to solve niche problems.

The passion economy that drives these platforms. The desire for freedom is propelling talent to go beyond their organizational boundaries and plant their own flags on digital platforms. From seeking flexibility to chasing personal desires through independent work, there's an almost-indomitable momentum driving the passion economy. With such autonomy comes an unprecedented say over your time and talent as treasured possessions to nurture at leisure. The benefit of such arrangements boosts comfort and quality of life—things companies cannot quite ignore. Leaders need to leverage the advantages that the passion economy presents for both companies and workers.

Case study from the front line of today's platform culture. Jimmy Chin is bringing many disruptive practices to the market, removing the barriers that traditional structures impose. But where can companies hire future Chins? Furthermore, what if those companies demand a freelancer's assistance for short bursts of time and for specific tasks? Organizations need to seriously consider open talent platforms if they are to move from fixed to variable costs in their budgets and stay relevant in the market.

A networked culture. Leaders should stop looking for a one-size-fits-all approach but should foster curiosity, which makes learning and experimentation paramount. The goal is to shift from a hierarchy to more-decentralized functions, where cross-collaboration is highly encouraged.

Quick wins to establish cultural credibility. Consider experimenting with open platforms as a parallel path on existing projects, not as a replacement. Solve the same problems using two processes (legacy and open) to compare results and experience. Either way, it's important to dip your toe by seeking shorter-term or smaller successes at first, not major long-term ones.

A growth mindset. Rethink how the culture can solve problems, and be careful not to be rooted in motivating your internal workforce to solve the problems. We recommend that you ask the right questions, ditch mindsets around scarcity, and help your own employees seek out solutions.

PART TWO

Integrating Open Talent Strategies in Organizations

Chapter 3

Design a Center of Excellence

In part 1 of this book, we saw how leaders can consider using open talent platforms and how they can help their company cultures embrace them. In part 2, we start thinking about strategies for making the shift to become fully networked organizations.

Open talent strategies should be designed to create a competitive advantage for your company in the future. Much like culture, strategies are all about people. Competitive advantages ignite ideas, technologies, and other intellectual property (IP), but people are key to all of these advantages since people create those ideas, technologies, and IP and make up the ecosystems in which they are used.

In today's fast-paced and dynamic business environment, small businesses, with their entrepreneurial nature, are increasingly adopting an open talent strategy to remain competitive. We saw the effects of this at Victors & Spoils, where the competitive environment dictated how quickly the agency moved to source the right talent. As a result, it didn't need to move through bureaucratic approval processes to get the accounts and deliver quickly. By leveraging a pool of freelancers and external resources, small and even midsize companies can maintain the agility and cleverness necessary to succeed in their target markets. This approach allows them to adapt to changing market demands and respond swiftly to customer needs without the burden of bloated fixed costs. Additionally, the very nature of their small size enables these companies to bring in highly skilled experts and creative ideas faster than larger organizations can do so. This heightened level of responsiveness and ability to tap into a global talent pool ensures that small businesses stay ahead of the curve, innovate continually, and drive growth.

For larger companies starting to strategize how to become more networked, your first main task will be establishing a center of excellence (COE) or some similarly named organization in your company. Your center might include dozens of people from various parts of the organization. Or it might consist of just a single person entirely focused on coordinating open talent solutions. Either way, you need a COE-type division that specifically takes on the task of developing and deploying open talent practices inside and outside the organization.

These centers play a crucial role in fostering communication and collaboration through their cross-functional approach, benefiting numerous internal stakeholders across verticals in the company. The COE highlights the retention of knowledge and skills so that they are not lost by the time the single users are done with a project. By encouraging the sharing of expertise, and promoting collaboration, both of which are facilitated by the COE, open talent initiatives significantly contribute to creating a dynamic environment where innovation can thrive and continue. Recall that mindset shifts needed to be reinforced with structure and reproducibility. We'll get into that more in the coming chapters.

Furthermore, COEs not only provide comprehensive guidance to organizations looking to implement challenge-based initiatives but also enable them to adopt emerging methods seamlessly. By offering support in areas like problem definition, incentive design, and post-submission evaluation, these centers empower companies to efficiently experiment with new strategies before incorporating them into their structure. The use of data-driven analysis, which is generally conducted by the COE, also ensures that the value of each tool is validated, enabling the implementation of more effective strategies. Ultimately, the centers help users navigate administrative bureaucracy, streamlining processes and contributing to the overall enhancement of operations and growth. The ability to function as a lifeline between talent seekers and emerging and evolving platforms also relies heavily on open talent strategies harnessed by the COE.

No doubt, any organization trying to adopt open talent solutions will face constraints from internal employees, who sometimes push back or try to undo any efforts to externalize aspects of their workflows and systems. The COE is the place where such constraints can be understood and solutions developed.

The biggest roadblocks to the growth of an open talent strategy are cultural rather than technical, so an essential task for the COE is to create a *cultural coalition* of support. Two other main tasks are to choose a leader of the center and to set your goals and timelines for meeting those goals. This chapter examines all those tasks and looks at some historical instances of COEs.

Early Setup of a Center of Excellence

Support from the C-suite, of course, is crucial. Executive sponsors can do more than talk about open talent. They can take direct action to ensure that people try this new tool. For example, Deloitte's Balaji Bondili had a number of senior sponsors, but it wasn't until Matt David and Pete Giorgio, two principals at the company, entered their leadership roles that he could accelerate Deloitte Pixel. They not only gave him air cover but also exerted top-down pressure by reducing hires in certain areas while insisting that every project contain a Deloitte Pixel solution.

After enlisting executive support, you will next want to convene an initial open talent workshop in which you include HR in your procurement leadership. The idea is to allow these people to cocreate your strategy. Unless they see open talent as a solution for their problems,

BUYING A CENTER OF EXCELLENCE IN A BOX

What happens when you don't have the time or political capital to build a COE? Rather than build one from scratch, you can opt to buy one instead.

Of course, we recommend that companies build their own COEs whenever possible, working with legal, procurement, HR, and finance to develop a seamless experience for vetting and onboarding. But those are large tasks and take much coordination and negotiating between departments that have a variety of agendas. After all, even staffing firms aren't always shouldering the responsibility. They too have outsourced everything to do with how workers are handled, including compliance, the risk of noncompliance, IP, insurance risk, unemployment risk, and unpaid tax. These many tasks of open talent have created layers on layers of providers. Many companies approach staffing vendors through a vendor management system; the staffing vendors then outsource the payroll, worker classification, and background checks. The experience is so intrusive and disorganized that most freelancers dread assignments at large organizations. Once they get through all those gauntlets, it takes another three or four weeks to be onboarded.

Millennials and Gen Z workers were born in the digital age; they simply don't have the patience to deal with bad systems. They've grown up in a world of seamless digital experiences like Instagram and TikTok, and they expect the same thing from everything else they do. That's why, when working with freelancers, not only do you need a centralized platform that can find the talent you need, but you also need new ways of taking care of governance issues, including compliance, IP protection, and risk.

That's where platforms like Worksome and Utmost can help. Think of them as a COE operating system, or a COE in a box. With these platforms, you can onboard a freelancer in three or four hours instead of three or four weeks. That's because they not only pull together these disparate systems but also provide a better data platform that knows where every worker comes from and how they integrate into the talent ecosystem.

"Companies like Google now have more than 60 percent of their workforce made up of external workers," says Sam Orrin of Worksome. "They've outsourced the relationship between the worker and the company and lack the data to really know them."[1]

Dan Beck, CEO of Utmost (which was since acquired by Beeline), told a story about working with a pharmaceutical company: "When we started working with them, they had data on 6,000 folks that worked externally to the company. When we started modeling the ecosystem, we realized that they actually had over 30,000 external talent working with the company. You've got to have the data first to understand the ecosystem before you can start managing the work and finding efficient ways to engage with talent to get the work done."[2]

Whether you build one yourself or use the services of a platform like Utmost, the power of a COE model is clear. Simply put, it removes the friction of working with freelancers, giving them one seamless experience that works for both the company and the freelancer.

they will not fully support it. You should bring in some experts to help you run these workshops.

Your company's COE will be able to focus on the questions that people at various levels in the organization have about open talent solutions. For the C-suite, it might be questions like, Do employees trust managers enough to understand that exploring an open talent strategy does not mean that workers are being replaced? At a project level, managers will want to trust that their IP and data are safe. And your HR folks will want to know things like whether these freelancers really are who they say they are. The COE must work to develop these areas of trust by creating airtight systems. (See the sidebar "Buying a Center of Excellence in a Box" for a completely different approach to establishing a COE.)

How Is an Open Talent Center of Excellence Different?

The overarching goal of a COE is to ensure that an organization is taking full advantage of all the skills, talent, and knowledge that it can harness. The center does this by ensuring that all the procedural roadblocks and blind spots that stand in the way of open talent adoption are openly acknowledged and addressed. We will look at the steps outlined here more closely in chapter 4, but the basic idea is that the COE, working closely with senior management, takes several steps toward a fully networked organization. First, the center assesses the organization's needs and capabilities and learns what it has to know about platforms, "taskification" (breaking things down to smaller tasks to be done rather than positions to be filled), and compliance. Next, the center experiments with smaller-scale initiatives. It then builds and scales three structures: (1) an external talent cloud (ETC), (2) an open innovation capability that uses crowds and contests, and (3) an internal talent marketplace (ITM). The ultimate goal, which only a few nondigitally native enterprises of scale have yet to achieve, is *transformation*, the fully networked state of the whole organization.

A COE provides expertise, collects and retains institutional knowledge, shapes and molds culture, tackles roadblocks in processes and procedures, and bridges services with platforms. Most importantly, the center provides stability by creating processes uniquely adapted to your organization's abilities and appetites. Essentially, it acts as a platform of platforms, ensuring that you will go to the right place to secure the right talent. Done right, the COE becomes an airtight system with repeatable procedures, so that your IP and data will remain safe, especially on sensitive projects. And it creates trust that external workers are really who they say they are. When the time comes to scale open talent, your internal people will be its chief advocates. (For a brief history on dedicated innovation centers, see the sidebar "Centers of Excellence in History.")

NASA created its CoECI when the White House's Office of Science and Technology Policy recognized NASA's success with pilots. The department wanted other government agencies to replicate that success using the knowledge, expertise, and experience NASA had gained. At the time, LISH's Karim Lakhani proposed that organizations like NASA needed to engage a global pool of talent—at scale—to work on the global problems it was grappling with. A dedicated team at such a center could educate and evangelize for open talent approaches and then oversee their development and implementation. Finding the best talent is about exposing the internal process to complementary resources.

Karim, Jin, and the team at LISH have changed the game again and again, working extensively to bridge connections between paradigms. As a result, NASA has developed a healthy cultural ecosystem. Although NASA has 17,000 employees, it has created NASA@Work, a platform that allows 43,000 contractors to tap into its community. And to extend the network even further, NASA's CoECI built a network of fifty platforms that focus on technology search and matching, expert talent matching, and various other forms of crowdsourcing. In turn, the access

CENTERS OF EXCELLENCE IN HISTORY

The idea for a dedicated innovation center within a corporation or another organization dates back to 1880. After the French government awarded Alexander Graham Bell the Volta Prize for the invention of the telephone, he dedicated the 50,000 francs of the prize money (the equivalent of about $300,000 dollars today) to advanced research on the analysis, recording, and transmission of sound and "for the increase and diffusion of knowledge relating to the Deaf."[3] The laboratory he built to do this in Washington, DC, was variously known as the Volta Bureau, the Bell Carriage House, the Bell Laboratory, and the Volta Laboratory. In 1925, three years after Bell died, it became Bell Telephone Laboratories. Over the next seventy years, Bell Labs researchers pioneered the development of radio astronomy, the transistor, the laser, the photovoltaic cell, the charge-coupled device, information theory, the Unix operating system, and the programming languages B, C, C++, S, SNOBOL, AWK, AMPL, and others. Fourteen

gives NASA the ability to tap into 200,000,000 brains. Depending on the frame, you could say that NASA has 60,000 members and access to 200,060,000 as needed. LISH has executed more than 750 open talent projects, including a study of 400 projects that NASA has done over eight years and key advancements at the Harvard Medical School and with other commercial partners. Along with these elite institutions, many more, including startups, have come out of the woods to transform their organizations to establish network principles.

Strangely enough, the more success LISH had, the more resistance it encountered at NASA, especially during the first four years of the pro-

scientists won Nobel Prizes for work they completed at Bell Laboratories.

Though Bell Labs set the standard for centers for corporate innovation, it was not unique. Many companies set up labs, Skunk Works, innovation centers, or other hubs to explore emerging technologies and organizational processes. Most of the early innovators in the open talent space that we have worked with also set up special organizations to incubate and introduce talent innovations to their organizations without disrupting their existing business models. GE had GeniusLink, Deloitte has Deloitte Pixel, and NASA has the Center of Excellence for Collaborative Innovation (CoECI). The model is consistent with Michael Tushman and Charles O'Reilly's work on ambidextrous organizations in *Lead and Disrupt* and Vijay Govindarajan's on innovation leadership in *The Three-Box Solution*, which advocates for the creation of separate innovation organizations outside the core, to ensure that their new ideas and business models can be incubated safely.

gram. In response, researchers at LISH, led by Hila Lifshitz-Assaf, studied the sources of this resistance. LISH and NASA learned about the not-invented-here syndrome across different organizations, the stubbornness of organizational culture, and how the fragility of talented people's egos threatened their professional identities.[4] People's resistance to change was frustrating but understandable.

As described in chapter 2, when LISH collaborated with the Broad Institute of MIT and Harvard to task contest participants to develop an algorithm that aligned DNA sequences faster and more accurately, the winner was a Polish machine-learning specialist with no experience in the life sciences. Just imagine if you were a computational biologist at Harvard or MIT, and you and your team had thought that your algorithm was fully optimized. The project would be your identity. Now imagine there was a contest, and an unknown amateur accomplished in a matter of weeks what you and your team had failed to do in ten years. It's only natural that you would feel threatened.

But here's the thing: as Jin told those discontented internal team members, platforms can be used by *anyone*. Platforms aren't just for the C-suite. In the networked organization with a healthy COE to coordinate projects, internal employees can use platforms to tap into new ideas that help their own teams solve problems. It provides equitable access to those willing and curious to dive into new ways of innovation.

Who Should Lead Your Center of Excellence?

Historically, leadership has been viewed through the lens of music, where a conductor leads a group of musicians through a symphonic arrangement. This type of orchestration is steeped in tradition and specific rules, much like those that most companies have for working with talent. Leading an open talent COE is like leading a jazz band; the task is based on the art of improvisation. Sometimes a center needs the structure of a conductor-led orchestra; at other times, it needs the space and flexibility to allow for creativity and innovation to flow through the organization more intuitively and spontaneously. Like a community of musicians, the COE must create the right types of collaboration and coordination to produce inspired work. To do that, it needs the right kind of leader—one who is adept at selecting, guiding, and coordinating the various moving pieces of talent, both internally and externally, to complete tasks and projects.

Who is the best person to lead a COE, and what kind of style works best? We've seen different approaches and personalities. The leaders who use a slow and steady approach, like the team at NASA, are trying to set up long-term success that drives projects year after year. As described earlier, NASA's Human Health and Performance Directorate got going with initial pilots by working with LISH. Two of the NASA program's directors—Jason Crusan, who headed NASA's Advanced Exploration Systems, and Jeffrey Davis, director of astronaut safety and chief medical officer at Johnson Space Center—were forward-thinking about bringing innovation into their existing technology development processes. But they needed someone who could take their experiments and put systems and contracting mechanisms into place to scale the operation.

That's where Lynn Buquo came into the picture. When she started as the inaugural manager of the CoECI in 2012, only 10 percent of the agency was interested in using open talent. When she retired a decade later, "more than 50 percent of the agency" was aware of its successes.[5] How did she do it? From the outset, Buquo aligned herself strategically with NASA's procurement and legal departments, because she understood that the center would need the right administrative allies. She didn't hesitate to turn away projects that were not the right fit, but she also fought to keep ones that would potentially have real impact.

Choosing and winning the right battles was key. Buquo and her team masterfully spearheaded a bottom-up grassroots campaign to get people to use platforms while it messaged to NASA executives that their top-down support was needed. It didn't matter if Buquo and the rest of her team had the best talent platforms working with them; they needed to do the work in ways that NASA employees understood. Every conversation with potential clients at NASA would end with a discussion of the platform's ability to execute on the promise of open talent rather than just say it could be done. The process needed to be seamless for their NASA partners. People didn't want to think about whether they could do it or if it was some hack.

Buquo's success was highlighted by two developments. First, after ten years at this, the CoECI's contract ceiling to work with platforms was increased to seven times its original ceiling (from $25 million to $175 million). (This number was based on projected use across both NASA and other federal agencies.) Though its operating budget has remained the same, the increase signals that the entire agency was considering CoECI a viable option. Second, in March 2022, NASA awarded its Distinguished Service Medal to Buquo.[6] This amazing achievement is only awarded to five to fifteen people per year, usually for technological achievements, not innovative business processes.

Buquo used a slow but thoughtful approach to align with the departments around her to succeed. The trouble with scaling fast, however, is the need for quick and significant buy-in from the organization. Otherwise, the COE can be squashed fast. Many business leaders take this speedy angle to get things going with tremendous momentum, but they struggle to get the infrastructure in place for the long haul.

Paul Estes is one such center of excellence leader who started out with great momentum. While he was still at Microsoft, he took his personal passion for open talent and let it drive his business strategy. A productive video producer on his team could create a polished how-to video within a week. Estes introduced him to the Upwork platform and challenged him to tap its talent to create twenty great videos a week. At first, the producer was reluctant to do so, as he would go from being a producer to a curator of other producers' work. But once he started, the project worked so well that he became something of a folk hero inside Microsoft and spent much of his time traveling the world teaching other people how to take advantage of open talent.

Soon after, Estes and his team launched Microsoft's 365 freelance toolkit, a set of tools, templates, and best practices to help the 47 percent of hiring managers who are utilizing freelancers to launch, execute, and manage open talent programs at scale. By then, he was effectively running Microsoft's open talent operation, which was his version of a COE. Then he wrote and published *The Gig Mindset*. That was when Microsoft's traditional talent procurement organization took notice. Although contingent and outsourced talent had been a big part of the Microsoft workforce for a long time, the company had suffered a legal setback in 2000, when it lost a lawsuit regarding the classification of temporary workers and had been required to pay a $97 million settlement.

Estes's use of the word *gig* troubled company leaders, especially given Uber's bad reputation for exploiting its drivers. Estes ended up leaving Microsoft.

What Are the Goals of Your Center of Excellence?

A COE's overarching goal should be to take full advantage of all the talent opportunities that are available. Every organization is unique, but we suggest you start with these three principles:

- **Understand your readiness.** While many people inside your organization may be using open talent already, there can be, as we've seen, many blind spots and roadblocks when you try to institutionalize it. The better you understand your readiness, the better your chances of a successful adoption.

- **Be prepared; things evolve rapidly.** Understand that the ecosystem of open talent is quickly evolving, just as technology is. With the emergence of VDI (virtual desktop infrastructure), there has been a profusion of solutions to compliance concerns and security issues. These solutions dramatically remove the friction of adoption. A COE is necessary to stay on top of these changes and be ready to implement those that best address the needs of the organization.

- **Fit your digital transformation to your talent strategy.** In many companies, talent acquisition is siloed between HR, procurement, and innovation. The COE should digitally transform all these silos by using internal and external platforms.

At the core of building a COE is the ability to get internal alignment around goals. Goal alignment needs to be explicitly managed, crossing several senior stakeholder domains, including creative talent, operations, the legal department, procurement, and client-facing leaders.

This kind of alignment usually takes some education in the art of the possible. Open Assembly has built out our early-stage methodology to ensure that an agreed-on set of positive outcomes for open talent is established in week one of our engagements. We also make sure that those outcomes are translated directly into measurable data that is developed during pilots and are clearly communicated in the company. Remember, key performance metrics matter even with early wins.

A successful COE must get alignment around its objectives. In the end, while every organization wants to solve the big problems with home runs, a center needs to focus on solutions that are more sustainable and that come from singles and doubles, much in the way that NASA and Deloitte did.

KEY IDEAS

We recommended setting up a COE for open talent that fits within the existing corporate culture. The center should help establish administrative protocols and foster a learning culture around the different players in the ecosystem. Make sure that your open talent strategy fits your organization's larger talent strategy. You never want to stray too far from companywide goals.

Early setup of a COE. The vision for a COE starts with leveraging the organization's abilities and desire for open talent. The center should provide coaching that works with institutional knowledge and bridging services with platforms while building a sustainable culture.

How is an open talent COE different? It's about harnessing skill and talent tailored for the situation. Repeatable processes can help navigate a large world of platform vendors, which are growing in number by the day. Also, remind your employees that these platforms are for everyone's use.

Who should lead your COE? To find a leader, look for someone who is clever enough to navigate your bureaucracy but with thick enough skin to stay the course. (When it's time to scale, you might need to look for someone else.) Find an executive sponsor to support the mission and objectives.

What are the goals of your COE? The three goals are understanding readiness, shifting rapidly with technology changes and platform offerings, and aligning digital transformation strategies with talent strategy.

Chapter 4

Assess, Learn, and Experiment

When Wipro purchased Appirio in 2016, the goal of then-CEO Abidali Z. Neemuchwala was to create one of the world's largest cloud transformation practices, a game changer in today's economy. Appirio came with a little-known subsidiary, Topcoder, an open talent platform with more than 1.5 million members and which had hosted some twenty-five thousand contests for clients like Wellmark, T-Mobile, and NASA. Intrigued, Neemuchwala wondered how many of Wipro's 200,000-plus employees were members. After some investigation, he discovered that they numbered in the thousands.

A traditional CEO might have been chagrined or even angry. Such an executive might have accused the employees who were working on the Topcoder platform of double-dipping and punished or even fired them. But Neemuchwala held an all-company meeting instead. There, he celebrated the employees who had taken it on themselves to learn new skills and make new discoveries through their participation in Topcoder's open model. Not only had these Wipro employees sought alternative sources of income, but by working on the Topcoder platform and doing contests, they could also learn and expand their skills. He went even further and gave them bonuses and encouraged everyone else in the company to follow their lead. Anyone who did would also be compensated, he promised.

Leaders set the tone for the culture, and Neemuchwala's open mind-set ensured two things—that Topcoder was in good hands and that Wipro's own transition to open talent would go smoothly. Modeling that kind of mindset is not only important at the very top of an organization but is also the sine qua non for a center of excellence (COE). As we described in chapter 3, ideally your organization will set up a COE to lead and manage the transformation of the organization's open talent practice from start to finish.

When it comes to implementing a talent strategy, however, the old adage "Start with the end in mind" does not apply. Instead, every organization must find its own path to whatever endpoint is appropriate for the individual business. Reinvention is hard, and any new systems will need to use language that can be integrated with current business systems, whatever those might be. In other words, you have to start from where you are. And since every participant—whether that's an internal employee or an external worker hired from a platform—will begin their journey from a different place, your COE should include multiple ways and places to jump onto projects in the organization.

Remember that open talent is about removing friction. It frees your people from the bureaucratic encumbrances that prevent them from moving faster than your competitors, from getting help from outsiders when they need it, and from capturing and applying the wisdom of crowds to the toughest problems. Companies that use those capabilities are like boxers, bobbing and weaving through punches, agilely side-stepping disruptions, and continually floating and testing new ideas and approaches.

Accordingly, when developing your open talent strategy, keep in mind the following elements: responsiveness, agility, speed, efficiency, commitment, and staying emergent. These are attributes as opposed to goals; think of them as benchmarks to guide your decision-making.

Responsiveness comes first, because you want to stay attuned to changes in your ecosystem and adapt quickly to them. Measure your outputs against your expectations, and make changes. What ultimately matters is how good your response is, and for that, you will need sound metrics that capture your weaknesses and strengths to track your improvements.

Next comes *agility*, which is an indicator of how much you're increasing the speed of your business. *Speed* is a function of pull, as in how much motivation and creativity you can pull out of your ecosystem. It's about building a system that can anticipate and respond to market demands. It means encouraging people to come to you and tell you what they want to do instead of waiting to receive their marching orders. *Efficiency* is about allocating resources, expanding and contracting them to reflect changes in the world and your organization.

Commitment is essential: your firm is lost if your people don't have it. Increase employee motivation by making them a part of strategic decision-making through bottom-up analysis. Build a high-performance culture that rewards people for doing great work and gives them opportunities to grow into better jobs—whether at your own organization or at your competitors.

Finally, *staying emergent* means that you are always developing new things to enhance, supplement, and eventually replace your core business. Have one strategy to drive your current business objectives while exploring other strategies that react to and drive change.

Elite organizations such as Siemens, IBM, and Unilever have begun deploying open talent solutions over the past fifteen years, but too many of these efforts at enterprise-sized companies lose steam. Although executives get excited by the possibilities that successful pilots point to, innovation managers often leave, and then funding runs dry. This loss of momentum over time is one of the many reasons we recommend that companies establish the kinds of COEs we described in the last chapter.

A strong COE can both guide and sustain a company's efforts as it works through five distinct phases of its transformation: assess, learn, experiment, build, and scale.[1] In this chapter, we look at the first three of these phases:

- **Assess.** Before you can figure out where you're going, you must know where you are. By asking the right questions, the COE leads the assessment process by helping leaders understand the organizational changes that are needed to develop open talent solutions.

- **Learn.** This phase aims to use education, culture, and communications to create a coalition of the curious and willing. It's easy, especially for talent innovators, to race ahead quickly with new ideas or models. But such speed only works when a single entrepreneur is leading the charge or needs convincing. When the proposed changes are companywide, people need to understand what they are getting into and why. The COE lays the groundwork for the program through workshops and formal and informal communications.

- **Experiment.** The goal of this phase is to gain experience using new tools and systems and to have measurable results to share both to problem-solve and gain buy-in. Experimental initiatives should only begin after an organization has spent ample time in the learn phase. Operationally, this is when leaders test, refine, and lock down business systems and talent network platforms.

The Assessment Phase

Before getting started on the path to open talent systems, most companies will want first to determine their readiness for such a move. We created a five-step assessment model that allows companies to look at things like their risk tolerance and to find out to what extent open talent is already being used in the business. Likewise, an assessment can help you identify which areas of your organization need to be upgraded or reconfigured. When assessing your organization, make sure that its softer dimensions such as open talent vision and risk tolerance are in balance with its more tangible attributes such as its open talent operating model and internal mobility. In addition, clarity of purpose, leadership support, and open risk appetite must be in place to accelerate the inevitable changes to your organization's processes, platforms, and strategy.

Below this summary level, organizations must assess everything. To measure how much the stakeholders approve of your open talent approach, for example, you will need a clear set of agreed-on outcomes, how to track benefits, and an understanding of how all of the processes line up with your organization's overarching purpose and goals. Among the many questions to explore in the assessment phase are these:

- What are our goals for using open talent?

- How will we measure these goals, and how often should they be measured?

- Who are the key internal and external players that need to be involved, and what are their roles and responsibilities?

- How long will it take to get buy-in from stakeholders?

- What is the timeline for implementing each component of the open talent initiative once it has gained executive approval?

- Who will be responsible for determining the metrics and overseeing data collection, analysis, and reporting?

We start the assessment by interviewing stakeholders. These are portfolio managers and employees who are volunteering to go on the initial journey with full support from the organization's leadership. We also conduct desk-based research to assess each of the dimensions as set out in the risk model (figure 4-1). We map a simple rating for each, using a database of models and standards as a baseline. At the other end of the process, the assessment can be used as a dashboard to track the

FIGURE 4-1

Open talent (OT) risk assessment model

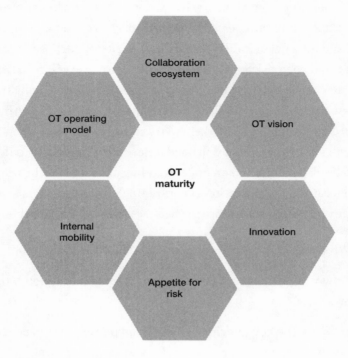

Source: Open Assembly.

organization's ongoing development. If there is a need for further investment in change management or if priorities need to be changed, the assessment gives you a firm baseline and a business-case-based perspective. Now let's examine the six main parts of the risk assessment model, as highlighted in the figure.

1. Assess your collaboration ecosystem

As you assess your organization's readiness, probe to gain a general understanding of how your people are using open talent already. As Wipro's CEO discovered, chances are good that someone somewhere in your company is using open talent solutions now. One way to find out is to send out surveys that your employees can respond to anonymously: First, ask how many of them are hiring outsiders to complete projects, and if so, which platforms they are using. Second, you could ask your internal employees whether they are considering working for outside companies via platforms as a second job. Be sure to mention that you are only doing this for informational purposes. Or you can bring in a third party to do this assessment to address employees' fears concerning losing their jobs. The assessment establishes a good baseline for you to better understand how your internal employees use their skills outside regular work hours. Also, it helps you know whether they have learned and developed other skills outside their job and are now making a few extra dollars. If that is the case, you can start to plan for an internal marketplace to give them new opportunities within your company.

Part of your assessment needs to look at what those existing relationships are and how they can be changed or leveraged. Do your business units share vendors, sourcing strategies, and portfolios with each other and with other firms? For example, NASA's largest contractors are California Institute of Technology, Boeing, and Lockheed Martin. When Jin was helping build NASA's CoECI, he looked at how the organization used (or could use) open talent that was not offered by the big contractors. NASA tackled some critical questions: How much internal mobility do your people have? Are they offered lots of opportunities to change roles so that they can learn and stretch, or are they actively discouraged from doing so? Are there mentorships, job swaps, and innovation initiatives they can participate in?

These are important questions, considering that large enterprises can lose up to $500 million a year from employee attrition alone. When companies encourage and support mobility within the organization, employees feel more valued and empowered to develop their skills continually—and therefore more likely to stay on the job. Over the last few years, companies we've worked with to develop internal marketplaces tell us that they are filling nearly half of their openings internally (as compared with a national average of just 20 percent) and that their employee engagement has risen more than 25 percent.[2]

Next, explore a few relevant platforms yourself to see how many of their users have your corporate email address. You'll be surprised. In our research, while only 350 companies have an enterprise relationship with platforms, institutionalizing their open talent strategy, over 2 million companies have someone in the company using an open talent platform. This statistic is evidenced by the work-related emails that people use when hiring platform talent. For example, when we spoke to representatives at Freelancer.com, they reported that despite having only a couple of dozen *Fortune* 500 clients with formal enterprise-level accounts, close to 70 percent of all *Fortune* 500 companies have employees with active corporate emails using the platform to get work done on a monthly basis. We're not insinuating that these employees are doing anything wrong. In fact, they have no problem using their business emails. These companies, however, have not fully assessed why and how this platform practice should work at the company level.

2. Assess your open talent vision

We recommend that you create an open talent vision document and have it approved by senior leadership, preferably at the C-suite level. It should be based on several inputs: general objectives of the project, the organization's strategic plan, company competencies, and specific technology challenges or research and development (R&D) needs. The COE will need to budget time and resources for annual updates, which can be used to provide a clear compass for the efforts and to communicate their progress.

You need to define success metrics clearly and share them early. Identify what your big goal is. Top line? Bottom line? Make sure to choose the right ones, by asking questions like these:

- What are the primary metrics—the firm's or organization's top-line and bottom-line goals?

- What are the shadow metrics—the longer-term metrics that make you think about your goal as more of a long-term story?

Full buy-in will be required from a broad range of actors, including HR, finance, procurement, IT, sales and marketing, and legal. Leaders and the COE need to clearly communicate the changes they will have to make. They should map out these changes and build an engagement plan to drive excitement rather than fear.

Your open talent vision needs to align with your stakeholders' objectives. Early on at NASA, Jin saw problems with getting repeat users of open talent tools, not because the pilots were unsuccessful but because the users still failed to understand how these tools fit into the larger scheme of their work. Many of them saw the pilots as one-offs, means to specific ends rather than repeatable processes that drive efficiencies and results and that should be written into budgets year after year.

That's why you should develop a value proposition for senior management when requesting funds for a pilot program. Pilots are proofs of concepts; communications to senior leaders should emphasize that they may not provide complete solutions. The proposals can be scoped modestly but should include both internal and external projects. To reduce resistance, we recommend running internal challenges first. While the pilots can be planned and executed quickly, it's likely that only a few will be deployed and scaled. When selecting problems for the pilots, challenge owners to clearly define the criteria for success. When recruiting staff, make it clear that they will be expected to become champions for open talent and to engage in peer teaching.

3. Assess your talent innovation

It's highly likely you'll need to change processes, systems, and accountabilities to enable open talent—even for pilots. Engage your talent acquisition teams early on to assess the probable scale of these changes and prioritize short-, medium-, and long-term solutions. HR and procurement already have a way of acquiring talent and you're not going to overtake them. Instead, you need to work side by side with these groups and innovate with them through open conversations about how bringing on additional open talent capabilities will affect their workload. These critical conversations promote transparency and assure your colleagues so that the COE's momentum is not stopped. Innovation can be scary, so find a way to build on what's already there.

To do this, you'll need to define your current onboarding procedures for external workers across the key metrics of speed, scale, quality, and cost. (In chapter 5, we look at this process in detail.) If you have a one-size-fits-all approach to connecting with talent, consider whether you should orchestrate different processes for different talent or work archetypes.

A company can lose good open talent candidates if it has rigid onboarding processes, especially those that take twelve weeks or longer. If at all possible, rearchitect your internal procedures such as background checks, drug testing, and IT security protocols to cut down on time—or allow the platform to carry out some of this due diligence. For example, at Altruistic, the data science talent provides digitally certified credentials, which most companies want to see.

4. Assess your risk appetite

Define the key dimensions of your appetite for risk with regard to talent. Consider both the operational impacts of doing without specific kinds of talent and the impacts of bringing the wrong talent in. Protecting your data, IP, client confidentiality obligations, and operational integrity and open talent are *not* mutually exclusive. You don't need to sacrifice security if you address the issues proactively and build them into your open talent operating system. For example, Deloitte Pixel used crowdsourcing to resolve some of its security questions, uncovering several approaches and comparing them. Historically, each platform has its own way of solving these issues. There is now an effort by the industry to reduce that friction by creating common language and processes across the leading platforms.

Assess your internal mobility

The biggest opportunity for you when you start your open talent journey is to tap into your current team to help you solve problems and do the tasks you need. There is always a combination of cognitive surplus and people inside your organization looking for mobility with upskilling and project work. NASA has found that one of its most important open talent tools is its NASA@Work internal talent platform. Every company can offer more mobility opportunities for current staff, allowing them to take control of their careers. We'll explain the use of internal marketplaces for talent in more detail in chapter 7. But until then, start talking to people inside your organization. Are they really doing what they love? What skills do they want to develop? Are they willing to help out on a project in another division?

5. Assess your open talent operating model

You'll want to develop an open talent playbook. It can start small and evolve, but the framework should be there from the get-go. Strive for clarity on the role you envision for open talent, who will make the decisions about platforms and freelancer engagements, and how you will handle the technology and data implications. Over time, the COE will have the policies and institutional knowledge to provide this information quickly and help evaluate how a potential platform might solve a problem.

Gauge how closely your company's capacity for innovation, its internal talent mobility, and any current relationship with external open talent align with your business's overall strategic goals. Then make sure you shift your attack to address any misalignment. Where do you score on the critical dashboards of mobility, engagement, and onboarding across full-time, full-time equivalent, and contract workers? Where do you need to shift the dial? Look to complement rather than replace your internal talent, but be attentive to how open talent is disrupting your internal people.

Consider a formal methodology for determining whether problems are amenable to open talent solutions. Which skills are the hardest for you to find? Which ones turn over the fastest or give you the biggest headache when you look toward tomorrow's demand profile? Alternatively, what problems are you struggling to solve, and do you have the resources to crack them? Can a problem be defined and abstracted for an external solver and the data and tools made available to them, or is it too sensitive to be shared outside the organization? Does your in-house expert have the budget to conduct the challenge and implement the solutions or apply the knowledge gained? The best problems to tackle initially are generally low-hanging fruit and can go a long way toward establishing the right mindset for success with open talent.

. . .

Once you've made a clear assessment that your enterprise is ready to become a networked organization, you can begin learning about and experimenting with how to get there.

The Learn and Experiment Phases

While learning and experimentation seem like two different activities, you'll want to put them together to create a flywheel that will help you build timely momentum. The Wright brothers knew this. They are known for being first in flight, but they also accomplished another feat that improved the learning curve for everyone else: creating an early free-exchange network of knowledge.

Wilbur and Orville Wright were bicycle mechanics when they began learning and experimenting with the concept of mechanical flight in 1899. While they worked in obscurity, the Smithsonian's Samuel Langley's quest to conquer the skies, which was underwritten by the US War Department, was covered by an avid press. It turned out to be the classic story of David versus Goliath. Though Langley had unlimited resources, his rivals—who he didn't even know he was in a race with—won the day.

What gave the Wright brothers their edge was their recognition that flying machines would have to be flown by humans—that the problems of flight could not be solved on the ground, from behind a desk. Their success also came from their endurance and dogged determination, as they launched more than a thousand flights with their gliders from atop Big Kill Devil Hill in North Carolina. In Wilbur's words, "It is possible to fly without motors, but not without knowledge and skill."[3] Before they attempted powered flight, the Wright brothers had made themselves masters of the air. Finally, after four years of study and thousands of controlled experiments, on December 17, 1903, the brothers took turns behind the controls getting airborne on four separate flights, the last of which covered an impressive 852 feet in fifty-nine seconds.

Within the decade, the brothers shared with everyone exactly how they did it. In 1910, the *Bibliography of Aeronautics* listed thirteen thousand pieces of published work by the Wright brothers. In a time and age when information and knowledge flow was limited, the Wrights thought it prudent to share their knowledge publicly, even without the prospect of monetary gains. Back then as it is today, people who loved experiments also loved the challenge of solving tough problems. To overcome the barriers to knowledge sharing, they built networks through print journals, clubs, and letters. Through such networks, people learned together.

Langley's efforts excepted, most aerial science and technology research received scant institutional support, as the financing prospects were so uncertain. Patents were considered more like publications than IP. Australian scientist Lawrence Hargrave, who spent years perfecting designs for aero foils, box kites, and rotary engines, opted to forgo patents altogether and contribute his designs to the public, knowing that the open network could advance his work more than he could. Elon Musk made a similar decision on July 12, 2014, when he decided to make all his battery patents open source: "We believe that Tesla, other companies making electric cars, and the world would all benefit from a common, rapidly evolving technology platform."[4]

In his important books *Free Innovation* and *Democratizing Innovation*, Eric von Hippel has made a similar case for the benefits of a "free innovation paradigm" in which innovators are self-rewarded for their efforts. The drawback, however, is that intrinsically motivated inventors are less inspired to scale or diffuse their ideas to economies of scale. While open-source innovation has encouraged a huge amount of valuable learning and experimentation in the software industry, IP is still a critical area of protection for most organizations. If those organizations want to truly innovate their talent practices, however, they must rethink their stance on IP and its protection.

To get the most out of open talent platforms, you'll need to learn what categories of platforms cater to various capabilities you might seek. For example, Torc, Turing AI, and Braintrust focus on finding freelance tech talent. Topcoder and Kaggle specialize in software and algorithm development. Wazoku and HeroX launch ideation exercises. Gloat and Eightfold AI provide software as a service (SAAS) for internal markets. As a result of their research, Jin and associate director Steven Randazzo at LISH built a platform aggregator funded by Schmidt Futures and hosted on the Harvard website. The aggregator is the first of its kind to explain the sorts of problems that people can solve using budget parameters and to access multiple talent platforms simultaneously. (You can find the aggregator on the Innovation Science Guide web page, at https://innovationscienceguide.org.) From that academic endeavor, Open Assembly is now building the same type of technology at scale to API in platforms; this aggregator technology allows for direct access into platforms.

Let's now look at some of the lessons that companies have learned to get us all to this point in the platform revolution. Established platforms like Uber, Airbnb, Etsy, and Upwork redefine who can be producers and how they can interact with consumers while bringing structure and formality to previously less organized nonglobal work.

Today, a baker in Paris can have a global customer base. At the same time, the increase in speed and reduction in complexity by the internet has drastically reduced the cost of collaboration in every industry. For these reasons, people can set up their own networks of collaboration and become micro-entrepreneurs.

Platforms and ecosystems depend on individual users' abilities to create, contribute to, and extend networks. Social platforms link people to their interests. Networked organizations must similarly tap into talent markets by aligning their company interests with potential workers' passions. As we covered in an earlier chapter, one of the best ways to feed your employees' passions is by giving them opportunities to upskill. In most companies, the learning-and-working cycle currently places working and learning too far apart. The traditional paradigm is for companies to give employees feedback at their annual reviews and to leave it up to the person to find ways to improve themselves. The average freelancer in a skilled profession spends 15 percent of their time learning, and many spend a lot more. For example, one coder based in Eastern Europe makes close to $1 million per year competing in software engineering and data science contests. While this amount seems fantastical, it's much like a high schooler who plays pickup basketball and who is inspired by NBA stars making millions in his first year playing on a college team. Surprisingly, this coder spends 40 percent of his time on the platform for the sole purpose of learning.

As we mentioned in the assessment phase, your employees are probably already out there trying to upskill and reskill to adjust to new digital jobs. It's the organization that needs to assess how it will work with this new reality. Not only does the company need to develop a learning culture internally, but it will also have to see what types of external workers can potentially contribute to projects as well.

We've come up with three steps that your company's COE can take to expedite and increase its acquired knowledge. Each of these steps will be explored in more detail in the coming chapters.

1. Learn about platforms

Learning any new system can be hard, and it's often emotional too. We've frequently heard how confusing the world of platforms is. A while back, we spoke with a Nike executive who said that he had tried an open platform that promised solutions, but he never discovered how it worked. Out of frustration, he quit and moved on to another project. He prefers to do rather than learn.

When it comes to using open talent, however, you cannot skip the learning phase. You need to decide for yourself whether learning about platforms is worth it to you and your business. For example, when someone purchases a desk from IKEA, they decide whether the time investment in learning how to assemble the piece correctly is worth the enjoyment of the product later. Michael Norton, Daniel Mochon, and Dan Ariely examined people working through Lego building projects, origami, and IKEA purchases and classified this emotional entanglement with labor as the "IKEA effect."[5] For many people, the time and effort invested in a product or process give it more value.

Of course, a segment of the market does not enjoy these tasks at all. That's why IKEA bought TaskRabbit: a platform that allows owners to hire a local handy worker to assemble their purchases. Rather than change the model so that in-house employees build the furniture, IKEA offers their customers assembly contracts with people it has coached and vetted.

Similarly, platforms are full of people who want to do the tasks for which you lack either the desire or the time. At LISH, we work with companies to see what's bothering them and help them partner with platforms that can take away those worries. Here's what they usually tell us:

- I don't have the time to do this.

- I don't have enough budget to pull this off.

- I can't find the right expert for this.

- I need to know that what I have is good enough.

Even if you don't want to invest the time and energy to learn about platforms, it will be worth it. Ultimately, finding workers through platforms will save you from doing many tasks you'd rather not do.

2. Learn how others have managed external, internal, and open innovation talent

As we discussed earlier, the creation of a COE is the best way to start organizing open talent activities. With our experience of building NASA's CoECI and V&S's platform, we know that any integration with the larger workforce ecosystem starts with building a COE. There's no other way to assess where you are now; what you need to learn; and how to experiment, build an open talent system, and then scale the system using examples from leading organizations like NASA and Deloitte.

We made a good-faith effort to get the lay of the open talent landscape. First we developed a guide to cover white papers, videos, and case studies at LISH (see our Innovative Science Guide at https://innovationscienceguide.org). Then we mapped out the entire ecosystem in detail to see how large organizations manage outside talent. Through this research, we've found over a thousand external platforms for open talent, covering every industry. These can be broken down into external platforms, idea management through open innovation, and internal platforms:

- **External talent clouds (ETCs):** External platforms (such as Upwork, Freelancer.com, Toptal, Altruistic, Fiverr, and 99designs) provide companies with everything from temporary bookkeepers to highly skilled data scientists and software engineers, and they provide workers with feedback, training, and educational opportunities, and exposure to new challenges that ensure their further development. Think of these ETC platforms as a more efficient way to hire talent for a role to be filled. Our research shows that hiring talent from an ETC platform is more efficient and more cost-effective than using a contingent workforce solution. They cover a wide variety of domains, from the low end (driving, customer service) to the high (data science, strategy development, AI).

- **Open innovation and crowdsourcing:** Many of these are external platforms (such as Wazoku, Topcoder, and Kaggle) that connect businesses to global networks of subject matter experts, bringing crowds together in a competitive format to solve difficult problems. For example, they facilitate contests and other methods of crowdsourcing by developing communities of open talent workers with shared interests and skills and matching them to potential employers. Some are solution generation contests with practical implementation goals. Others are idea management catalysts. Idea management platforms specialize in process improvements, market opportunities, cost savings, technology improvement, and innovation. In some cases, they supply broad thinking that a company can then develop; in others, they deliver a product ready to be licensed. Companies looking for technology partners or licensing technology can find matches through these platforms.

- **Internal talent marketplaces (ITMs):** Organizations on the journey to becoming networked use internal platforms—such as Workday's plug-in and the startups Hitch Works (acquired by ServiceNow) and Gloat—to allow existing employees to work collaboratively, enhancing their ideas and results. These internal platforms give workers more control over what they do within their own organizations and whom they do it for, essentially eliminating silos and enabling dialogues. Hallmarks of good internal platforms are software that automates all aspects of the process, for example, allowing employees to comment and vote on ideas as they develop.

Below we look at a few cases and explore how platforms work in the ETC, in open innovation, and in the ITM.

Learn to digitally transform contingent and outsourced work. The lion's share of the open talent ecosystem is external and freelance. This is the focus of all the larger open talent platforms, such as Upwork, Freelancer.com, Torc, and Toptal. Theses platforms got off the ground slowly, as they needed to develop technologies that allowed them to verify workers' identities in real time, ensure quality, and protect IP security. But the real opportunity for these platforms is to challenge the current outsourcing and contingent-work industries.

Despite the immense potential of open talent platforms, the traditional $100 billion outsourcing industry (including such companies as Wipro and Infosys) has mostly brushed them off as existential threats. This attitude is unfortunate, because open platforms and the outsourcing industry stand to learn a lot from each other (Wipro's acquisition of Topcoder may signal a change).

Traditional outsourcing firms are best at aggregating the supply of workers at the low end of the marketplace—for example, recruiting fifteen hundred English-speaking customer service professionals in India for a new venture—while open talent platforms are best suited to recruiting a couple of dozen data scientists. We provide details on building the ETC arm of the COE in chapter 5.

Learn to tap the power of crowds. Though many people use the terms *open talent* and *crowdsourcing* interchangeably, there are clear differences. While freelancing (which is at the core of open talent) is about hiring people's capabilities on a project basis, crowdsourcing is about buying outcomes. In the early Web 2.0 days, it was hard to verify temp workers' identities, ensure quality, and protect IP securely. Crowdsourcing was a clever way around that, as you can limit how much information you expose to contest participants. Furthermore, participants grant IP to the platform, which assigns it to the company in turn. It's still an effective tool to get around IP issues.

In 2017, NASA and HeroX, the platform that was developed for XPrize competitions (XPrize is a nonprofit that designs public competitions for technological development to benefit humanity), launched the Space Poop Challenge. The challenge was to develop a hands-free system that could collect human waste from space-suited astronauts and hold it away from their bodies for 144 hours. The state of the art at the time was a diaper that lasted about a day. NASA needed a solution that was a level 4 on the ready-for-flight scale, which meant that winning solutions could be tested in a year and be ready for use in three years. Out of over twenty thousand participants, the winners came up with novel ideas for drainage systems. The top winner, Thatcher Cardon, an air force surgeon, said, "[I] spent some time lying down, eyes closed, just visualizing different solutions and modelling them mentally. Over time, the winning system of ideas coalesced. Then, I packed up the family, and we drove around Del Rio, Texas, to dollar stores, thrift stores, craft stores, clothing and hardware stores to get materials for mock-ups."[6]

Another crowd contest has reached iconic status in the open talent industry. A few years ago, a large US-based snack food company learned that customers preferred potato chips that were less oily than its own product. But after a couple of years of trying to find a solution, the company hit a roadblock. Historically, it had vibrated the racks as the chips came out of the oil and into the dryer. But if the equipment shook them any harder than it did, an unacceptable number of the chips would break.

The company decided to put the challenge out on a platform. To ensure as wide a scope of expertise as possible, the platform suggested that the company reframe the question from "How do you remove excess oil from potato chips?" to "How do you remove a viscous fluid from a thin, delicate wafer?" Now it wasn't just a problem for food scientists and food production engineers. It was a problem for anyone who knew about physics (people working with silicon wafers, for example) or who, like experimental biologists, routinely dealt with the removal of viscous fluids in their work. Simply by changing a few words, the platform ensured that the company was harnessing as many people and perspectives as possible.

Within a couple of weeks, it got a solution that worked, and the idea came from as unlikely a source as you could imagine. A violinist saw the problem and connected it with sympathetic vibration. She knew that if she played certain notes, they would cause some substances, like glass, to vibrate. She proposed that the company broadcast a sound at a frequency that would create a harmonic in the oil, causing it to fly off the chips. The mechanical engineers who designed the machines that shook the racks knew that vibration was the answer, but they hadn't thought of nonmechanical ways to produce it, because that was outside of their specific experience. We will go into detail on building the mechanics of contests in chapter 6.

Learn about ITMs. Internal platforms allow people in your organization to be mobilized as crowds in some circumstances, but more generally they create vital marketplaces of people and ideas. Usually, there is a tremendous amount of cognitive surplus in organizations; internal platforms harvest it and put it to use. ITMs can start very simply. Sanjay Sharma, the chief technology officer of SEI, created such a marketplace when he published an Excel spreadsheet with a list of problems. Within the first six months, the responses it garnered gave rise to seventy-five fully deployed projects. Since then, Sharma has scaled the company's ITM even to the point where SEI's clients can use the platform to get work done directly.

SEI didn't need advanced matching technology to launch its simple talent marketplace, and neither do you. Using our "start to start" motto, which encourages leaders to take a small but simple approach, you can get going while thinking about which platforms might offer the best software capabilities to organize as you scale.

Once you get started, you'll want to engage SAAS models. Jeroen Wels, Unilever's head of talent, is using Gloat's AI-powered technology to run the multinational's FLEX (short for flexible) program. Users from across Unilever's sixty-five offices in sixty-three countries post purpose statements and share their skills online, allowing any manager or team to "shop for skills." A full 95 percent of Unilever employees have endorsed the system; thirty thousand are using it. In its first few years, it unlocked more than sixty thousand hours of productive work that people wanted to do, breaking down silos and hierarchies and unleashing creativity, productivity, and growth.

The NASA@Work platform is another perfect example of a more sophisticated internal platform. In this online community, NASA employees can connect with internal experts to find quick solutions to complex problems, collaborate directly with colleagues, search for high-quality data, and find people for projects that require particular knowledge sets. For example, in a NASA@Work project from a few years ago, a scientist needed to measure the amount of water in urine to ensure that astronauts were not becoming too dehydrated. But he found that existing processes took far too long. A notice went up on NASA@Work, and the network responded by creating a machine that could measure the water in male astronauts' urine much faster.

A few weeks later, another request was posted to NASA@Work: "We need a better way to measure water in urine for astronauts." During space flight, NASA needs biomarkers and ways to track health, so they collect urine. Because the existing method created lots of waste and lacked any capability for real-time analysis, NASA stored the urine until the astronauts returned to earth. What's more, the procedure was time-consuming for the crew. The organization was looking both for real-time in-flight measurements and for the ability to store the urine. Using suggestions from the internal experts, NASA found $1.3 million in savings and reduced the time to develop by three to five years.

The same NASA scientists collaborated with in-house experts in a variety of fields to develop yet another solution for the urine storage and analysis problem. An added benefit was that the scientific thinking that informed it was posted on NASA@Work for anyone else to use. The network facilitated not only brainstorming but also the diffusion of useful knowledge.

NASA@Work is run by IdeaScale software but managed by NASA's CoECI. The effort started with a platform built by Wazoku and then switched to IdeaScale once it got its feet wet and wanted different features in light of the community's requests. There are many SAAS models out there, but the key is to have a process for engagement. We offer details on operational elements of a scaled ITM in chapter 7.

3. Experiment

Next, it's time to put your new insight into practice through small pilots. In this early stage, organizations can largely rely on the platforms for security, IP protection, and administrative challenges. Your overarching goals are to form a plan for moving forward and then to share the plan and create alignment with stakeholders. Next you finalize the identification of each problem and select the appropriate platform to solve each one, using the open systems and tools. Finally, you will capture and measure your results and communicate them widely to get stakeholders' buy-in to continue. When sharing results with senior management, you need to make sure that they understand that learning metrics rather than mature business metrics are the appropriate measures of success.

Dyan Finkhousen, the founder and director of GE's global innovation accelerator GeniusLink, has worked with enterprise clients that are navigating the adoption of open talent. "It's important to have innovation budgets that are retained and controlled by the operating units that own the customers," she notes. "But if you are a large conglomerate, it's also important to retain an innovation budget at corporate for the longer-term, riskier, more disruptive investments. You lay down a portfolio of bets, and some will come back with modest returns, others with no returns or, if you get it right, large returns. That to me is a healthy structure for a budget."[7]

Although you should make sure that business units have a budget for innovation, Finkhousen says, you should also include a budget for longer-term or more disruptive innovation that could provide more widespread benefits. Moreover, your evaluation criteria should be clear and your deployment strategies thought out in advance. Just as critically, there should be a clear plan for failure. Many projects will end up on the cutting room floor, and the reason is seldom poor work. They are experiments and perhaps cannot be reframed as problems for nonexperts. (See the sidebar "Focusing on Pain Points Rather Than Solutions.")

COEs and other owners of specific problems can use a variety of communications strategies to get buy-in. Our research suggests that you especially need to target the following four groups:

- The expert community that will solve the problem and that you will want to motivate to work with the program

- The leadership group that will be interested in the impact that the solution will have on the company's performance

- Stakeholders, who will be interested in how the approach will solve their specific problems

- A general audience who will create buzz and awareness of the mission

Once the problem owner and the COE identify these four key groups, the communication campaign should promote the launch, the work itself, and the results. It's also a good idea to hold webinars with the groups that will be the most affected by any changes.

Even with the best communications, some resistance is inevitable. To help contain negative spillover, you'll want to acknowledge within the organization that open talent solutions do threaten existing structures to some extent. But as noted earlier, organizations should educate internal employees about the many ways open talent works as a complementary approach—not a replacement for all that exists today. Even so, sometimes

FOCUSING ON PAIN POINTS RATHER THAN SOLUTIONS

A simple exercise Jin conducts in workshops in organizations is asking people to identify pain points. His one rule is that they are not allowed to propose solutions at the same time. Most people—especially the decision-makers, who tend to have firm convictions—struggle with this rule. During a session with an energy company, we watched as one of the participants literally rocked back and forth in his chair as he struggled to not give answers.

People's biases are so strong that they affect the way they formulate problems and hence limit their scope of solutions. For example, if you see a child bleeding, your first thought might be, "The child needs a bandage." The bandage is a possible solution, but the pain point is the bleeding. There are in fact many other ways to stanch a bleed. Subsequent questions might be, "Does the need to quickly stop the bleeding outweigh the need to stop it in a sterile way? Would stitches or medical glue work better than a bandage? What can we do to avoid a scar?" Or perhaps most important of all is the question that comes after the immediate problem is resolved: "What can we do to prevent the accident that caused the bleed from happening again?"

Another example is one that carpenters love. When contemplating a project, they might say, "I need a half-inch drill bit," and everyone agrees. But that's a solution. The pain point is "I need a hole that's a half-inch round."

(continued)

Pain points can easily fall into one of the following buckets or a combination of them:

- **Economics.** Are we spending too much money on our current provider or product; can we reduce our spending or lower our costs?

- **Effectiveness.** Using what we have, can we get everything done that we need to? Are we doing the right things? Are we productive?

- **Efficiency.** Are we doing things in the best way? Are we identifying bottlenecks and redundancies? Do we have the right processes?

- **Innovation.** Do we need something completely different?

- **Support.** Are we receiving the right support at critical stages?

We have developed this pain-point mindset at LISH to continually refine problems and to avoid jumping to conclusions as soon as we think we see a plausible solution.

it's less alarming to your people if experiments are carried out in a separate Skunk Works operating outside the corporate membrane.

A final note: Open talent can yield impressive results. That's why managers need to be especially careful to tell the right stories about the right people in their communication campaigns. When your experimenting is complete, be sure to give credit to the inside team.

During the early days of another NASA initiative, its Tournament Lab, a joint collaboration between NASA and Harvard to host a series of open innovation challenges, chief medical officer Jeff Davis and senior strategist Elizabeth Richard thought it would be interesting to share stories about the winners of the competitions. The idea was to inspire people who worked at NASA to try crowdsourcing themselves. But the two leaders quickly realized their mistake: open talent tools can cause long-term employees to feel devalued or disposable. Davis and Richard needed to change their approach. Rather than focusing the story on the outside person or people who had won the competitions, they focused on the skills of the NASA employees who had curated the solutions. Employee attitudes and openness to change improved considerably once Davis and Richard began to shift their focus. The leaders recognized how the internal teams zeroed in on the pain points, broke the problems into understandable chunks, coordinated with the platform to manage the process, evaluated the results, and posed new sets of questions to further refine the results. Davis and Richard still emphasized the good results but, by flipping the focus, also assured employees that their roles in the organization would be elevated and not replaced by this new approach to work. Later research from LISH confirmed that managerial recognition of existing employees' efforts was key to the acceptance of open talent approaches.[8]

As with many innovations, leaders are often tempted to close their open talent projects too early and bring them back inside, before all the good ideas have been captured. When things get difficult, leaders often want to jump ship—it's important to remind them that experimentation is by definition about learning. Sticking with the plan from start to finish will yield more actionable results.

. . .

Whatever else happens in your journey to using open talent solutions, don't skip the learning phase. LISH recently got a call from the innovation department of a large pharmaceutical company. After a new board member had sung the praises of open talent and innovation, the CEO tasked the innovation department in Boston to begin applying open talent solutions. A problem was quickly formulated, and a platform was picked. Six weeks later, after the company had gotten only a couple of subpar submissions, it decided to call us at Open Assembly. With the executive meeting coming up, the company would have to report on the status of the project. The leaders were hoping we could help them salvage their effort. Unfortunately, we had to tell them that the project was beyond saving. Since they hadn't completed the assessment phase, they had no idea of how the organization might use open talent strategically or how it would be culturally accepted. Second, the leaders had used the "ready, fire, aim" approach instead of a learning phase: they had picked a platform without a clear assessment of how and why it was best suited to solve their problem.

Innovators are bullish by nature; they are temperamentally inclined to "move fast and break things," to borrow the cliché. That approach works when only one person is leading the charge or needs convincing but not when there are many stakeholders. LISH researcher and Harvard Business School professor Jacqueline Ng Lane says, "The experts are not the final decision makers. It's really the innovation manager, or the person who's in charge of the project, who's going to say, 'OK, these are the reviews that I got, and these are the ones that I'm going to go forward with.' But they're going to be informed by the experts that they select to evaluate."[9]

No matter how nimble or adaptive, most company cultures need to understand what they are getting into and why. A company's ability to understand these aspects of a project early on demonstrates the importance of the learning and experimental phases. It means the difference between a successful program and a program that ultimately founders. Goals are set and disseminated via dedicated communications, which gain buy-in and support from key players. At the same time, these phases shouldn't take forever. We typically limit it to six to eight weeks.

In part 3, we'll explore in detail how we set up the ETC, open innovation capability, and the ITM, among other things.

KEY IDEAS

This chapter looked at the actions your company can take before building a COE. Assessment, learning, and experimentation are core to mapping out a strategy for the long term. As we've discussed, ambitious attempts at enterprise-level implementation too often fail in the long term because of waning enthusiasm (highlighting a need for robust COEs with dedicated staff to provide continual support over time). The way to mitigate failure is to assess organizational challenges, learn to create a curious and willing culture by seeing what's out there and what's possible, and experiment by using tools and systems readily available through existing talent platforms.

The assessment phase. By deploying our six-step assessment model, companies now have the power to evaluate their risk tolerance level and uncover areas in which open talent can enable them to maximize operational efficiencies. We recommend the following six steps, which can be done in any order: (1) assessing your collaboration ecosystem, (2) creating an open talent vision, (3) assessing your talent innovation by reviewing your onboarding processes, (4) defining your appetite for risk, (5) assessing your internal mobility, and (6) assessing your operating model for open talent.

The learn and experiment phases. We recommend learning about what's happening out in the world and tapping into a rich ecosystem of companies, talent platforms, and users. Companies can turbocharge their learning by following the steps associated with finding out what platforms do and how they can help, seeing how other pioneers have managed their COEs, and looking closely at changes in ETCs, open innovation capabilities, and ITMs. Once you begin to learn, then small experiments help map out the next steps to building a proper COE.

PART THREE

Developing Operations and Leadership for Open Talent

Chapter 5

Build an External Talent Cloud

As described in the introduction, Ryan Hicke's problem at SEI was not that he didn't know about using freelancers. Most companies have some way to find and hire freelancers. In fact, with today's rapid digital transformation, more and more businesses are coming to platforms to hire in bulk. The problem was that most companies that hired freelancers were doing it in secret. The use of outside talent is the secret sauce we alluded to in earlier chapters. Someone at a company we worked with used platforms like Freelancer.com or Upwork to advance their careers, and they saw no need to share this insight in the pre-pandemic world.

Today, because of the tremendous pressure to move more fixed costs to variable costs, it's neither prudent nor possible to keep your use of external talent to yourself. Instead, you will need to build an external talent cloud (ETC), which allows your organization to develop a full, scalable strategy to deploy hundreds of freelance workers into your firm routinely.

ETCs are the fastest and the most economical way for companies to resolve their talent crisis, even at the high end of the market. Other benefits include increased productivity of talent and speed to solutions, decreased cost of talent, and the ability to move more fixed costs to variable costs to allow for flexibility when disruptions occur. To set up an ETC, your center of excellence (COE) should assess your internal needs, learn about the platform ecosystem, and start experimenting through pilots by launching fifty to one hundred freelancing projects on established platforms and building enterprise relationships with others who are using these platforms.

This chapter begins part 3, which discusses how to weave the efficiency of open talent solutions into everything your company does to keep the business up and running day-to-day. In this chapter, we will cover the first of the three building phases needed to transform your company into a networked organization. We will look at the other two phases in subsequent chapters.

The build phase is where the juiciest, most fulfilling learning takes place. It is also where the most exciting results can occur as companies construct the infrastructure and systems they will need to host new programs and expand on existing ones. Let's begin with some definitions and then move into how ETCs work, how to choose the kinds of platforms you'll work with, and finally, how to build your own cloud.

External Talent Clouds for Strategic Advantages, Cost Savings, and Flexibility

At its most basic level, an ETC is simply the pool of people who can be accessed for temporary employment. In the analog era, companies turned to agencies when they needed temps for routine jobs and to consultancies when they required highly skilled ones. Now there are digital platforms that match the supply of talent to demand instantly, precisely, and in an orderly, transparent way, providing job ratings, trust scales, skills certifications, and more.

We use the term ETC to give an organizational lens to freelancing in the digital economy. Freelancing is a quickly expanding way of working with talent who choose to work on several projects from several organizations via platforms. Every organization faces skills gaps at one time or another. They can be transitory, because of seasonal demand or a big crunch after an acquisition or a successful product launch, or endemic, like the global tech talent shortage we face today. Although companies will still compete for the best permanent talent, the typical workforce of the future will be a blend of permanent employees and freelancers, and many of these freelancers will be highly skilled and well paid.

Our research shows that, using platforms, it typically takes four days to hire a freelancer to do the work you need instead of the average two-plus months to find the right talent in this talent-constrained environment through traditional methods. We also find that the freelance talent you hire on a platform is typically 30 percent less expensive and 40 percent more productive than the internal employee performing the same tasks. You see this massive gain in productivity because you're hiring freelancers to do a task, not to play a role in the company. You are paying them to do the work you want, not to spend time at corporate meetings, office gatherings, and the like.

Companies' relationships with their ETCs can run in two directions, using them either as a strategic advantage or as a cost savings and flexibility measure. IBM, for example, looked at the growth of the open talent economy and saw an opportunity to create network effects that would boost both the demand for the IBM Cloud, one of its flagship products, and the supply of people who know how to use it. To do that, the company began promoting the IBM Cloud and its certification program through Freelancer.com, a platform with more than fifty-six million registered users across 247 countries, supplying about 80 percent of the *Fortune* 500 with workers.[1] For example, a job on the platform that tasked people to create an infographic for the IBM Center for Cloud Training attracted more than a thousand participants. While the job posting was live, IBM saw a 65 percent increase in web traffic on the center's landing page. Five months later, the number of freelancers with certified IBM Cloud skills had risen by 15 percent, with a 28 percent increase in IBM Cloud projects being posted.[2]

Freelancer.com's AI-driven technology matches the right talent with the right tasks, allowing companies to find and hire 40 percent faster than they can through traditional temp agencies—sometimes as fast as in two hours. And as we have seen, Freelancer.com is just one of the hundreds of talent platforms that companies could use. But how did platform-based solutions first grow and expand?

The story begin in 2009, when low barriers to entry and rapidly evolving technologies made the competition in the online, on-demand labor space quite fierce indeed. Around that time, an entrepreneur named Matt Barrie began a site called BidItOut. To build scale, he contacted all his competitors that didn't have institutional or venture capital backing and asked them if they were willing to sell. One of the first he called was GetAFreelancer, owned by Magnus Tibell, a Swede living in the island nation of Vanuatu. GetAFreelancer was the world's five-thousandth biggest website at the time, with half a million users and about $1 million in annual revenue. To Barrie's surprise, Tibell quoted a price much lower than the $4 million Barrie had estimated he would have needed to raise to build his business up to that level from scratch. Barrie immediately agreed to the deal with the contingency that if he could not pay in full within forty-five days, he would help Tibell sell the site to another buyer for twice as much. After obtaining backing from Simon Clausen, a friend who had received a substantial payout after selling his startup PC Tools to Symantec, Barrie made the acquisition, and the combined companies became Freelancer.com.

As CEO, Barrie built data analytics into every facet of Freelancer.com's site to provide insights into what changes improved site traffic and user registrations. Every new user profile or project page raised the site's page rank in search engines, driving new users to it. By the end of 2009, the company had registered over a million new users. Freelancer.com also acquired several other highly ranked online freelancing platforms, including EUFreelance, LimeExchange, Scriptlance, and Rent-A-Coder (vWorker). To reduce churn, Freelancer.com transported users from the acquired sites over to its own platform quickly and seamlessly. As Barrie described it, "I did it within 24 hours so that before [users on] the old website knew what was going on, they had a new account on the new website, and everything was there. This would minimize angst about the acquisition and churn. Their projects, their money, their reputation, their feedback, their messaging, et cetera. It was all there."[3]

The growth of enterprise users on these marketplace platforms for short-term talent has driven companies like Freelancer.com to adopt a comprehensive enterprise strategy. As we've seen, talent cloud platforms provide a range of services that allow companies to access the best available skills.

Note that very large enterprises can work with freelance platforms at the enterprise level to access the skills they need. Arrow Electronics offers a case in point. With $30 billion in annual sales, the company guides innovation for more than two hundred thousand technology manufacturers and service providers. In 2019 Arrow and Freelancer .com partnered to launch ArrowPlus, a platform that allows access to half a million skilled electronic and electrical engineers to find solutions for technology needs across industries, including consumer electronics, transportation, health care, manufacturing, the internet of things, telecommunications, biomedical, cloud security, firmware, and hardware.

How Does an External Talent Cloud Work?

Most of the companies that we work with us tell us they are most interested in digitizing their permanent workforces. But given the severity of the tech talent crisis, most jump into building an ETC first without fully understanding how things work. One single platform cannot provide you with all the talent you need. You have probably already reached this conclusion through the learning and experimenting you did in chapter 4. This phase of building an ETC requires deeper trust between the organization and its platform partners—a trust acquired by knowing which platforms can provide the right talent for your needs. As with most things in life, you must first form deep and trusting relationships with the people who can help you get through your biggest challenges. Organizations that view platforms as potential partners have the best outcomes.

Once you've established trust with platform partners, the next step is to become an agile, well-networked organization that can take full advantage of the ETC. We recommended a two-pronged approach. First, think back on how you once assessed the roles of your full-time workforce (because this approach will need to change!). Once you have a sense of what these roles were, look again at which staff members have nonmanagerial, task-oriented jobs. You may find that these positions are better suited for freelancer workers. The goal here is to become agile, not to think about eliminating all positions. Be thoughtful about which positions are absolutely critical to make the company's operations run smoothly.

Second, you'll want to change how your organization thinks more broadly about tasks and repeatable tasks. The ETC will be great at completing tasks but not if you cannot clearly define what they need to be. Let's take accounting for example. A group of freelancers from a platform like Amazon's MTurk can help digitize receipts, another group from a different platform can populate spreadsheets, and freelancers responding to Upwork can provide financial analysis. However, they won't be able to access your systems unless you allow them to. If your organization had problems with granting this access to freelancers, then create a subset of tasks to work around this challenge. The key is to have tasks that are replicable and fast. You need to get away from thinking about one-offs and plan strategically about how to minimize training and simplify processes for new workers.

Choosing Your Platforms

As noted, enterprise-ready platforms, those that are seamlessly integrated into your workforce platforms through advanced technology like API and AI features for matching, are in development but still rare. Most enterprise-ready platforms are much smaller. The following platforms are a sample of the more than one thousand platforms you can use for your ETC:

- **Altruistic.** With a global crowd of four thousand data science and AI professionals with hundreds of skills, Altruistic collaborates with enterprises to solve real-world problems, providing end-to-end analytics and software development services. The platform specializes in assessing workers through scientific testing, and then matching client needs to talent through the power of AI. Companies can innovate faster by building better cutting-edge technology.

- **Braintrust.** User-owned through tokens and blockchain-driven, Braintrust aims to benefit technology talent and enterprises alike by limiting fees and aligning incentives through tokens. Users are fully vetted and live in more than a hundred countries. Braintrust Academy provides certifications and badges, and community roundtables and workshops offer advice from industry experts (more on Braintrust and Turing later in this chapter).

- **Distributed.** A UK-based platform in the market since 2018, Distributed is an enterprise-focused private talent cloud that has enjoyed triple-digit growth every year since its launch. Its customers include large UK private and public companies such as BT Group, Capita, and the BBC. In the platform's own words, its mission is to enable independent software careers with more benefits than those found in permanent employment.

- **Field Nation.** The platform helps companies build freelance field service teams on demand. Today, with fast-changing technology, most companies struggle to hire, train, and deploy teams quickly. Using Field Nation's variable-cost freelance community, companies can find expert technicians who are already in the field and who can do a variety of tasks to ensure time to market for things like networking, cabling, security, or point-of-sale equipment installation or repair.

- **Freelancer.com.** Founded in 2009, Freelancer.com is headquartered in Sydney. Employers post work on the site, and members place bids in a competitive tender process. On completion, both sides write reviews of the iteration. Freelancer.com charges freelancers a 10 percent fee, which can be reduced with a paid monthly membership. The site also hosts contests as an alternative to bid work.

- **Fiverr.** A two-sided marketplace where people can buy and sell services, Fiverr allows users to post gigs ranging in technical ability, from "produce a well-designed business card" to "help with HTML, JavaScript, CSS, and jQuery." Other services offered include writing, translation, video editing, and programming.

- **Toptal.** Its name derived from "top talent," Toptal claims to be the world's largest fully remote company. It screens its community of software developers, designers, finance experts, and project and product managers so rigorously that only 3 percent of applicants are accepted. Its clients run the gamut of *Fortune* 500 companies, startups, and universities in ninety-plus countries. One of its programs is a partnership with education company General Assembly to develop intern programs that give its students real-world experience and a track record that they can point to once they are certified.

- **Torc.** A talent marketplace for software developers, Torc is geared to meet the heightened procurement, HR, legal, and security demands of enterprises while providing coaching and accelerator programs for talent. Its focus is on measurable skills and productivity stats.

- **Turing AI.** Based in Palo Alto, California, Turing is a data-science-driven jobs platform that allows companies to hire teams of vetted Silicon Valley–caliber software talent across a hundred-plus skills in as little as three to five days. More than one million developers worldwide belong to its community.

- **Upwork.** The product of the merger of Elance and oDesk, the US-based Upwork Global Inc. has a community of thirty-five million freelancers. Clients post descriptions of their jobs and a price range. They may invite specific freelancers to apply or invite anyone to apply. Once they have made their choice, they send the freelancer a contract with rates and a deadline. The Upwork platform includes a real-time chat feature that clients and freelancers can use to message prospects. A time tracker application records the freelancer's keystrokes and mouse movements and takes screenshots, which it shares with the client.

Building an External Talent Cloud

Individuals, startups, and smaller companies generally rely on third-party platforms to find, vet, and secure external talent. Larger and mid-size companies will probably also depend on platforms in the early stages of their open talent experiments, but as they scale their strategies, most will want to build their own ETCs to take firmer control of security and compliance and to save on fees.

But they needn't start from scratch. As we've already seen, both companies and freelancers can use Microsoft's 365 freelance toolkit to manage any work that is already compatible with Microsoft's 365 software. Microsoft developed its tools with Upwork but has now made it generally available. The toolkit includes four major offerings:

- **Communications.** Microsoft allows internal teams to share knowledge about the ETC through SharePoint. This knowledge includes use cases, policies, tips, tricks, pricing, and anything else that requires nuanced know-how that can be shared throughout the organization. This level of communication helps orchestrate the learning culture.

- **Collaboration.** How do you work with both internal employees and freelancers? Microsoft uses the Teams platform to work on a secure network. Teams allows all members to hold discussions, track progress, and share files using intelligent search tools. The network also allows you to add external parties to your organization and remove them when projects are completed. Moreover, by granting guest access to freelancers at no cost to them, you are letting them work for you without burdening them with having to pay for necessary tools. This capability is a big cultural shift in making work more inclusive for external talent.

- **Success measurement.** Microsoft leverages Power BI, which captures analytics for work performed. Dashboard features allow real-time visualization of a freelancer's key performance indicators, while the underlying analytics help the internal teams know how they are performing.

- **Repeat-task management.** Everyone wants a seamless way to repurpose or rerun tasks, and Microsoft does this through Power Automate. Rather than using a clunky manual, the toolkit provides workflows for automation and bases them on budget, compliance, and monitoring preferences. It uses if-then, or Boolean, logic to capture the essence of a repeatable project. Features include sending notices, synchronizing files, collecting data, and creating ad hoc reports with the help of an AI copilot.

Despite its fraught corporate history with contract workers, Microsoft uses a lot of freelance talent itself. Liane Scult heads up Microsoft's equivalent of a COE, which is developing open talent strategies throughout the company. "Like most transformations," she admits, "this [is] disruptive."[4] She speaks daily with managers, helping them identify tasks that could be performed by freelancers. The biggest difficulty, she says, is getting managers to take that first step into something they've never tried before. She draws a useful analogy when she says, "It's just like when people take their first ride-share or sleep in their first VRBO."

Here are the top three questions she asks managers when she is trying to determine whether integrating open talent into their projects would be a good fit:

- At the end of the month, are there still unfinished items on your to-do list?

- Could you make better decisions if you had more research?

- Are you having trouble catching up? Are you missing deadlines or working nights and weekends to complete something? What are those projects?

Running an ETC workshop

Our research has shown that the best place to start is where there is the greatest pain. Your COE should run workshops for key functional owners, including HR, talent acquisition, legal, procurement, IT, security, compliance, and client delivery. The workshops should focus on three tasks: objectives, strategy, and goals for changing operational models.

The first task is to agree on your objectives; be very specific about what an ETC can deliver and why. A keen understanding of your objectives will allow you to benchmark your success or failure later on.

The second task is to look at strategy, as defined by the following:

- The exact problem external talent is solving

- The business case or other success metrics

- Priority areas to focus a pilot project on

- The range of ETC solution options

- The likely ETC solution model for a pilot

- The range of ETC platforms to partner with

- The type of talent, role, or skills required

- The location of the activity and any worker compliance constraints

- Systems access required

- Security constraints and solutions to consider

- Communications and change management

Regarding the security aspect of your open talent strategy, see the sidebar "Making Sure Things Are Secure: Using a Virtual Desktop Infrastructure."

The third and final task of the workshop focuses on goals you have for changing your operating model to an open talent approach and how that aligns with your organizational values. This task centers on taskification—as described earlier, the shifting of your mindset from positions and roles to tasks. Specifying tasks is one of the most critical things to do as you create your ETC, so you should be as specific as possible. For example, will your freelancers need to write a certain amount of code? How much? What are your productivity expectations, and how do they differ from those for internal employees?

A simple example of the importance of task-based thinking comes from one of our clients, which was looking to reduce the workload of its IT service desk. Historically, the company had hired expensive specialists on a full-time basis. Through taskification, it was able to categorize incidents into narrow categories (training needs, hardware problems, backup failures, etc.) and bring in additional people with appropriate skill sets to manage the problems on an as-needed basis. Even if you rely on a platform to acquire and vet your outside talent, you will need to make exceptions or changes in your standard contracts, background checking procedures, insurance and indemnities, and quality control and risk management methodologies, especially when it comes to confidentiality and IP protection.

Once you have alignment on your objectives, strategy, and goals for changing your operational models, it's time to assess the platforms you are thinking of working with to ensure they are capable of meeting all your requirements. These requirements might range from security and compliance capabilities to the kinds of sectors it focuses on.

Every platform is a little bit different. Compare how each works and what the process feels like. Reach out to the platforms you are interested in working with, and ask them questions. Make sure they understand your industry category and your goals.

We've found that it is best to build a business case not only for the overall open talent effort but also for each of the platforms that will be involved in the pilot. For example, NASA chose platforms that could generate software engineering and creative and design elements for marketing. It needed the engineering capabilities because much of what the space agency developed required technology builds, and NASA sought out the creative and design talent because many of the agency's smaller teams couldn't assess creatives for marketing needs.

The platforms must have the freedom to work the way they work best. But your COE must also be able to create the right business case with the right metrics to ensure that your organization understands the results that your program can produce.

Here are some of the suggested key performance indicators we look at when helping companies choose platforms:

MAKING SURE THINGS ARE SECURE: USING A VIRTUAL DESKTOP INFRASTRUCTURE

There are three ways to work with freelancers. One of them doesn't require any systems access at all. It's really easy. You assign a freelancer a task, and they complete it. They don't need access to your systems or IP. Let's say you want them to turn your document into a PowerPoint presentation. All you have to do is look at their portfolio to see if they're good, describe what you need, and see what they deliver. A full 80 percent of the enterprise gig economy is done in this way.

The second scenario requires the freelancer to access your systems. Providing external access to internal systems is quite risky. If you're an insider at Wipro, Accenture, UST, or Capgemini, giving a freelancer access to your systems and data is something that you're not going to do lightly. The freelancer could do something that would be very detrimental to your core systems or client relationships. Therefore, companies have

- **Time to hire.** The time can be as short as hours; it should never be more than a few days.

- **Cost to hire.** Typically, using an agency to hire a full-time employee costs 20 percent of their salary and the time it costs to recruit them. On average, using an ETC platform reduces this cost to about 10 percent of the freelancer's pay.

- **Cost.** Our research shows that a typical full-time tech employee costs 30 percent more than a similarly skilled freelancer.

strict rules in place about outside talent. Sometimes these rules forbid the use of freelancers, but more typically, companies require strict background checks to ensure that freelancers are who they say they are. You might want to send freelancers a laptop that is firewalled to prevent them from looking at more than you want them to. But today, as most work goes remote, there needs to be a more straightforward, cheaper solution.

Enter the VDI, or virtual desktop infrastructure. It's akin to having a laptop in the cloud. The infrastructure is completely configurable. If the freelancer is using a VDI, they log in using a web interface and they see only what they need to. The applications they use are completely controlled and restricted by the enterprise. Not only is this restriction in place, but the work is also recorded and auditable.

Although VDI systems are not new, they have been cumbersome and difficult to use. Newer systems, like UST's CloudDesk or Simple Cloud, are much simpler. They can even be configured so that different freelancers on a team see different things, depending on their need to know.

- **Productivity.** Our research has shown that an average employee works on the project they've been hired to work on five hours a day, while a freelancer works for eight hours. This difference means a 40 percent increase in productivity.

Be sure to create standards to ensure that the data your pilot projects produce is scalable and sharable throughout the organization. Before you begin to build in earnest, stop and make a map. Figures 5-1 and 5-2 show ways to map out your pilot project with platforms.

FIGURE 5-1

A linear method for mapping out two separate pilots for a project in open talent

Parameter and steps to address it	Pilot 1	Pilot 2
Requirements: Detailing specific activities or roles that will prove that the skills can be accessed at scale to meet the project's criteria		
Contracts: Identifying the constraints in any contracts between the company and each client, and enabling suitable solutions		
Screening: Understanding which roles or tasks require specific screening, and implementing an open talent solution for this screening		
Access: Understanding the requirements for systems access and the constraints and supporting solutions		
Process: Outlining the major process changes associated with open talent, for example, interviewing and CV review		
Coordination: Establishing rules for managing open resources in each pilot project		
Quality: Agreeing on quality and risk management measures for each pilot project		

Source: Open Assembly.

Your COE needs to lead a coherent assessment of all these processes and then map them into your strategy. This process should involve everyone who has traditionally been involved with the hiring of external talent, especially the procurement leadership that works with contingent-talent vendors for traditional outsourcing. Pay special attention to typical areas of friction, such as demand forecasting and talent reporting, onboarding, IT security (will you need to send out laptops?), billing, and cost-center alignment.

You will also need to think about your organization going forward, which may require you to formalize and extend the responsibilities of the COE, and governance. Both figures 5-1 and 5-2 represent an example of a step-by-step process that you can use when you're running a pilot. In figure 5-2, these steps of value—service catalog, process landscape, organization, operating system, people, and governance—help you use

FIGURE 5-2

A circular method for mapping out the iterative nature of a pilot project in open talent

Value
Align your **drivers, objectives and performance** with stakeholder needs and enterprise goals

Service catalog
Integrate a cohesive set of outcomes to **drive the right stakeholder experience**

Process landscape
Identify critical enabling work practices and establish clear **roles and responsibilities**

Organization
Create the structure to enable people to efficiently conduct operations

Operating system
Enable visibility of performance and **integration of data and technology**

People
Align and enable a **skilled workforce** to achieve enterprise objectives

Governance
Enable ongoing **strategic alignment** and control of performance and risks

Iterative

Iterative

Iterative

Organizational change

Source: Open Assembly.

a pilot to plan for later measurable success that can be shared with the rest of the organization. Once you've begun to actively build your ETC and are collecting data, you can iterate your operating model further.

The assessment model in figure 5-3, which looks at the primary characteristics we've seen in enterprises showing high maturity with regard to open talent, maps out an ideal timeline for this preliminary work. Note in particular the initial four-week sprint to get to a high-level view of the changes required, which gives you a useful go/no-go checkpoint before you embark on detailed design and physical implementation activities. While you are piloting and then building your ETC strategy, the most effective internal communications plan is one that reassures full-time employees that their jobs are safe and that the changes will be for the better. In general, the more transparency the better—especially as you move to scale your open talent and become a fully networked organization.

FIGURE 5-3

Ideal timeline for an assessment model

The recommendations in the road map can help guide implementation.

	High-level design (4 weeks)	Detailed design (12–16 weeks)	Activation planning
Organization change management	Stakeholder assessment; Change readiness assessment	Define change strategy; Assess workforce impact; Agree comms plan; Training strategies; Design comms events	Design training; Communications toolkit creation
Value	Analyze current state information; Draft charter	Define financial model	Define performance management system
Service catalog	Identify services	Document business services; Document IT components	
Process landscape	Define process landscape & priorities	Conduct process integration workshops; Define process roles & responsibilities	Develop process training materials
Organization	Identify required functions & roles	Select logical org model; Define size & value of the organization	Create physical org structure
Operating system	Determine scope, gaps & needs; Outline strategy for technologies	Develop detailed requirements	Plan releases & user migrations
People	Determine skill capability requirements; Perform gap analysis	Document job descriptions	Create development plans
Governance	Define high-level decision matrix	Define reporting structure; Define escalation principles & process	

Source: Open Assembly.

Upwork and the evolving acceptance of open talent

In September 2013, both Elance and oDesk (which would merge to become Upwork later that same year) announced new services for enterprise clients—Private Talent Cloud and Private Workplace, respectively. Elance, the first of its kind—a platform to hire freelance talent—was founded in 1998. While the traditional contingent-work model was well established, most organizations looked at open talent with a skeptical eye. Enterprise buyers saw it as a solution for small startup companies that couldn't afford full-time employees. John experienced that same attitude when he bought *Women's Sports and Fitness* and had to rely on freelance writers and photographers instead of creatives on staff. Although the use of freelancers was a necessity for him, by the time Elance started, the use of freelance writers and photographers in the magazine industry was well established. At the time, only the oldest and the most established magazines eschewed freelance talent.

Back in 2009, oDesk (the other half of what would become Upwork), was founded by Odysseas Tsatalos and Stratis Karamanlakis, who wanted to work together despite their geographic distance (one was in the United States and the other in Greece). Shifting from the original intent to service enterprises as a staffing platform, oDesk built an online marketplace that allowed registered users to search and hire remote workers. That same year, 2009, Freelancer.com got started in Sydney.

While Elance, oDesk, and Freelancer.com found some early success, their growth was hindered because the public didn't yet trust in online services. For example, do you remember the days when it was common thinking that you couldn't order shoes or clothes online? Zappos changed the paradigm by offering free returns, a policy that allowed people to order multiple styles and sizes at once and try things on in the comfort of their own homes.

In talent, issues around security, IP protection, and compliance created headwinds. (See the sidebar "What about Compliance?") For example, in 1989 and 1990, the Internal Revenue Service ruled that

WHAT ABOUT COMPLIANCE?

Historically, open talent has been relatively straightforward when used for simple tasks. But as enterprises engage open talent for more and more tasks, some challenges are arising. Suppose you're a company already effectively outsourcing activities and you are now starting to use open talent that could be on the other side of the world. In that case, you, as a responsible customer, need to be concerned about things like security, compliance, background checking, quality, cost, and all the other things that your organization considers when hiring other internal and external talent.

One of the big areas of compliance is verifying the freelancer who's doing some work for you. Are they who they say they are? Can they work for you as a freelancer? Are they set up to work as a freelancer? Are they working for somebody else at the same time? Is your IP protected? These are all fundamental questions that need to be answered.

Ensuring that the freelancers working for you are paying taxes in the right way is a compliance function typically carried out in an organization's COE, but specialist companies like CXC, MBO Partners, and others can support you with this and other functions. Likewise, as platforms move from servicing consumers and small businesses to larger enterprises, they are beginning to adopt compliance processes.

"It's a really complicated process," Barry Matthews, CEO of Open Assembly, told us. "If you're in the UK, you could be accessing freelancers from anywhere in the world via Upwork or Freelancer.com, or any of the big global platforms. Suppose they don't take responsibility for ensuring that the freelancer is who they say they are. How do you know that you're not giving work to a terrorist or a criminal or someone working for my competitor?"

Put simply, the compliance function of your ETC is essential for the enterprise. Compliance will typically work the same way a bank would when it makes sure it knows its customers and takes other anti-money-laundering measures. Some platforms provide the compliance function themselves, and some don't. You need to find out which platforms do it well and which platforms don't and where else to go for compliance. Likewise, many countries have legislation that prohibits a freelancer from paying less tax than an employee would pay if the freelancer is working as an employee. And in the United States, the tax laws vary by state.

The United Kingdom implemented IR 35, a law designed to prevent freelancers from working for a single client for an extended period, paying themselves a tiny salary with a small tax burden, and then paying themselves dividends and therefore paying half the tax that an employee would pay. So an employer then has to think carefully about whether they are treating a freelancer like an employee.

"Microsoft misclassified certain workers as independent contractors. Following this ruling, approximately 10,000 current and former contingent workers sued Microsoft for benefits, including the ability to participate in its lucrative stock-purchase plan."[5]

The Microsoft lawsuit, combined with the lack of verification of online freelance talent, meant that using open talent was too risky for many large organizations. Still, like so many other categories where digital technologies transformed industries, it would only be a matter of time before the worlds of digital, networks, and platforms would catch up to the historically analog world of HR.

In 2013, oDesk and Elance combined forces, as described earlier, to become the dynamic platform known as Upwork. Pulling out all the stops postmerger, oDesk received quite an overhaul and a fresh new look. The decision that Elance would be gradually replaced in turn created one platform for freelancers. Here's how it works: clients put up a description of the work they need to have done, along with their best offer. They then either handpick specific freelancers or open it up to anyone interested. Once the client had chosen its ideal candidate, it locks the person in by sending a custom contract to ensure everything runs smoothly.

A big advancement in the adoption of ETC has been the advent of the Upwork Enterprise solution, started in 2015. This platform enables companies to use Upwork more efficiently as they seek solutions on how to integrate their insights and develop a better user experience. "One of the things we noticed and continue to notice," Hayden Brown, Upwork's CEO, told us, "is that while many employees inside *Fortune* 500 companies were using Upwork, they weren't sharing the results. It was their secret sauce that was accelerating their careers."

Our research aligns with Brown's insight. While there are only a few dozen *Fortune* 500 clients on any given platform, more than 80 percent of *Fortune* 500 companies have an active account on open talent platforms. And this doesn't count the workers who are using open talent platforms from their personal emails. While most C-suite talent leaders are unaware of their companies' usage of open talent platforms, it's happening under their noses and making their employees more efficient and productive.

Upwork Enterprise helps large companies identify and hire freelance workers in a more systemic way that addresses the risks inherent in working with external talent. The platform is designed to simplify the tasks involved with centrally managing a remote, freelance workforce strategy while accessing talent. Such an ETC was a great solution for companies as they shifted to remote work in the midst of the Covid-19 pandemic. Upwork is positioning itself to be one answer to the various technical, logistic, and operational challenges that come with managing a combined force of off-site workers. The platform includes features like Bring Your Own Talent, which enables companies to onboard their existing, non-Upwork freelance and contingent workers for centralized management. This service includes payroll, collaboration, cost management, and reporting. Upwork Enterprise has also added a feature called Work Protection, which helps customers resolve any issues on work done.

To address the higher level of needs from enterprise clients, Upwork Enterprise focuses on everything from sourcing experts who provide extra assistance in finding talent to on-platform onboarding and contracting processes that allow professionals to start work with minimal administrative delays. Most promising, the addition of Upwork Enterprise and the cultural shift brought on by the pandemic has brought Upwork an annual revenue growth of 30 percent. (See the sidebar "How Flexera Uses Upwork.")

The Future of External Talent Clouds

Building an ETC is just beginning to be understood by most organizations and, like so many other technology-based transformations, open talent and ETCs continue to morph and grow on a monthly basis. We briefly described Braintrust and Turing earlier in this chapter.

HOW FLEXERA USES UPWORK

Even HR functions are moving toward using platforms like Upwork to build a COE. That was the case when Flexera found its business growing and needed help to keep up with the changes in technologies it uses. Help was especially needed because of the nature of the software company: Flexera assists companies in their tracking of data across multiple platforms.

As a first step, Flexera's leadership tapped Elizabeth Lages, senior vice president of culture, and Jennifer Matsuoka, a project management director in HR, to create a COE and to drive the process. After they ran their assessment, they realized that their biggest challenge was to ensure data security. The second hurdle was to overcome employees' fears that outside talent would dilute the quality of the company's work while threatening their own jobs. For both concerns, Matsuoka enlisted Upwork's services.

Though the CEO made it clear from the outset that he backed the program, Matsuoka didn't rely on a top-down mandate from his office; instead, she inspired usage through example. Her own function, HR, was the program's first user. She purposely chose a large important project that required talent to work with highly sensitive data so that she could show that reliable safeguards had been established. The project's success "lifted the veil of uncertainty and showed other

While Upwork, Toptal, and Freelancer.com still dominate the market for digital talent clouds, they are version 1.0. With their reliance on AI and Web 3.0, Braintrust and Turing are version 2.0.

We're in a shift with the internet. In the original Web 1.0 paradigm, information flowed in one direction, from sites to users, and it was

teams they can trust Upwork," she says. From there, functions with immediate needs, like marketing and engineering, began experimenting. Matsuoka gained still more users by sharing use cases. "People saw what could have happened if we didn't have Upwork in place, the losses we avoided, and the gains we got," she says.[a]

The results have been impressive. With the help of Upwork, Flexera has created a system that onboards talent twenty-four times faster than traditional talent acquisition methods and has saved more than 60 percent of traditional costs.

"Having access to that flexible workforce is a huge competitive advantage for us," says Jim Ryan, president and CEO of Flexera. "To stay ahead of the curve, there are areas we do need to access outside of our existing employee base. We have needs that transcend just here in the United States. We need to find the very best in Belfast, to Bangalore, to Melbourne, to Santa Barbara."[b]

Ryan had hoped to integrate the use of Upwork so deeply into Flexera's culture that it became "part of the water supply," and it has.

a. "Upwork Customer Highlight: Flexera," YouTube, https://www.youtube.com/watch?v=BsDNpFlr3Hs, accessed July 26, 2023.

b. "How Flexera Overcame Security Concerns When Engaging Independent Talent at Scale," Upwork, https://content-static.upwork.com/blog/uploads/sites/11/2020/04/14182918/Flexera-security-case-study.pdf, accessed July 26, 2023.

static. Think of the old landing pages where people only received published information but had little interaction. In Web 2.0, information started to become bidirectional. Users interacted with apps, feeding them data (uploading photos, creating content, sharing, etc.). The downside to Web 2.0 is that the dream of a democratized web was quickly overwhelmed by a few global platforms—Google, Apple, Facebook, Amazon—that not only devastated traditional media and brick-and-mortar retail, but also upended our collective property rights. For example, under its current terms and conditions, Facebook can grant free licensing on pictures posted without getting further consent than what you agreed to as you joined the platform. That's a steep price to pay for access.

Decentralized autonomous organizations, or DAOs, are a new way to finance projects, govern communities, and share value. Instead of a top-down hierarchical structure, they use Web3 technology and rapidly evolving governance and incentive systems to distribute decision-making authority and financial rewards.

Braintrust, which operates as a Web3-based DAO that runs on the Ethereum blockchain, was started by Adam Jackson and Gabriel Luna-Ostaseski in 2018 to disrupt the open talent economy by giving more control and greater rewards to freelancers. It has launched a token or an incentive for participating in a decentralized network as part of a reward system called BTRST, which in time will allow its users rather than a central corporation to become its owners.

If we look at early versions of talent processes that create friction and inequities, Uber is the poster child for these disparities of rewards in the gig economy marketplace. If you invested $1 million in the first round of venture funding in Uber, your stock would have been worth $25 million when it went public nine years later. At the same time, Uber drivers continue to make minimum wage.

Braintrust represents a new model, ensuring that everyone benefits from the success of the platform. The company has kept its core team small, with only thirty-five employees, while its network is powered by more than seven hundred thousand community members who earn tokens for recruiting new members and clients, as well as perks and privileges. Thanks to its Web3 DAO-based business model, Braintrust can reduce costs for both sides of the market, eliminating talent's fees altogether and reducing clients' fees by as much as 50 to 75 percent compared to other platforms. Time will tell if Braintrust and blockchain will own the future. In the meantime, these kinds of bold experiments signal a healthy, evolving market.

In order for ETCs to thrive, they must match skills with tasks and consider how freelancers can contribute to capturing and perhaps even owning part of the company's IP. With the emergence of Web3, free-lancers will be able to showcase their skills and jump from platform to platform with ease, collecting skills and credits along the way. Perhaps we'll even see a new era of badges that, like LinkedIn badges but with more precise verification, will make it even easier for valuable freelanc-ers to find their place in the workforce.

The push for action is growing stronger as various platforms seek to validate specific skill sets and create technology that predicts collab-oration opportunities between workers. Despite the current manual and crude approach to pairing users according to their skills, platforms are now investing in the development of technology that tracks skill and performance in greater detail, beyond mere user ratings. What's more, workers can share knowledge and experiences and find ways to work together as the nature of collaboration and teaming evolves.

. . .

ETCs are the fastest and the most economical way for companies to resolve their talent crises, even at the high end of the market. Your COE should assess your internal needs and use platforms to their maximum capability by looking at their many offerings aside from talent supply. In the next chapter, we'll uncover the secrets to crowdsourcing as we explore how to operationalize open innovation capabilities into your organization.

KEY IDEAS

Companies can quickly acquire the highly sought-after talent they need to stay competitive by leveraging ETCs. To keep up with the rapid digital transformation of today's economy, organizations are now leveraging freelancers to fill short-term skills gaps. Your center of excellence should assess your internal needs, learn about the platform ecosystem, and start experimenting by conducting pilot projects and building enterprise relationships.

External talent clouds for strategic advantages, cost savings, and flexibility. The ETC is a term we use for this growing practice; it's an efficient and cost-effective way that companies can obtain the specialized talents they need from outside sources without sacrificing quality or productivity.

How does an ETC work? The key to success in this phase rests on strong and trusting relationships with the right platform partners. Our recommendation is to take a two-fold approach. Revisit how you managed your full-time staff and determine which of these roles are better suited for freelance workers. The goal here should be to become agile yet to remain focused on the indispensability of certain positions for the company's operations to run smoothly.

Choosing your platforms. We describe the various kinds of platforms you will need to build your ETC. You should consider the different features of these platforms and which ones have more niche workers (e.g., data science) or a broad range of skills.

Building an ETC. As we saw with the Microsoft 365 Toolkit, use off-the-shelf products to get going. Also run workshops with key stakeholders to identify pain points. Task management has evolved, and so should your organization. To maximize efficiency with minimal training, try skewing toward replicable tasks. Be sure to include communication strategies that reassure full-time employees that their jobs are safe and that the changes will help them.

The future of ETCs. In the future, ETCs will empower workers to become a part of more than just a paying gig and a rating on the platform. Web3 and tokens allow people to earn money from referrals and to enjoy various perks, including potential ownership of the IP related to the work performed. Think critically about what your company can offer in this space as you work with platforms.

Chapter 6

Build an Open Innovation Capability

Albert Lin is something of a modern-day Indiana Jones. He's not a treasure hunter, but as a research scientist, he relishes opportunities to work in the field as a National Geographic explorer, riding through the Gobi Desert on horseback in search of ancient structures. It's not an easy life; he has had to use a high-tech prosthetic leg since he lost his own after an accident in an off-road vehicle in 2016. Undaunted, he recently signed on with Disney+ to document his travels and discoveries.

In 2012, when LISH's Karim Lakhani and Jin Paik first met Lin, he was on a quest to find the lost tomb of Genghis Khan, an interest he'd developed on an early trip to Mongolia as a student. It soon became clear, however, that he'd have to find evidence of the buried structures he sought without actually excavating on-site. The people of the Mongolian desert are wary of foreigners, and many scientists had been expelled from the country for desecrating historic sites. So Lin would need the help of advanced cutting-edge satellite technologies to investigate artifacts in situ without compromising their integrity.[1]

The trouble was that the target area in Mongolia was vast; it would take Lin decades just to look through the satellite footage, much less to zero in on areas where any human-made features might indicate the possible site of the tomb. It occurred to Lin that by using crowdsourcing, he could find the needle in the haystack. That's when he pulled together an online platform sponsored by National Geographic and tasked people to help him look through satellite imagery and tag whatever evidence of human-constructed features turned up.

Lin's story offers a good example of the kinds of challenging problems that open innovation can solve. Building an open innovation capability in your organization—the topic of this chapter—is all about mobilizing crowds to solve difficult problems. As we'll see, organizations are using crowds to solve some of the most intransigent problems, including challenges in archaeology and medical research.

Among other advantages, open innovation practices can result in shorter product and technology development cycles. These practices often turn conventional wisdom on its head. Closed and top-down methodologies assume that successful innovation relies solely on ideas that originate in-house, within the full control of the organization. But the kind of bottom-up insights that open innovation capabilities offer can originate at any level and then build their way throughout the organization.

Often, organizations are already using open innovation to do such things as searching for already-existing advances that they could use or license and cultivating communities around topics of interest (e.g., open-source software). This chapter will focus more on how open innovation capabilities are most commonly used: to solve problems by way of contests. We'll begin with the ins and outs of running contests before moving on to ways to measure and evaluate success.

Open Innovation as a Contest

Although the use of contests to solve problems had been largely overlooked until the rise of the internet, contests are not an entirely new tool when it comes to innovation. For example, in the 1400s, when the

Florence Cathedral, under construction since the year 1296, was nearly complete, its builders envisioned a dome that was higher and wider than any known structure. Not knowing exactly how to pull off such a vision, the Arte della Lana, Florence's powerful wool guild, sponsored a competition. Filippo Brunelleschi—whose career as a sculptor had been advanced decades before, when he tied for first place in a contest to design the doors to the Florence Baptistery—won the contest and the contract. In another contest centuries later, Napoléon Bonaparte offered twelve thousand francs to the inventor who could devise a better food ration for his troops. A confectioner named Nicolas François Appert came through with a method of boiling and sealing food in jars—the basic technology that is still used in canning today.

In today's open innovation contests, a problem is typically posed online, and individuals and teams compete to find a solution that is judged according to a clearly specified set of criteria. Some of these contests are winner take all; others have multiple winners. In many cases, contests are used to gather resources and ideas for larger projects. For example, the Defense Advanced Research Projects Agency got pretty good at sponsoring contests for autonomous vehicles, starting in 2005. Fully autonomous vehicles are still a long way away, but we can see some of the technologies that came out of those contests in Tesla's and other auto companies' efforts to introduce self-driving features to their cars. In many ways, contests have been used to validate talent and in particular to validate how open talent can perform using emerging technology. Running a contest is one of the fastest ways to assess open talent skills, but in doing so, we need to classify the types of contests.

Contests fall under three broad categories: ideation (idea generation), solution generation, and grand challenges. In an idea generation contest, a question—either defined or open-ended—is posed. Suitable answers can run the gamut from casual suggestions to formal proposals, full-blown designs, and even videos. See table 6-1 for the pros and cons of this type of contest.

The second category, solution generation contests, draws on the cognitive diversity of different disciplines and industries in search of a

TABLE 6-1

Pros and cons of an idea generation contest

Pros	Cons
• Low barrier to entry for both participants and organizations	• Potentially lengthy review period
• For organizations, lower cost than other contests	• Subjective evaluation
• Fast, easy to set up, and with quick results	• Results highly variable in terms of quality and scope

specific outcome or sets of outcomes that can be deployed to revamp or replace existing processes. Examples of outcomes are algorithms, new software designs, or the harmonic solution for greasy potato chips we discussed in chapter 4. (See table 6-2.)

The third category, grand challenges, generally takes much longer than do ideation or solution contests and is more expensive to run. Examples of grand challenges include many of the XPrize competitions, the Netflix Prize for a new collaborative filtering algorithm, and the Defense Advanced Research Projects Agency's Autonomous Vehicles Challenge. In grand challenges, teams submit one-size-fits-all solutions for ambitious but achievable goals for national or global problems. The

TABLE 6-2

Pros and cons of a solution generation contest

Pros	Cons
• Access to experts (e.g., architects, designers, data scientists, marketing specialists)	• Need to break down the complexity of the problem
• Objective and subjective scoring	• More expensive, especially if a prototype is needed
• Well-defined	• Setting up a contest takes longer than other projects because of trade-offs in defining specifics for a nonexpert crowd

TABLE 6-3

Pros and cons of a grand challenge

Pros	Cons
• High visibility	• Costly, resource intensive
• High participation	• Long setup and execution times
• Ability to take on large problem spaces	• Solvers often bear additional costs

solutions might capture the public's imagination and draw attention to a specific topic, push the boundaries of discovery, or build toward a larger goal. Although grand challenges clearly have their place in the ecosystem, few organizations have the capacity, time, and resources to run them since they can take many years to develop and execute. (See table 6-3.)

Can Crowds Really Perform Better?

Let's go a little deeper into the practicality of using crowds to devise solutions via contests.

With crowds, you see all the bad ideas, but you get all the brilliant ones as well. It's all about seeing every possible idea and then picking the right fit. We call this approach the *extreme value solution*, which is what most companies are looking for. The sponsor company gets literally thousands of hours of people's engagement on the problem but pays only the winners.

Even the bad ideas that come in may have some value. By giving you a landscape view of potential solutions, a contest offers much insight into what isn't working and why. Just think how many initially discarded ideas that, when someone else reframed them, suddenly sounded a lot more interesting. Sometimes you can resolve your problem not by the suggestion itself but by the way you implement it. And the top-tier solutions are often simply cheaper, faster, and better than anything you could have thought up yourself. Figures 6-1, 6-2, and 6-3 help explain the probability of finding solutions using crowds.

On the *x* axis in figure 6-1 is the value that a firm places on an idea, or the quality of the idea. On the *y* axis is the number of people or the number of solutions you can get. In this distribution, the dot shows you what you're likely to get on average from your own employees and contractors. You usually get the best of what's available, but don't have access to what's possible. With the contest model (figure 6-2), you enjoy not only the benefit of your own people's knowledge and insights but also the benefit of everyone else's. In particular, you are looking for what's at the tail end of the distribution, in the box. These solutions are the best in terms of value, although they are the least likely.

Based on our analysis of research conducted by Michael Menietti and Karim Lakhani on Topcoder contest submissions across a range of software development projects, we've found that you don't need hundreds of submissions to obtain that extreme value. You only need about twenty-two entrants.

FIGURE 6-1

Probability of finding a great idea using traditional methods

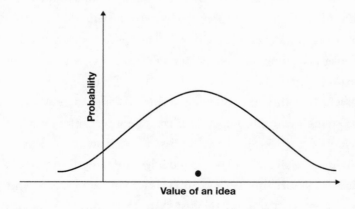

Source: Jin Paik adapted this graph from his research at LISH with Karim Lakhani.

FIGURE 6-2

Probability of finding a great idea using contests

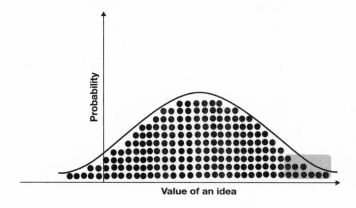

Source: Jin Paik adapted this graph from his research at LISH with Karim Lakhani.

But can crowds really beat, say, the Harvard doctor you have on staff? Or the scientists employed at NASA? These are difficult questions, but again our research has a simple explanation. The Harvard or NASA expertise would shift the curve in figure 6-2 to the right. As indicated by the gray rectangle, on average, the experts would do much better than the crowd. But you're only getting the best from Harvard or NASA, not from the whole world. So yes, Harvard is smarter, but it's going to lack the depth of knowledge and the perspective that you can get from the left-shifted crowd.

In short, with crowds, you get the worst of the worst ideas, the average ideas, *and* the best ones. So, if you want the expertise of the top performers that you don't own or normally have access to, crowds are the way to go. The extreme value of the crowd supersedes the average value of the experts as the gray rectangle in figure 6-3 shows.

As a humorous but revealing aside, let's consider a recent ideation contest from Great Britain. In 2016, the Natural Environment Research Council, an agency of the UK government, asked the public to help name a new state-of-the-art $287 million polar research vessel. Entries

FIGURE 6-3

Probability of finding a solution: Experts versus crowds

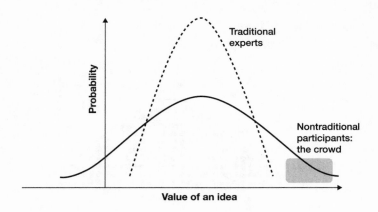

Source: Jin Paik adapted this graph from his research at LISH with Karim Lakhani.

had to satisfy three requirements: the name must use the convention RRS *Name* (RRS for royal research ship); it should be inspirational and related to the environment; and it should not be a name already in use in the fleet (eliminating such obvious entries as *James Cook, Ernest Shackleton, Discovery,* and *James Clark Ross*). About seven thousand entries came in, including a number of oddball choices that clearly weren't meant to be taken seriously. After the public voted, these were the results:[2]

1. RRS *Boaty McBoatface*: 124,109

2. RRS *Poppy-Mai*: 34,371

3. RRS *Henry Worsley*: 15,231

4. RRS *It's bloody cold here*: 10,679

5. RRS *David Attenborough*: 10,248

RRS *Boaty McBoatface* routed the competition, earning as many votes as the next nineteen names combined. It was so popular it appeared twice in the top twenty, with RRS *Boaty McBoatface the Return* placing thirteenth.

Skeptics of crowdsourcing often bring up this story, asking, "How can we trust the crowd with our most pressing challenges when it can't even name a boat?"

In fact, the public didn't name the boat. At the end of the day, the research council opted for RRS *Attenborough*, which ranked fifth. It had every right to do so; the rules of the contest made it clear that the council reserved the right to the final say, and the winner fit two of its three criteria (which *Boaty McBoatface* decidedly did not). The experience of the research council speaks to the reason that contests generally work so well: you get to see all the submissions, good and bad. Every contest produces its share of bad entries; the real moral of the story is that you have to be transparent about the contest's rules and frame things properly. We'll explore these recommendations in the next section.

Case study: crowds develop solutions for cancer diagnostics

In 2017 we received a grant at LISH to tackle a big bottleneck issue in cancer research. There were many directions we could go, but we lacked the funds to launch a grand challenge. Nor did we want to. The goal was to partner with the crowd, not replace the existing experts. We wanted to launch a solution contest that would demonstrate that even small-scale crowds can still make a significant impact. While we hoped to bring science a little closer to a cure for lung cancer, we also knew that, at the very least, a contest would yield tangible insight and increase the likelihood of success through collaboration. Furthermore, any resulting ideas could be refined and developed over many more iterative contests.

Lung cancer is a problem that persists despite a steady reduction in tobacco use, the main contributor to the disease. With two million new cases a year, lung cancer is the most commonly occurring cancer worldwide in men and the third most common in women. At 17.8 percent, its five-year survival rate is one of the lowest among the leading cancers.

Survival is affected by a number of factors, including age, prior health conditions, stage of the disease at diagnosis, access to health-care providers, and efficacy of treatment.

The treatments for lung cancer and the outcomes of those treatments aren't a single problem but are instead a large problem space with multiple interconnected problems that affect each other. The diversity of challenges provides an opportunity for different approaches and touchpoints for solution development—a point brought home to us when we sat down with Raymond Mak and Eva Guinan, physicians and professors at Harvard Medical School who understood the problems in medical practice.[3]

As our conversation proceeded, we tried to imagine a contest that might help not only Harvard doctors but also your average radiation oncologist in rural America or sub-Saharan Africa—people who didn't have access to the best education or resources. Rather than asking how we could solve the global lung cancer problem for everyone, we wondered how to replicate what Harvard doctors might do regarding treatment. We needed specificity, which is where most crowdsourced contests fall short. It's OK to run a blue-sky ideation contest, where you might get the out-of-the-box answers, but how can you increase your odds of getting good ones? You don't start by asking how to boil the ocean—you need to narrow your focus and ask about something much more concrete to get you results you can test and learn from. It takes at least a few brainstorming sessions to get there.

Gradually, we began to home in on just such a problem. The challenge for radiation therapists is to kill off cancer cells without harming healthy cells. If the tumor is in the lung, for example, the therapists have to be careful not to deliver radiation to the heart or spinal column. This level of precision is difficult. It's not quite a guessing game but having a tool that could help the health professionals analyze the visual data would certainly help—perhaps an AI-based approach, in which the software analyzes millions of pixels to learn which cells are cancerous and which are not.

The two doctors told us about the National Lung Screening Trial, a robust study of fifty-three thousand high-risk patients at thirty-three cancer centers. The study, conducted between 2004 and 2009, investigated whether low-dose helical computerized tomography (CT) scans of high-risk patients could catch enough early-stage cancers to reduce overall death rates. The results were generally good: the scans reduced lung cancer deaths by 20 percent. But the approach had a downside: a 96.4 percent false-positive rate. This rate meant that less than 4 percent of the early-stage cancers found through this screening were actual cancers.

High error rates in diagnosis are inefficient but not likely to be fatal. But targeting the radiation treatment at misidentified healthy cells is disastrous. So, the question became, What problems would you need to solve to create a digital assistant that is better at identifying cancer cells than a typical oncologist is? Unlike cancer image analysis for diagnostic purposes, which produces a single binary yes-or-no answer to a single question (Is a mass present?), therapeutic tumor segmentation involves the interpretation of medical imaging. The challenge is to precisely trace the outline of the tumor. Commercial software that does this is cumbersome and time-consuming to use and requires doctors to think in three dimensions. Outlining an image can take between thirty seconds and thirty minutes, depending on a doctor's training, skill, experience, and intuition—all factors that can have an impact on patient outcomes.

We decided to challenge the crowd to develop AI algorithms that could replicate expert skill and knowledge so that this expertise could be transferred to under-resourced health-care settings and improve the quality of radiation therapy. Mak was familiar with the commercial software and understood what an expert typically gets right or wrong. We recruited data scientists who had run similar competitions, and we engaged the platform Topcoder because we knew it had the deepest pool of data scientists. (For more on platforms and contests, see the sidebar "Types of Contest Platforms.") Then, to help the crowd contestants develop the algorithms, we ultimately provided them with the following:

- A well-curated lung tumor dataset that was segmented by an expert clinician and that the contestants could train and test their algorithms on

TYPES OF CONTEST PLATFORMS

There are many contest platforms for small challenges (offering usually less than $100,000 in prizes) that attract different types of solvers. Grand challenges (offering millions of dollars in prizes) are generally run through the organization's own platform. We recommend mixing and matching platforms according to your needs. Most contests will not attract thousands, but even ten to one hundred participants can generate a handful of very good solutions. The following are some of the most commonly used contest platforms for solving difficult technical and business problems. Many of them charge a single contest fee, which is a percentage of the target prize purse or yearly subscriptions to launch unlimited contests. Contestants are only paid through the platform if they achieve a desired result that is acceptable to the sponsor.

Topcoder. The Topcoder community consists of 1.5 million designers, software programmers, and data scientists. Some firms require community members to sign nondisclosure agreements and seldom reveal their identities publicly. The IP for the winning submissions passes from the contestants to the client in exchange for the monetary prizes.

- An objective scoring system for evaluating the submitted algorithms

- Information sharing and access to feedback from expert clinicians to guide the work

- A total prize purse of $55,000 to be distributed to the top five to eight entrants after each round, according to performance

Kaggle. This platform allows its eight million data scientists and machine-learning practitioners to find and publish datasets, explore and build models, collaborate in teams, and enter competitions to solve challenges. Work is shared publicly through a portal called Kaggle Kernels to achieve better benchmarks and inspire new ideas.

HeroX. A spin-off from the XPrize contest, HeroX's primary focus is idea generation contests for a wide range of challenges, including engineering problems, design and content creation, consumer product development, and market research. Part of the engagement process includes the recruitment of flash crowds, or quickly assembled crowds, to move faster. Unlike Kaggle and Topcoder, this community has a wide set of specializations.

Wazoku. In 2020, Wazoku bought InnoCentive, an early crowdsourcing company. The idea for InnoCentive came to Alpheus Bingham and Aaron Schacht in 1998, when they were working at the pharmaceutical giant Eli Lilly, and the new company was spun off in 2005. In 2020, after InnoCentive had run some twenty-five hundred challenges and had captured two hundred thousand innovations, Wazoku acquired it and integrated it into Wazoku's own offerings for enterprise innovation management.

Crowdsourcing results

Contests allow for flexibility and solutions sprints, similar to what you would see in agile development. Our contest around lung cancer therapy had three phases. During each phase, the contestants produced segmentations using their algorithms on the validation set and received real-time evaluation of their algorithm's performance on a public leaderboard. The contestants then used the feedback to modify their solutions or to generate new approaches to improve their scores. At the end of each phase, the participants submitted their final algorithms for independent evaluation. Then the study team, including the clinical expert, reviewed the winning algorithms' performance and segmentations on individual patient scans to revise the contest design and objectives in each subsequent phase.

After phase 1, our team went back and reformulated the problem, focusing on the contouring of the tumors instead of their identification, since an oncologist would know where the tumor is in a real-life situation. Instead, we dropped a marker on randomly generated seed points within each tumor. We ran the contest under these new conditions in phase 2 and saw a 40 percent improvement in results. This improvement shows the power of giving feedback as contestants worked through their problems.

In preparation for phase 3, Guinan and the team worked with Topcoder to further refine the contest. Top competitors, who had already been awarded prizes, were offered an additional incremental prize to work collaboratively with each other and the contest expert to recombine some of the data and solutions. From phase 2 to phase 3, the results improved by another 10 percent. Remarkably, the final algorithm had an accuracy rate equal to that of the human thoracic oncologist—only it produced results much faster. The expert took eight minutes to perform a manual segmentation, whereas the algorithm took between fifteen seconds and two minutes.

A total of 564 contestants from sixty-two countries registered for the challenge, and 34 (6 percent) submitted algorithms. The top contestants used a variety of approaches, including convolutional neural networks, cluster growth, and random-forest algorithms. Some of the solutions had been originally developed for other purposes—facial detection, biomedical image segmentation, and road-scene segmentation for autonomous-vehicle research—and adapted for the present task. This borrowing from other domains was precisely what the commercial approaches had been missing. The contest had unlocked the benefits of *adjacency knowledge*, new insights gained from outside the group of folks who would typically be the people involved in the work.

. . .

Now that we've explored this case, let's go deeper into how we assess when to run a contest.

When to Run a Contest: Some Frameworks to Consider

When developing innovation strategies, firms must consider whether to make or buy them. In general, companies do not rely on any one strategy exclusively. One study found that 72 percent of firms that describe themselves as innovative actually rely on both making strategies and buying them.[4] But there's a third possible approach. *Innovation contests* add a fresh perspective to the make-or-buy discussion (figure 6-4).[5]

When assessing how the contest will perform against traditional sourcing, we recommend a counterfactual analysis. Such an analysis compares what actually happened with what would have happened without the contest. The comparison considers three categories, as seen in figure 6-5:

- *Cost comparisons* measure traditional methods of procuring ideas or solutions against the contest model. Traditional business acquisition estimates can also include how much it would cost to solve the problem internally.

FIGURE 6-4

Innovation contests offer a third possibility beyond making or buying innovations

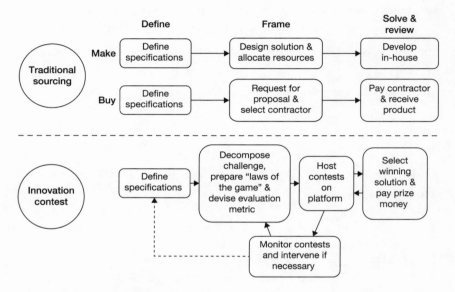

Source: Adapted from Jin H. Paik, Martin Scholl, Rinat Sergeev, Steven Randazzo, and Karim R. Lakhani, "Innovation Contests for High-Tech Procurement," *Research-Technology Management* 63, no. 2 (2020): 36–45.

- *Benefits* to contests include both hard facts like improvements in performance and soft facts like increased awareness of the problem.

- *Managerial lessons* should include best practices, "watch outs" or cautions, and further process improvements.

Roles and Responsibilities When You Are Running a Contest

When setting out to create and execute a contest, you'll want to consider several issues about the different roles and responsibilities for platforms and the internal teams at your company. The following questions might help.

FIGURE 6-5

Framework for comparing contests with traditional sourcing

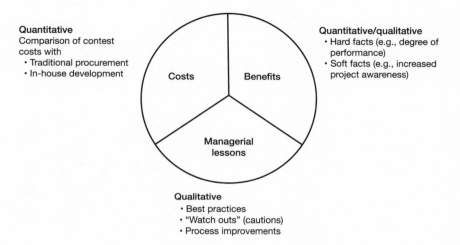

Quantitative
Comparison of contest
costs with
- Traditional procurement
- In-house development

Quantitative/qualitative
- Hard facts (e.g., degree of
  performance)
- Soft facts (e.g., increased
  project awareness)

Qualitative
- Best practices
- "Watch outs" (cautions)
- Process improvements

Source: Adapted from Jin H. Paik, Martin Scholl, Rinat Sergeev, Steven Randazzo, and Karim R. Lakhani, "Innovation Contests for High-Tech Procurement," *Research-Technology Management* 63, no. 2 (2020): 36–45.

Who will design and manage the contest?

Though the owners and judges of a challenge are almost always the end users, the contest itself should be designed and managed by people with expertise and experience in running contests. They could constitute a center of excellence (COE), if your organization already has one, or they could be outside consultants or people from the platform. The contest's results are largely determined by the quality of the question posed.

Most contests are short-term efforts, but how the process is communicated internally, documented, and showcased will matter—especially if it is a part of a larger open talent effort, since its results are likely to exceed expectations. HeroX cites that 90 percent of its clients get great results.

The first step is to prepare an agreement with a platform. We recommend creating a master service agreement to make this process go as smoothly as possible. NASA has master service agreements with thirty-two crowd platforms with the ceiling of $175 million for all platforms over an allotted time period. When it needs a crowdsourced project, NASA issues a request for proposal to the platforms on contract, and they respond with proposals on how they would meet that request for proposal. NASA selects the proposal that it believes has the highest chance of success and that provides the most value to the government.

With experience, you will get a sense for what to expect from each platform. Also, you should consider asking platforms to collaborate as a team. NASA has been successful having Topcoder and DrivenData run data science challenges together, with HeroX handling marketing and outreach.

Who is responsible for this problem or opportunity?

We label the person or department responsible for the problem the *challenge owner*. This person or group is often the end user or the representative of the end users and carries the day-to-day responsibility of working with the COE. It's not enough to get a management person to sponsor a contest. You must have someone who thoroughly understands the kind of data they'll be receiving from the platforms and how it will be used. Steve Rader at NASA says, "We try to focus [the challenge owner] not on what the method is, or the contractor or the vendor or the crowd. We tune in on what the problem is."[6] With this in mind, make sure that your challenge owner is someone who fully understands the problem that they'll be asking crowds on platforms to solve.

We know from experience that if you are not the problem owner or the one who can implement the solution, then you need to ensure that whoever you make responsible for doing the work is involved. Defining the requirements usually helps keep people involved. For example, at NASA, if the person receiving the software code for a new app won't be responsible for implementing or deploying it, then we ask that person to find the stakeholders who will deploy that software and to include them in the definition of the problem and the development of the requirements.

Do you have an executive sponsor?

It's important to get executive support that leads the organization's innovation efforts. You will need to discuss with these leaders how and why the project is important and what will be done with the results. Unlike external talent clouds, these contests will not be ongoing engagements. There's a good chance that they will be run as a short series or one-off efforts, but how the process is communicated internally, documented, and showcased will matter. You need to make sure the executive sponsor understands the impact of the contest and how the impact is relayed back to the organization. Be sure to ask your sponsors why they care about the contest and how it aligns with the overall business or R&D strategy. The sponsor will also commit to the budget needed to drive the results from the contest forward for internal development or rollout.

Do you have a multivendor contract in place?

As already mentioned, most organizations struggle to get contracts with platforms. We recommend working with the top platforms to get them on a vendor list quickly, using some kind of master service agreement such as the one NASA uses (described earlier in this section). To recap, the contest idea usually starts as a challenge form that is then generated into a formal request for proposals for the preapproved platforms. When you receive the platforms' proposals, you should examine their approach to the problem (length of contest, contest type, and marketing) and what their crowd can offer (specialty). The purpose is not just to see who's going to do the best job; you need to know *how* the platform is going to carry out the job. Then your COE can look at them and see who can perform the best or offer the best value, given any resource or schedule constraints.

Once you run a subset of these platform engagements, you will get a sense for various platforms' performance and what to expect. You should also consider having the vendor platforms work together as teams. As mentioned earlier, on NASA's contract, Topcoder and Driven-Data have both partnered with HeroX to do marketing and outreach on data science challenges.

How Will You Measure Success?

You will also need to consider ways that you'll review your contest and determine its value. Unlike a traditional approach to problem-solving, there are winners and losers in a contest. As a consequence, solutions are evaluated according to a set of criteria. Once the problem statement is clearly defined, you need to think about how you will evaluate the solutions developed by the crowd. Our research shows that the following questions are the most important metrics in helping define success initially:

- How many people are you looking to engage in your challenge?

- How many ideas would you like to take forward to implementation?

- What type of benefits would you like to track from the implemented ideas?

These questions not only help set expectations for the challenge owner but also help hold the executor sponsor accountable.

We also recommend tracking programmatic data. This information includes the number of problems solved, time saved, cost savings, and revenue generated.

How Will You Evaluate Your Contest?

Just as you need to be very clear in the questions you pose to contest participants, you need to be very clear about the criteria you will use to evaluate their answers. In most cases, scores will feed into the areas listed in table 6-4.

Judges should be recruited before the contest is launched and, for continuity, should participate from end to end. The last thing you need is for someone to come in at the last minute and blow up the criteria or shake up the contest description. You should recruit at least three judges but can have up to a dozen. They will generally come from your industry or inside the company. Keep in mind that coordinating time is difficult and judges may expect to be compensated if they are not in your own company.

For idea generation contests, your evaluation metric may be subjective. Some categories can be weighted more than others, depending on the desired solution outcomes. To avoid bias, judgment criteria should align with your desired outcomes and the panel should be diverse.

For solution generation contests, the evaluation criteria should be objective. This is the approach that Eva Guinan and her team took for their lung cancer contest. Their evaluation metric was based on computational benchmarks for accuracy, speed, and computing resources.

Timelines for Carrying Out Your Contest

A contest generally runs for three to eight weeks, depending on its goals. In our experience, crowds generally submit solutions at the beginning and toward the end. Longer time frames are generally not helpful unless there are special circumstances. If the crowd is not responsive, there

TABLE 6-4

Criteria for evaluation

Criteria	Description
Impact	• Does the proposed solution help create a more effective system?
	• Does the proposed solution use existing methods, data, or research findings (e.g., knowledge from other domains and AI-based applications from other industries) to strengthen its validity?
Innovation	• Is the proposed solution an improvement over existing methods?
	• How unique or creative is the proposed solution?
Implementation	• Is there a viable path to implement the proposed solution?
	• If it uses new technology, is there a clear development path?
	• Does it list key milestones for development or include a project plan?
	• Does it say how long the implementation will take?
	• Does it list the skills, roles, and subject matter expertise that would be needed to implement the proposed solution?
	• Does it provide costs?
Ease of use	• To what extent does the proposal specifically address the design requirements described in the challenge? Consider the following:
	— Can the proposed solution be easily used without changes to policy?
	— Does it provide outputs that are easy to deploy (e.g., desktop, cloud-based, or mobile apps)?
	— Does it provide an interface?
	— Is it easily adoptable, regardless of tech-savviness?
	• Does it include details on how the proposed solution would be tested and implemented? Does it provide a pathway to collect more data?
Quality	• Are the explanations of the technical and nontechnical components clear?
	• Does it capture real-world use cases and data, or does it require more research and data collection because of the theoretical nature of the proposal?

are two ways to motivate people. First, you could offer a bonus to the first solver to reach an established benchmark (though this tactic is more practical for data science or software development challenges than ideation contests). Second, you could extend the deadline if the desired level of participation is not reached.

Contests should be announced no more than two months before contestants must submit their entries. The first month targets those who are not current members of a platform. For example, Wazoku/InnoCentive has around half a million members in its community; they will be notified that a new contest is upcoming, but you'll want to develop a marketing plan to get the word out there to experts who aren't regulars on the platform.

Consider setting up a virtual event where potential contestants can ask questions. When we ran the lung cancer challenge on Topcoder, we had Ray Mak walk through the exact process he faced as an oncologist trying to segment tumors. His sharing of this experience helped potential contestants get up to speed on the subject matter and forced our team to refine the problem statement even further.

Besides hosting a real-time virtual event, you'll want to set up a forum for contestants to post questions and other comments At LISH, we often have one to two hundred forum comments by the time the contest is finished. Afterward, people share ideas and talk about what they thought was useful. The forum is also the best mechanism to send out communications and reminders during the competitions. You need to establish who will answer questions. For most engagements, platform- and prize-related questions are handled by the platform, while the challenge owner monitors technical questions.

Now let's look at the two most common types of contests and the kinds of processes or phases you will set up for each.

For ideation contests, we recommend the following timeline once the challenge has gone live (see figure 6-6):

FIGURE 6-6

Processes for ideation contests

Week 1	Week 2	Week 3	Week 4	Week 5	Week 6	Week 7	Week 8	Week 9
Submission				Initial review		Final review		Selection & announce-ment

Submission (three to four weeks)

• Ideas are submitted by competitors.

• Ideas can be made visible, and people can comment and vote on ideas if desired.

Initial review (two weeks)

• Ideas are filtered according to their feasibility and strategic fit.

• A few solutions are selected for pitching to a panel.

Final review (two weeks)

• Ideas are pitched to a judging panel with the top three to five ideas being approved for implementation according to the judging criteria.

Idea selected and announced

• Ideas are taken forward for implementation, and winning idea creators receive some form of recognition or reward.

For solution generation (data science or algorithm) contests, we recommend the following timeline (see figure 6-7):

FIGURE 6-7

Processes for solution generation contests

Week 1	Week 2	Week 3	Week 4	Week 5	Week 6	Week 7	Week 8
Submission							

Week 9	Week 10	Week 11	Week 12	Week 13	Week 14
Final review	Selection & announce-ment	Internal testing			

Submission (four to eight weeks)

- Solutions are submitted as provisional scores.

- Leaderboards drive the competition.

Final contest review (one week)

- Solutions are tested against reserved datasets.

- Only the final submission counts.

Selection and announcement (one week)

- Winning solutions receive some form of recognition or reward.

Internal testing (four weeks)

- Contest awards are often different from internal systems testing, which could take weeks or months.

- Typically, awards are given on the parameters of the contest, not a systems integration success.

What can you expect in terms of how each of these phases will play out? The submission phase has the least amount of action. Use it to take a deep breath and prepare for the review process. Reviews will differ depending on whether the criteria are objective or subjective.

Objective benchmarks and scoring for software or data science contests are set before the contest by the platform, a member of the community known as a copilot (who helps develop the problem statement), and a community tester who has already seen the problem. Thresholds are based on how you think the crowd will perform. A live leaderboard gives a provisional score for contestants, though only their final submissions count. Companies may need to carry out additional testing within their own systems. The final review is solely to select a winner. Unlike in sports, the final winner may have to make some tweaks even after their victory is announced.

Subjective judging follows a slightly different format. There are no leaderboards or provisional scores. Submissions will either be due in waves or all at once, at the end. Initial reviews are simple screenings to ensure that all eligibility criteria have been met. The platforms usually help with this process and charge a nominal fee. Your committee, which should consist of members of your firm and a few experts, conducts the final evaluation. Be sure to communicate your expectations to the committee members clearly. We recommended holding one initial meeting to review the contest details, a training on scoring, and one longer meeting for the final deliberations. It's crucial to eliminate biases by having at least two judges see each submission so you can take the average of the two scores.

How to Gain Long-Term Traction Using Open Innovation Contests

Next, we pivot to see how the organization can build momentum to launch these smaller contests. Companies that implement these lessons can overcome some of the inevitable roadblocks.

In 2006, Jeff Davis, as the director of astronaut safety and chief medical officer at NASA's Johnson Space Center, faced an 80 percent budget cut. But his division's mission hadn't changed: he still needed to mitigate the health risks for astronauts for space missions. With only 20 percent of his budget to accomplish that goal, he had no choice but to get creative about solutions and adopt a growth mindset. He called Karim Lakhani, who had recently been appointed as a junior professor at the Harvard Business School. The two had met briefly during an executive education session at Harvard, where Karim's research presented the right theoretical concepts for Davis's managerial problem. Karim had been studying successful crowdsourcing cases in the industry and was looking to use that method to solve critical scientific problems.

Davis presented Karim with his problem: if astronauts were on a space walk outside the International Space Station and there was a solar flare, the spike in radiation from the event could be extremely dangerous, even life-threatening. NASA had been working on the issue for years—for ten years, in fact, with eight heliophysicists from NASA and a budget of $2 million annually. They had advanced an algorithm that could predict solar flares 1.5 hours in advance and with 50 percent accuracy. But to Davis, an hour and a half was cutting it close, considering the time the astronauts needed to move themselves from outside the space station to back inside, make it through the airlock, take off all their equipment, and get to a secure part of the space station.

Despite some reservations about the partnership (a NASA-Harvard collaboration with a crowd and not with scientists seemed odd in the eyes of both intuitions), Karim agreed to launch Davis's pilot. NASA and LISH used a crowdsourcing platform to ask the world, "How can we advance this algorithm to save astronauts' lives by protecting them against radiation?" They worked with InnoCentive, which amassed an online community of 250,000 scientific experts. Davis and Karim carefully framed the problem, posed it to the community, and curated the results.

Within two months and for $30,000 in prizes, they received many viable answers. Bruce Cragin provided the best. A retired radio-frequency engineer from New Hampshire, Cragin had played around with radiation and cell phone towers in the past. He developed an algorithm that could predict a solar flare up to eight hours in advance, with 85 percent accuracy—a far better solution to the same problem that the best minds at NASA had worked on for ten years at a cost of $20 million. Davis went on to run several more pilots.

Inspired by Davis's success, Jason Crusan, NASA's director of advanced exploration systems, decided to crowdsource a different problem. The International Space Station is powered by solar arrays on long, thin arms called longerons. It is hard to position them optimally for maximum power generation, and the shadowing of the structures causes extreme temperature differences that put strains on the materials. NASA engineers and contractors had kept the problem under control by steadily cranking out equations in Excel, but they lacked the skills, time, and money to develop a permanent fix. This issue was big enough that Crusan, Davis, and Karim launched the NASA Tournament Lab to experiment with these types of problems. (The success of the lab eventually launched NASA's Center of Excellence for Collaborative Innovation, or CoECI, which would service the entire US federal government at scale.)

As Crusan told Jin on his first day of work, "This is easily a million-dollar problem. If we can make any progress for less money or the same, it's still a success." Jin and researchers at Harvard organized a three-week contest for $30,000 on the Topcoder platform. With nearly five hundred competitors globally, the top winners came from China, Canada, Italy, Poland, Russia, and Romania. They submitted AI-based algorithms that NASA had not considered before, and about half of the submissions succeeded in improving on the agency's internal benchmarks.

Those contests were proofs of concepts, experiments that started to demonstrate that NASA's leaders had found a better way of doing things, by using crowdsourcing. Crusan puts it this way: "You find what works and what doesn't work, and you find the one in ten thousand shots. Some things fall back, but you don't get rid of them. It's a heat-map approach."[7]

Agility in organizations is measured by how quickly they can respond to challenges and iterate their way toward success. Similarly, the role of leaders in a networked organization is not just to be agile themselves but also to develop a workforce that is light and fast in both thought and action. These are leaders who are willing to introduce new talent processes, technologies, and ways of working and then create a path for others to follow. Moreover, these leaders understand that by extending their network outward, such as what Davis did at NASA, they can tap more skills and knowledge than they ever could before.

In a follow-up survey to the solar flare project, of the three thousand people who set eyes on trying to solve this problem, 81 percent reported that they had never engaged with NASA before this project. That's more than twenty-four hundred people who NASA could not have accessed otherwise and who the agency *did* access without having to "own" their talent.

Let's take a closer look at the hurdles the agency faced and how it's thinking about continually integrating contest-based work. NASA took five steps to propel the adoption of contests across the organization.

Be radical by reducing budgets

NASA had some difficulty getting traction, so it worked toward getting teams to use the Topcoder platform more frequently. One of the drastic decisions that Crusan made was cutting technology development budgets for his teams. Rather than forcing his teams to use open innovation, he simply took a percentage of their budget. He told them they could get it back if they worked with CoECI and launched a few contests.

This approach worked well in many instances. The Disruptive Tolerant Networking team, a space communications technology group at NASA, was tasked to figure out deep space internet protocol (emails from space can run into communications disruptions and delays). The team ran two or three contests in the first year. By the third year, a significant portion of its development work was being done using crowds.

The use of open innovation was never forced. The teams never went back to ask for more money. They were encouraged to try something they had never done before. It's a risky strategy, but it pushes people out of their badger holes. Can you think of how you can reduce your own team's budget but then offer it back to them if they run a contest?

Work with procurement, legal, and HR

NASA's stable infrastructure came with guaranteed work for the platforms. But teams that use platforms also need to coordinate with legal and procurement and quickly establish relationships with vendors. Getting platforms on a master service contract will show the broad range of problems they can solve and remove any friction from an internal client who wants to use them. For example, when the CoECI was sourcing goods and services, it needed to be clear on what was feasible and what jurisdiction its tools fell into.

Another consideration was that the more work the CoECI had, the more work it would be putting on procurement. It was essential to get complete alignment early on; otherwise, all the sales, training, and operational excellence would halt. Lynn Buquo, CoECI manager, said, "You have to know that you need them. They don't need you. Understanding that this doesn't work without procurement and legal was the best thing we did."[8]

For example, NASA could only onboard vendors for five years at a time. Knowing this, Buquo realized that considerable time from legal and procurement would be required and that she therefore needed to give them advance notice or risk making enemies.

As this example shows, leaders should always be thinking about how the use of open talent platforms affects other departments in their organization. While reflecting on this with Buquo at the ten-year anniversary of CoECI, we recognized that a huge misstep was the center's failure to get aligned with HR. Some of this shortcoming came about because open talent writ large had not taken root when CoECI started, and the focus was more on contests. But once the concept has been proven in your organization, alignment with HR and its strategies is critical.

Getting even more granular, proposal turnaround went from months to weeks with the help of procurement. While relationships with administrative departments in your organization may seem mundane, the COE needs these departments to create efficiency.

Provide a stable infrastructure for the entire organization

Davis and Crusan were working in silos, but they could see the benefit of open innovation to all of NASA, provided that the concept had more infrastructure. They encouraged Buquo to keep working at the agency-wide angle as well as within CoECI. There was a perception in the organization that the initial success of the center was more about NASA's goodwill in engaging the crowd rather than the actual benefits the agency received.

In any organization, leadership needs to acknowledge that open innovation works. This is fundamental: it doesn't matter how many contests you execute well, without proper support, people only see the success as a one-off. For example, to gain more momentum and make the idea of open innovation salient for all of NASA, the CoECI also moved away from overplayed terms like *innovation* and shifted the language to include terms like *technology development* and *talent*. Terms like these resonated far greater culturally both with potential client needs and with internal NASA teams.

Establish a rotational training program

In December 2021, after ten successful years leading CoECI, Buquo retired from NASA and handed over the reins to Steve Rader. Rader had been instrumental in marketing CoECI's efforts to gain internal traction and to encourage potential end users to use platforms. He pivoted to think about how else the organization could scale platforms so that they would get more users. Since its inception, the center had marketed itself by doing roadshows, visits Rader and his team members conducted at the different NASA centers to explain how to engage with platforms to run contests. The roadshows were helpful but contributed little toward the scaling of the overall model. The center needed to educate engineers and scientists not only on how to use crowdsourcing but also on how to actually do the work involved, so that execution could scale with demand. As this method has caught on around the space agency, the CoECI team has struggled to keep up with demand for helping teams execute open innovation projects (as demonstrated in the fall of 2021, when the team of ten was executing more than ninety open innovation projects at once).

Currently, the CoECI team is developing a training program that will not only train engineers and scientists on how to identify situations and problems where crowdsourcing can be useful but also teach them how to execute much of the work needed to develop contract requirements, work with vendors, and get results. This program will use rotations of people from throughout the organization and will grow a network of people who can execute at scale.

Develop better metrics

One metric to develop is related to your own data system: making it simpler, faster, and otherwise better and using more metrics. That entails leveraging more and more data, all the time. You should make sure that the data fits into an architecture that will allow you to build the kind of AI factories necessary to propel us into the future. They also have to be processes that digital natives can actually engage.

The teams for making this happen don't need to be large. CoECI operates with just four civil servants and a few contractors. They just got better at the process. They implemented templated challenge sheets for potential customers to fill out, and they started to retain the knowledge of how the process works and to get the timelines right. The center of excellence that NASA built depends on efficiency and not quantity. At the same time, the center's narrative must align with organizational goals and objectives—and constantly translate how your wins are contributing to the company at large.

. . .

Building your company's open innovation capability through the COE can help the company tap into external ideas and solutions that resonate in today's competitive business climate. In the next chapter, we look at ways to maximize the value of your internal resources. As technology is rapidly changing how we manage and access information, many companies are now turning to an internal talent marketplace platform as a solution for driving talent practices from within. Such platforms offer previously unavailable insights into employee skill sets and ways to manage talent more efficiently.

KEY IDEAS

Open innovation methodologies, in particular contests, challenge the traditional notions of top-down, in-house ideation. These practices have been gaining traction because they can result in shorter development cycles and foster a more inclusive approach to concept generation, drawing from every level of an organization or beyond its walls entirely. For these reasons, open innovation has become a go-to tool among organizations looking for novel ideas and dynamic methods of implementation.

> **Open innovation as a contest.** You need to think about idea generation versus solution generation and how each type of contest benefits your situation. Think of contests as ways to rapidly prototype or validate ideas and assumptions. Both are alternative to high-priced, all-in-one grand challenge models.

Can crowds really perform better? Crowds give you the full gamut of types of performance, but you generally only pay for the good ones. The competition aspect lets the best solutions surface to the top. You're looking to find top performers in a short period.

When to run a contest: some frameworks to consider. Consider a new option to the traditional make-or-buy paradigm. Performance metrics will differ, so be sure to include costs, benefits, and managerial lessons that you can share with the whole organization.

Roles and responsibilities when you are running a contest. It's imperative to have roles outlined at the beginning, including engaging someone who truly understands the technical and business implications of what's being asked.

How will you measure success? Plan for the success of a contest by looking hard at the evaluation of submissions. We recommend that you recruit judges who can comment on at least the following five criteria: impact, innovation, implementation, ease of use, and quality. Communicating the results back to your company is critical, but you need to clearly define the measures of success.

How will you evaluate your contest? Evaluations will be either subjective (for idea generation contests) or objective (for solution generation contests). For fairness and continuity, judges should be recruited before the contest launch and should participate throughout the contest.

Timelines for carrying out your contest. Three to eight weeks is generally a good duration for a contest, though it can go longer if needed. Set aside time for an initial review of the submissions, the final review, and the public awards announcement or ceremony. These phases will typically vary, depending on whether they are ideation or solution generation contests.

How to gain long-term traction using open innovation contests.
NASA was incredibly effective at continually building operating
capacity and momentum to get more and more users by aligning
with the larger organization. Recommendations included shifting
budgets to allocate more toward contest activities; continually
fostering relationships with procurement, legal, and HR; developing an infrastructure for repeatable processes; establishing new
training; and improving on long-term metrics.

Chapter 7

Build an Internal Talent Marketplace

When Vanessa Otake started at Unilever twenty years ago, she worked as an engineer in technically focused R&D roles. Over time, however, her interests shifted. She'd gotten to know the folks in HR, especially the diversity, equity, and inclusion team, and she'd gained a good understanding of their goals and what she could bring to the table. When a job became available on this team, Otake applied, and the team was eager to have her on board.

Otake's shift in roles was a win-win for everyone involved, and Unilever is one of the rare corporations where it could have happened: the company encourages employees to stretch themselves by spending 15 to 20 percent of their time on projects outside the boundaries of their normal jobs. What's more, Unilever managers can solicit help for projects from anyone in the company by writing task descriptions and posting them on an internal platform. Employees, in turn, are encouraged to create and post purpose statements that are then used to match them to projects, gigs, and mentorship opportunities that allow them to pursue more meaningful work within Unilever.

Since 2018, when the platform Unilever uses—flex-work—was launched, the company has unlocked half a million hours of employee engagement and has seen a 41 percent improvement in overall productivity. Flex-work offers other benefits as well, such as helping employees whose jobs are in jeopardy because of automation to seek out opportunities for reskilling. Retraining is a critical concern, given the World Economic Forum's prediction that 50 percent of the global workforce will need to reskill by 2025.

Flex-work is just one example of what we call an internal talent marketplace (ITM). Although some people in the HR industry look at ITMs as the next evolution of traditional HR technology, we see them more as a complement to HR departments—an important tool they can offer to employees. ITMs are one part of a fully digitally transformed talent practice that gives companies another platform to tap into an ecosystem of talent to work on specific tasks. Simply put, ITMs are two-sided platforms that allow the company to, as Unilever CEO Alan Jope says, "redeploy both temporary and permanent resources" in agile ways.[1] These marketplaces motivate and enable employees to develop new skills and help managers to tap skills, knowledge, and capabilities across organizational silos.

The flex-work platform was developed by Gloat and is used by over a hundred companies globally. Its founder, Ben Reuveni, got the idea for the platform when he was working at IBM and realized that it would be easier for him to find a job at a different company than it was to take his career in a new direction at IBM. "When everyone is really focused and has this structure of doing what they should do and only that, that creates less utilization, a less productive environment," he explains.[2]

Hiring and retaining talent is at the core of most organizations' growth concerns. But managing people goes beyond simple employee development or ensuring they achieve particular outcomes. Rather, talent management exists to support an organization's overall objectives, which ultimately boils down to generating ideas and helping the organization retain talent. But how do you ensure that the choices you make about talent align with this goal? The key is to make informed decisions that balance costs and benefits, all with the singular purpose of driving your organization forward. In short, investing in talent management can be a profitable decision, but only if it is done strategically.

There's a subtle yet important distinction between equity and equality. While equity rewards those who give more to the organization and therefore gets more out of those employees, equality means treating everyone the same. The equity-based approach to rewards, however, doesn't consider individuals' special abilities and talents. This is where the concept of an ITM comes in. By focusing on developing knowledge and promoting from within the ranks, companies can create a culture of investment in their people. And the benefits aren't just limited to higher job satisfaction and retention rates—an internal marketplace can boost an organization's brand as well. By breaking down larger training programs into more manageable segments, companies can take advantage of shorter, more responsive forecasts to get the most out of their workforce's potential.

But traditional HR models fail employees in other ways too. Traditional approaches can leave workers wasting their talent on jobs that are a poor fit, that require extra training, or that workers simply don't like. ITMs turn those models upside down. "It's a complete rewrite of HR," says Jean Pelletier, Schneider Electric's vice president of digital talent transformation. "You need to think differently about speed and how to go deep and broad in an organization using an internal talent marketplace, especially when it's fueled by AI."[3] Ultimately, ITMs strengthen the open talent capability of networked organizations, leveraging the power of your internal employees to get work done, whether it's on their own or working in teams that can include external workers on platforms.

This chapter explores the details of building an ITM—a key ingredient for the networked organization. Let's begin with a look at how some important internal platforms got started.

The Emergence of Talent Marketplace Platforms

While the work Jin and the rest of the LISH team did with CoECI (NASA's Center of Excellence for Collaborative Innovation) on external talent clouds (ETCs) and crowdsourcing has gotten the most attention in this book, we also put great effort into researching and helping develop: NASA@Work, the space agency's ITM. In 2010, NASA worked with Wazoku (formerly InnoCentive) to launch twenty internal challenges at the agency's ten centers. The effort initially met significant resistance from managers, who didn't want their employees working on outside projects. What they failed to see—and what CoECI ultimately showed them—was that the road ran both ways. Once the NASA@Work platform was fully established, managers could reach across silos for help on their own projects.

The technology organization SEI took a different path to develop its own brand of an ITM. At first, Ryan Hicke and Sanjay Sharma set out to build an internal marketplace by running three contests with Topcoder to find the best way to go about that task. The solutions they got were creative but difficult to implement. So, they did something much simpler. Sharma started an Excel spreadsheet with projects that his team needed help with and distributed it in a weekly email throughout the technology organization. Lo and behold, those projects were suddenly getting done—one hundred of them over two years, with a success rate of 95 percent. All that it required was getting the word out within SEI, says Sharma: "Now, managers start by looking for talent through a simple internal talent mechanism before they talk about going externally. And our talent is really engaged, as they have learned to use these projects as a way to learn and expand their career opportunities."[4] The ITM program at SEI has accelerated quickly in 2021 and 2022. Now its spreadsheet has been digitized, allowing easier direct access for clients to put up their own projects. Likewise, the supply side of the talent has begun to go beyond SEI employees to include outside team members, inside contractors, and SEI retirees.

Many companies have attempted to use ITMs to their advantage. SAP Blue was an internal platform that started in India to connect idea generators with developers at SAP. It could usually find a match within five minutes. French multinational advertising company Havas took still another approach to building an internal marketplace. Instead of creating something from scratch, it acquired Victors & Spoils to drive its open talent efforts. But as we'll describe more fully in the next chapter, the internal platform failed because it lacked buy-in from the relevant managers.

As with so many other things, the greatest drivers of innovative technologies are users, who know their own needs best of all. When buying or developing software for an ITM, you need to think about not only what you will need from it now but also where you are in the adoption process. If you're in the early days, a simple spreadsheet and email solution like SEI's will help you get started. But if your experiments are getting enough traction that you want to take them to the next level, read on.

The following are some of the leading ITM platforms and platform developers to consider. Each can be adapted to your organizational needs:

> **Gloat.** With its flagship platform InnerMobility, Gloat is the current leader in building robust ITM solutions. Among its clients are Unilever, Schneider Electric, Seagate, and ADP.

> **Fuel50.** This platform has been a pioneer in the marketplace. Founded by two well-known career coaches, the platform benefits from their deep experience in job and career models and competency management and assessment. Ingersoll Rand, Vanguard, and Mercer are some of Fuel50's leading clients.

> **Eightfold AI.** With its AI-based skills inference and analysis system, Eightfold AI is another platform to discover. The company's founders were among Google's original engineers.

> **Workday.** This platform has created a system to provide intelligent matching of people to opportunities for its 1,100-plus

clients and to manage gig-style work and projects. Workday could be a dominant player because of its large installed base of enterprise software.

Goals for Your Internal Talent Marketplace

Building an ITM can be a large undertaking. It helps to start with specific goals that your center of excellence (COE) will aim toward, for example:

- **Unlock agility in your internal talent.** While many organizations understand the importance of agility, especially in the context of digital transformation, they haven't yet applied it to talent. Leaders have been held hostage to traditional HR mindsets and culture; ITMs allow you to pivot at a moment's notice and redeploy your talent to where it's most needed. For example, you can shift your employees and their duties according to the organization's immediate requirements. Instead of laying off workers because of changing market needs, you may find that those employees already have developed some of the skills the company needs to pivot in the marketplace. The change happens frequently in startups and consulting companies. It also occurred at Commonwealth Bank of Australia during the pandemic, when its branch employees shifted to help the call center field questions.

- **Capture cognitive surplus.** Barry Matthews, CEO of Open Assembly, estimates that in most technology organizations, 20 percent of the staff are working on side projects. "There are two ways to approach it," he says. "Either you can try to kill people's side gigs or celebrate them. When you celebrate them, you can also ask people to use their creativity and passion to help your own organization out in different areas."[5] The key is to focus on finding the problems that people will be interested in and getting the word out internally.

- **Encourage high traffic in your ITM.** The problem with most internal platforms is that only a fraction of the community uses them. That's because it's a new way of working. Your chief metric of success will be how many people use your platform and how often. Increase internal traffic by sharing the stories of success widely throughout the organization.

- **Break down silos.** Traditional organizations have rigid talent hierarchies in which employees' skills are hoarded. This structure prevents the overall workforce from achieving its full potential. ITMs break down silos and allow for cross-fertilization.

- **Improve engagement and retention.** If people in your workforce don't see a future with your organization, they're going to find somewhere else to build one. ITMs empower employees to move laterally and vertically and to learn new skills and seek out new opportunities that align with their passion, skills, and ambition. Empowering your employees in this way helps your organization meet its goals.

- **Encourage experiential learning.** Traditional development efforts fall short because they fail to include experiential learning (such as offering ways to learn by doing, rather than just by reading or listening to someone else). These efforts also ignore the employee's acquired knowledge and ability to apply new skills in a real-time setting. ITMs create a unified workforce system that can act as a single source for skills management. Such a system is an important tool for organizations seeking to optimize their human resources and increase efficiency. By providing a consistent understanding of the internal roles, responsibilities, and relationships, organizations can ensure that processes are streamlined and everyone is working toward the same goals. In turn, HR departments will better understand how employees fit into the organizational structure and how they can work in areas that maximize their potential.

Laying the Foundation for an Internal Talent Marketplace

Once you have established the main goals of your ITM and the platform or platforms you'll enlist to help you, it's time to begin developing a robust internal marketplace. As a first step, your COE should do an in-depth assessment of the organization. Do employees take charge of their own career development by seeking out opportunities in other areas of the organization? How well do people in the company collaborate now, within and across departments? Do various parts of the company share talent, or do they hoard it?

Hoarding talent is one of the biggest barriers to internal mobility that we have seen in our research. It is only natural that managers want to keep talent to themselves. When a manager has created a great team and things are firing on all cylinders, it makes sense that they would want to keep the team together. Another barrier we see is fear, which also makes sense. As frustrated as some members of those teams may be with their lack of mobility, others may reject opportunities to move. If a pilot project goes south, or it turns out a person is not a good fit for a new role, they may not be able to get their old job back. But some of those psychological and practical barriers are falling, as the rise of remote work has made it necessary for companies to develop internal platforms and has given a huge impetus to work cultures that are much more flexible.

After doing an organizational assessment to ferret out problems like hoarding, make sure your ITM efforts have the backing of high-level executives, whose sponsorship will be key to success. Ideally, these people or this person will be deeply familiar with your organization's

HR functions. That said, the sponsor must see beyond traditional talent development methods like talent allocation and instead envision talent as personal career development.

Along with getting a sponsor, you'll need to involve key department heads from the beginning and get them to align on strategy. That's because an ITM is not just an incremental tweak to your HR structures; when done right, it fundamentally changes your organization's approach to talent. So, just as it did when building an ETC, your COE should start by holding a workshop with C-suite leaders, HR practitioners, and anyone else from domains where the changes that come with building an ITM will be felt most keenly. Be specific about what the marketplace will deliver and how. In doing so, you enable your team to set measurable objectives for activity against which success can be measured.

The strategy phase of the workshop should define the following:

- The exact problem that talent mobility is solving

- The business case or other success metrics

- The priority areas to focus your first ITM initiatives on

- The range of viable solution options, and the corresponding range of platforms to partner with

- The constraints your enterprise culture, policy, and structures will present

- How impacts on staff development, performance management, and succession planning should be managed in the short, medium, and long run

- The anticipated changes to talent allocation processes

- How you will use communications to shift managers' and employees' mindsets

The currency for success in ITMs is skills, not roles, so the second focus of the workshop should be on the skills map you will use to drive mobility. The map should include both the skills you have today and the skills you will need tomorrow. Most ITM platforms come with a skills catalog to support this today-and-tomorrow approach. If your existing HR technology has components of this as well, you may be able to trade up from a position of at least partial clarity.

ITMs and ETCs have huge parallels in that success at scale lies in the ability to reliably rent talent.* Since your current workforce management processes are geared around roles, you will need structures that are based on functions. The role of the line manager and HR support shift significantly in the new model as well, since talent today has much more say in where it works and what it pursues. Performance management may need a rewrite, resource planning will need a new dashboard, and your culture will need to become much more open and transparent. Given all that, the final focus of your workshop must be to envision the operating model required to deliver an ITM at scale. Most of our ITM consulting support falls into this area.

Launching and Monitoring Pilots

Once you've laid the needed groundwork, including workshopping ideas for your organization's ITM with the relevant department heads, you can start launching some trial balloons in the organization. Consider the following examples.

In 2014, Commonwealth Bank of Australia greenlit Unleashing Innovation, an internal innovation and collaboration program. Employees were invited to submit ideas to improve the bank's products, processes, systems, and services through a platform. Their submission were then evaluated by a panel of senior executives who moved the most promising ones into the bank's innovation lab for incubation. "The Unleashing Innovation platform makes it easier for teams and people across the

---

* Internal talent can also be considered rented when an employee temporarily works on a project outside their normal department or sphere.

bank to collaborate at scale, regardless of who they are, what they do, or where they're located," says Jesse Arundell, open innovation and partnerships lead. "Everyone is innovating and improving what we do for the benefit of the customers and communities we serve."[6]

When Jin met with the bank's executives, it occurred to him that the internal platform could also be used to serve customers in real time as the bank pivoted toward merging talent models with AI capabilities—a pivot many other large enterprises were making. The bank had three channels through which it interacted with customers—over eleven hundred branches, with forty-eight thousand staff, call centers with two thousand employees, and an online portal, including the mobile app. But because of a lack of coordination and communication between them, it had a one-size-fits-all approach to sales. The bank developed a customer engagement engine that captures customer data from all three channels, feeds it through 450 machine-learning models that extract insights from 157 billion data points, and then sends the results back to frontline bank employees, who use it to help customers. Imagine walking into a brick-and-mortar branch and finding out that the representative knows that you've been looking at a home equity loan with this bank, knows how much you can qualify for, or sees how the call center dealt with an erroneous transaction even before you mention the problem. Frontline workers even had prompts about birthdays and other special occasions, as that data was stored and given as suggestions, making customers feel welcome. This customer engagement engine turned everyone into better salespeople rather than just people selling generic products without context—all because of the internal focus on innovative collaborative tools.

NASA took a different approach when it started using NASA@Work. An internal medical team wanted to find a better way to measure astronauts' urine volume in zero-gravity environments. Existing methods were slow and complex and required large pieces of equipment. The team launched a challenge though NASA@Work. Interestingly, someone simply identified a working prototype that had already been developed in a lab at the Johnson Space Center, literally three hundred yards from the challenge owners' lab, for a different purpose. By avoiding the traditional IP acquisition process, the end user was able to skip his planned work and ultimately saved himself (and NASA) $1.3 million and three to five years.

Internal contest compensation and recognition

Because NASA is a government entity, it cannot give bonuses or cash for additional work or IP, even if it originates on internal platforms. So it offers other inducements for participation, such as what the agency called its "cool NASA experiences," like driving a Mars rover, participating in a virtual reality simulation, and having lunch with the director. (A fun fact about the "cool NASA experiences": ideas for those experiences were collected during an ideation contest on NASA@Work.)

From what we've observed at LISH over the years, nothing is as motivating as managerial or organizational recognition. That's why participation in internal contests and projects should be noted positively in formal employee evaluations. Moreover, as with external contests, it's important to be transparent about the evaluation criteria when you are running contests or hackathons. And remember, contestants want to improve. They want feedback. Put yourself in the shoes of someone who is dying to get their idea out there. Even if their idea isn't the best, they expect a response that's a little more useful than, "Sorry, that's not good enough." Offer at least a few kudos for what they got right and pointers on how they might improve.

Not long ago, Jin had an experience that hit close to home about the value of feedback. While watching his then eight-year-old daughter, Amelia, perform her floor routine at her first gymnastics meet of the year, he saw that she was clearly on her way to a score in the high 9s. Even the judges couldn't help but smile. Then, about two-thirds through her routine, she suddenly halted. The crowd gasped and craned their necks. But it wasn't an injury—she had forgotten her routine. It had been so perfect, yet for a split second, she had completely lost it. Then just like that, she picked right back up, tumbling her way to the finish. Her performance had been amazing, but we all knew it would fall short on the scoreboard. The judges gave her an 8.5, which was not good enough to place. Then, at the end of the trophy presentation, another award was announced. Amelia won the Most Fun and Exciting award. This wasn't some empty participation trophy. The judges and event coordinators understood the benefits of recognizing special efforts, and they had thought long and hard about how to honor them.

That kind of acknowledgment is especially important when it comes to efforts from your internal organization. Whether it's cash or some other recognition, leaders should put something on the table for internal efforts; it signals that they're being taken seriously. In situations where monetary prizes can be given, they should be the equivalent of a bonus or what a consultant or contract worker would have received for doing the same work. And senior management can show how seriously it takes the efforts in other ways. We saw a great example at Massachusetts General Hospital when the CEO of the heart center went door to door to make sure that everyone, including clerical staff and nurses, participated in the center's challenge to find the best ideas on high-quality patient care. Frontline employees' insights generated ideas that revealed real issues with operations and patient care. An added benefit: people who feel comfortable and secure in voicing new thoughts about problems on the job are often highly productive when it comes to thinking up creative solutions as well.

Promoting engagement while discouraging biases

One guaranteed mechanism for improving participation and engagement in internal contests—as well as visibility, transparency, and quality assurance—is crowd voting. Not everyone wants to contribute an idea, but many might be willing to evaluate other people's ideas. Crowd voting not only keeps the engagement level high but also ensures that all ideas are strongly considered and that management is not eliminating ones it simply doesn't like. A hybrid approach is the most helpful here—crowd voting to generate finalists, for example, and then an expert committee to choose the winner.

Of course, simply assigning an expert committee does not ensure that its judgments are free of biases. When Karim Lahkani and Eva Guinan were running a challenge on type 1 diabetes research at the Harvard Medical School, we had two panels evaluate the responses, one made up of diabetes experts, the other of nonexperts, and compared the results. This research was conducted through Harvard Catalyst, a networked center that fosters the translation of lab discoveries to patient care. The center adopted open and distributed innovation principles to break down the barriers between Harvard Medical School's various departments. We found that the experts were less open to novelty than nonexperts were, unless the ideas closely tracked their own. This is the innovator's conundrum—that having had breakthroughs themselves, innovators are often suspicious of other work that challenges their own and that could potentially lead to new breakthroughs.

Note too that when participation is low in any internal contest or vote, leaders can sometimes be too quick to close off the event, and they lose good ideas that could have been captured. Instead, they should consider that one phase can lead to another open phase. In the case of Harvard Medical School, it's much easier to have experts with biases evaluate ideas rather than leaning on others to judge novelty. Having a diverse set of inputs from a wide range of solvers is great, you need to make sure that the diversity doesn't end there. Leaders must continue to involve other evaluators to break the mental model of reverting to old, less-effective approaches.[7]

When running and judging contests, organizational leaders need to plan for success but also never underestimate the importance of shepherding along the way. Unfortunately, biases can and do creep into the process. Here are some key ways to control biases:

- **Actively manage the process.** People have an ingrained tendency to revert to old models, so each phase of any experiment should be closely monitored by both the problem owners and their superiors.

- **Don't close off input too early.** It's easy to close off an internal open talent project too early, before all the good ideas are captured.

- **Have a diversity of judges.** Having a diverse set of inputs from a wide range of *problem solvers* is great, but the diversity shouldn't end there. Having a broad range of *evaluators* makes it less likely that they will default to the current consensus.

Expanding the Internal Talent Marketplace

Building on the foundation you've created requires the right vision and communication for further growth. The point is not to stall after one or two successes. Here are five important considerations when you are establishing an ITM:

- **Advanced technology.** As we noted earlier in the chapter, SEI used a spreadsheet to get started, but building the ITM will require additional technological investments. The temptation to prioritize technology over people is real, but humans must always come first. Without the right people in place, technology is often a hollow solution that fails to drive productivity or spark meaningful change. Unfortunately, a focus on technological resources over human ones can lead to internal talent being undervalued and overlooked. To combat this risk, the COE can be responsible for driving change. However, in doing so, the center may inadvertently break the connection between innovation and the rest of the business. It's a tricky balance but one that's crucial to strike if you want to create lasting change through your technology investments.

- **How to use the data.** Internal talent innovation often starts
  with identifying inefficiencies and fixing them. But how do you
  find those problem spots? The answer is simple: data. Start
  collecting information on your current processes, and analyze it
  to see what's working and what's not. Look for areas that stand
  out as particularly inefficient, and brainstorm ways to address
  them. Don't forget to train your team on data literacy to get the
  most accurate results. With a data-driven approach, you'll
  identify problem areas and implement solutions more
  effectively—the key to successful innovation.

- **Time quotas.** Building an ITM is going to put a strain on your
  employees. They'll need to do something they don't normally
  do, so be sure to clearly express your reasoning regarding its
  value. One big factor that companies ignore is the extra time,
  attention, and resources that such initiatives need to succeed.
  Depending on employees' roles, they may have little downtime
  to work on ITM initiatives, and so this new way of work will
  always take a backseat. That's why managers need to think
  about how to allocate ongoing resources to ensure that these
  initiatives get the attention they deserve.

- **Sensitive topics and tacit knowledge.** While an ETC has its
  place, some delicate tasks require a more nuanced approach—
  especially when sensitive information is involved. An ITM is
  better suited for these kinds of tasks, which demand specific
  expertise and can require you to develop new business areas,
  scout for incremental talents, or define enterprise strategy. Of
  course, you need to balance your use of inside and outside
  talent. For example, you shouldn't task internal "volunteers" on
  heavy IT development projects since they don't have the time to
  look into how these systems function. Most want to contribute
  to be part of a bigger process but may unlikely be folded in as a
  main contributor because they have no skin in the game. Plus,
  unlike the situation with an ETC, you don't have to worry as

much about IP rights with an ITM. You are freer to focus on the big picture.

- **Innovation and entrepreneurial thinking.** The purpose of an ITM is to generate creativity and innovation, so be sure to foster the right environment for these ideas to grow into something meaningful. Inclusion and recognition are key to engaging employees in internal projects. Otherwise, resentment and feelings of alienation can breed among team members, creating a divide that stifles innovation. That's why it's important to build systematic touchpoints that blur the lines between internal and external work. The good news is that by encouraging entrepreneurial thinking, companies that can use ITMs are creating a more fertile ground for innovation. Instead of viewing the time spent on campaigns as a waste, your people will come to see it as an investment in the future.

. . .

When it comes to decisions on whether to access the ITM or run an ETC project, use discernment. There's a perception to overcome that people in an ITM can be a plug-and-play fix for everything without the context of business use cases. Some companies look to use an ITM for large-scale projects that require inside knowledge of the company and its technology for technical development projects rather than for suggestions on design features. Design projects can be better suited for an ETC.

ITMs often begin with contests, but their most powerful and long-lasting effect is the way they break down vertical hierarchies and silos, allowing companies to become networks rather than pyramids.

Next we will dive into putting all the pieces together to help you digitally transform your talent strategy and become a networked organization at scale. We will look at a few brave organizations that have gotten to the scale phase and explore what they're learning at this frontier.

KEY IDEAS

ITMs are not merely the next evolution of HR technology. They transform organizations by offering employees who have a cognitive surplus the opportunity to work on projects they desire. In effect, these marketplaces also help employees with upskilling and reskilling while allowing them to maintain a sense of innovation and opportunities for professional growth. The ITM is best used to retain employees and can be quite powerful when combined with remote work and skill-building opportunities. For the enterprise, unlocking agility, breaking down silos, and capturing the cognitive surplus are just a few benefits.

The first goal of the ITM is to make room for renting talent, which means the organizational structure and culture pivot toward skills, not roles. Accordingly, operating models will need to change. We recommend initially holding a leadership workshop to address these ideas and map out the process. The second goal leverages the internal contest platform. Include a good communication strategy, ensure visibility and transparency, and encourage wide-scale engagement. Crowd voting is a tool that organizations have used to extend continual engagement and allow for a collective voice.

The emergence of talent marketplace platforms. To make sure you set yourself up properly from the start, you'll need to take stock of how far along your organization is in its adoption process. This assessment will determine which software solution is most suited toward your goals. Platforms offer software, but only you can know how the software will fit in with your organization's internal needs.

Goals for your ITM. Employee engagement is key. To unlock untapped resources, push for agility. Some people may already have the skills you are looking for, and you need to capture the cognitive surplus. Encouraging continual learning will break down silos and improve engagement.

Laying the foundation for an ITM. Don't revert to hoarding talent. Instead, senior executives need to continually push the message about reinventing structures around functions rather than roles. The backing of executive sponsorship helps with talent renting.

Launching and monitoring pilots. Even in a pilot, inherent biases will creep up, and you'll have the tendency to revert to the old way of doing things. Input and talent sharing can come from anywhere in the organization, not just from the experts or the best performers overall. Be sure to think about incentives for participation. Recognition and rewards, even something as small as badges on your platform, go a long way.

Expanding the ITM. The temptation to prioritize technology over people is real, with potential risks that internal talent will be undervalued and overlooked. Look for inefficiencies that could be improved on, and brainstorm solutions to address them. Then find data that helps measure these inefficiencies. When it comes to participation on projects, time management is a major factor that companies overlook, as it can be difficult for employees to give ITM initiatives the resources and attention they deserve. Managers need to ensure that these initiatives are allocated the ongoing resources and attention they need. For tasks requiring specialized knowledge, such as expanding into new business areas, talent scouting, and enterprise strategy, an ITM may be a better choice than an ETC.

Chapter 8

Scale Your Networked Organization

When Havas bought John Winsor's company, Victors & Spoils, John had high hopes that the new owner would catalyze and scale change throughout the entire enterprise. To kick off the change effort, V&S had introduced into the organization a new internal marketplace platform, called Havas Crowd. The idea was simple: anyone inside Havas could upload a brief onto the platform, describing a problem that needed solving or a project on which they needed help or input. And anyone in the organization could respond to any brief. Yet the platform was dead on arrival. Not one of Havas's three hundred local CEOs would allow its use. Why?

This book in part has been our attempt to answer that question. So many lessons came out of that failed change program. Namely, don't try to run before you can walk. Havas leadership had tried to force the company into a 400-meter sprint from a seated position on the ground. But as we've described in these pages, change is a process—primarily a process of changing mindsets. Before attempting to scale Havas Crowd organizationally, the company didn't take its executives through the process to help change their mindsets, change the culture, and then to assess, learn about, and build open talent solutions. The platform was introduced into the organization at scale before any of those three hundred CEOs were given a chance to learn about the benefits of having an internal open talent mechanism.

The platform's failure brings us to another key lesson learned from the Havas change effort: the ideas and the process lacked a home. Before a company can shift to a networked organization, you need to establish a center of excellence (COE). Preferably your center will consist of a team drawn from various parts of the organization. But in a pinch, even just one focused person can do the work of designing, leading, and managing the change process if that person has enough leadership backing.

With a COE, your open talent journey has a structure to support it. That's what we saw at places like NASA, Deloitte, and GE. But at Havas, without a process to shift the mindsets of the people and the organization as a whole—and lacking a COE to lead that process—the chances of the new platform's ever getting to the building phases, much less to a scaling phase, were slim to none.

To be sure, scaling will be the most difficult undertaking of all the phases we've described in the transition to a fully networked organization. You need to look back at what worked in previous phases—at the assess, learn, and build phases of the journey—and then replicate those things across various parts of the organization, one at a time rather than all at once—unless your company is small.

Small companies can scale open talent more easily. We've already described companies like Victors & Spoils, which used platforms somewhat haphazardly before focusing on a strategy to weave open talent throughout the company. These smaller enterprises not only transformed themselves digitally but also benefited from efficiently working with talent both internally and externally to reach for higher and higher goals.

Most users of open talent today are precisely these small to midsize businesses, according to our research. These include one-person shops spending $50 dollars on a graphic design project and larger companies spending more than $1 million. The average annual spend for these businesses using direct self-service platforms is $8,000. That includes the cost to do project work on the platforms; this cost includes payment to the talent and fees to the platforms.

While many large companies also configure open talent solutions on their own, only a handful of those—0.03 percent of the customer base for platforms—are building a scalable open talent enterprise solution. That number is shockingly low, given the trajectory we see for the next frontier of growth in digital and AI. This forecast points precisely to why technology startups can scale quickly and increase their valuation exponentially. Many large organizations need to use this strategy to become more agile and adopt more startup-type mindsets by shifting workforces to adopt to task-based work. In ten years, everyone will be on the path to becoming a networked organization.

In this chapter, we will look at scaling and expanding your digital network, internally and externally. Let's start with a look at some companies that have scaled successfully.

Scaling Open Talent at Deloitte and NASA

Unlike what occurred at Havas, the approach to scaling that Balaji Bondili took at Deloitte was process-based and process-focused and was supported by the structure of Bondili's own COE, Deloitte Pixel. In the midst of the tech talent shortage, which hit Deloitte and its clients hardest in the areas of analytics and data science, Bondili and his team saw that the platform Experfy could play a role in its worldwide operations. Experfy has forty thousand data scientists on tap, so Deloitte decided to make a significant investment in the platform to ensure maximum access to talent. But instead of imposing Experfy on Deloitte departments and clients from the top down, Bondili's team sold it "door to door," using word of mouth from satisfied users to tell others and to create network effects. The team also relied on carrots, introducing into staff performance evaluations explicit goals and rewards for using open talent approaches in their projects. And the team used sticks, too, by withholding approval of projects unless they at least included some consideration of using open talent. Moreover, in evaluating partners' performance, Deloitte started focusing on margins rather than revenues, because use of platforms like Experfy lowers revenue but improves margins.

What ultimately tipped things toward platform usage was the Covid-19 pandemic, which quadrupled the amount of open talent being used across the board. Working remotely rewired many people's thinking about whether workers really needed to be on-site—or, for that matter, permanently employed. With the success Deloitte has had with Deloitte Pixel and Experfy, Bondili has been tapped to expand his role and become the managing director of new product and asset innovations, strategy, and analytics at Deloitte, overseeing all of open talent and contingent-talent relationships.

Along with having the right person to lead the scale phase, the organization is creating a model that has fully integrated open talent thinking throughout its entire culture and systems. NASA's Jenn Gustetic, the director of early-stage innovations and partnerships, is bringing together different parts of the organization's open talent ecosystem, including its CoECI and large-scale open R&D programs like Centennial Challenges, to create a culture of innovation that promotes the development of new ideas from within and without.

As Gustetic notes, open talent ecosystems offer opportunities beyond what is available daily within the organization. For example, upskilling of people's talents, knowledge, and networks happens much more widely because everyone is aware of all the available options, inside and outside of NASA. Moreover, with open systems, employees are encouraged to take ownership of their projects and not simply execute the tasks given to them. People then have a wider range of creativity in how they approach problems and how quickly they can reach a successful outcome.

Gustetic recalls how the culture shift at NASA is what allowed for the scaling of open tools and the CoECI: "When I started at NASA, all of our best tech tools were only available internally, and if you wanted something that would help you do your job better—or something completely new—then it was going to take five years for you to get it. Even then, you didn't know if the project would be completed—so it was best to just do what you were told."

What are some lessons to take from NASA and Deloitte? First, the freedom to use internal and external platforms allows employees to think strategically about planning for the possibilities rather than just doing the work in front of them. As a result, technology development at these organizations has happened much quicker with light and fast strategies for improving systems. It's embedded in how they move quickly now and how they plan for the future. And second, when an internal staff member acquires a new project, they should aim to establish a healthy balance between outside-the-box thinking about goals and the actual execution of the steps toward those goals. Without goals and execution plans, open tools are a means to develop ideas but are nothing tangible. Then, communicating objectives and tasks with both internal and external teams helps minimize friction. Bringing the internal staff along is paramount to changing the corporate culture, especially when difficulties arise.

Most important, before attempting to scale open talent across the company, leaders need to think through, clarify, and communicate the role of internal and external platform workers and what that means for the broad direction of their workforce architecture. An example is a dental business we studied. The owners wanted to grow the business and saw the potential to expand the dental services they offered by drawing on freelance specialists. The move significantly improved both the quality of patient care and the practice's growth and financial performance.

Scaling with the COLOR Spectrum

So how can your organization introduce and scale open talent approaches? To ensure that everything runs smoothly, we devised guidelines that we call the COLOR spectrum (communications, organizational structure, leadership, operations, and relationships).

Communications

Open talent leaders focused on scaling their strategy should be keenly aware of how quickly the culture can reject new ideas (as executives at Havas did). As we discussed, people view open talent as an existential threat to the organization. That's why you need to be thoughtful about the kind of story you want to communicate. More than data analysis or number crunching, it's the story that will drive your outcomes. Communication is about storytelling, and storytelling is about getting people to care. And to get people to care, you need to build emotion.

For years, we talked to organizations about how great the NASA contest work was since it yielded extreme value solutions. While this outcome resonated with some people, others saw it as off-putting. Why? Unbeknownst to us, those people weren't looking for a result that was ten times faster or a hundred times better. They just wanted a way to find solutions that were manageable or comparable to what they already knew how to do. Lesson learned: know your audience, and craft the narrative to fit those people. The metrics involved in open talent are many, and the benefits are vast.

What's more, just circulating your message is not enough. Effective communication requires follow-up to answer questions and clear up any misunderstandings. Secrets or the appearance of secrets can destroy any chance of trust. Accordingly, if a key decision-maker misses a presentation, don't assume they will get an accurate accounting of it. Seek them out to make sure they understand how they will be affected. Corporate communications can be like a game of Telephone. People repeat messages in their own words after refracting them through their own thought processes.

Active communication, together with reactive responses, enables leaders to address resistance head-on. Constantly telling people how great open talent is can backfire—what's most important is that they understand that it is needed and that it works. Here are a few more tips on how to communicate your company's intentions to scale open talent:

- **Create common standards.** Use common language, values, and frameworks to align people and objectives. Introducing new language and jargon can create unnecessary friction.

- **Collaborate at the speed of trust.** Invite a level of transparency in which honest criticism and conflict can occur without bringing harm.

- **Build on a defined purpose.** Work to develop a common understanding and agreement among team members about what they are trying to accomplish and how it connects with the organization's mission and strategic goals.

- **Use a data-driven approach.** Teams should focus their efforts on the data that matters most, seeking quantitative information that will drive decisions and actions in the effort—and serve as a benchmark to define progress later on.

- **Walk the talk.** Don't delegate too much. Having skin in the game shows your confidence in open talent.

- **Foster autonomy and empowerment.** You will develop trust and draw out people's intelligence by encouraging them to make their own decisions.

- **Identify ambassadors.** As external talent plans unfold, identify, and empower internal ambassadors.

- **Be transparent.** Use every opportunity to update your team, other employees, and external partners on progress, hurdles, and lessons learned.

- **Reframe and address concerns.** Openly engage with critics. You and they will learn from the effort.

- **Focus on results.** Be relentless in your focus on results. Nothing else matters, especially chatter about who said what or why a decision was made. All that matters is whether you are accomplishing your goals.

- **Communicate with clarity and vision.** Communicate a vision that is easy to understand, enjoys broad support, and aligns everyone on the team.

- **Celebrate solution seekers.** Highlight the rewards of collaboration.

Organizational structure

Trying to persuade people to change their behavior won't work unless the fundamentals of structure, reward systems, operations, and training are redesigned to support them. Even when the formal structures and tools needed to scale open talent are in place, the established culture can still undermine them if people revert to long-held beliefs and ways of behaving. Consider recent McKinsey & Company research, which reported that 85 percent of executives polled said their organizations were afraid to innovate, to implement new ideas, or to change the culture.[1]

To better your odds, follow these five guidelines:

- **Start at the top.** Talent is every CEO's biggest priority. It's important to engage employees at every level, but we've observed that all successful open talent scaling initiatives start at the top, with a committed and well-aligned group of executives strongly supported by the CEO.

- **Involve every layer.** The path to open talent is always smoother if people are tapped for input on issues that will affect their jobs. This means you have to go slow to go fast. Steve Rader at NASA says, "I have to be walking the halls of NASA and always be telling people about the transformative work we're doing at CoECI. The adoption of open talent is a one-on-one process."

- **Act your way into new thinking.** Many change initiatives assume that people will begin to shift their behaviors once formal elements like directives and incentives have been put in place. But leaders must also model the behavior by using open talent themselves.

- **Seek out continuous engagement.** Scaling open talent is not a one-and-done effort. It takes continuous engagement. Vinod Kartha, UST's vice president of strategic initiatives, and his team have a weekly newsletter that keeps everyone in the company up to speed about open talent.

- **Lead outside the lines.** Think about who the informal influencers are, inside and outside your organization, and approach them. Influence is many times more important than structural adoption. If the right partner, director, or internal leader says that open talent works and would be transformative for the organization, then make sure they are heard.

Let's look at an example from a large consumer bank, the Commonwealth Bank of Australia, which we discussed in chapter 7. It illustrates how a flexible organization can leverage both internal and external ideas to build products while promoting engagement. The bank does this structurally in the way it innovates, employs technology, and executes on its plans.

Innovation. After succeeding in connecting silos through networks of platforms, Commonwealth Bank of Australia continued to explore ways to grow the network. For example, its internal digital platform, called Unleashing Innovation, hosted crowdsourcing contests and always-on continuous improvement channels aligned to its businesses. The platform has provided a pathway for employees across the bank to collaborate by improving efficiencies in their internal operations.

In fiscal year 2020 alone, over 25 percent of the bank's employees had actively used the platform, which led to the submission of 8,664 ideas and a collection of 42,948 votes cast and comments submitted on ideas raised. What's more, the bank was also able to track the delivery of 1,276 ideas through the platform—meaning that nearly 15 percent of all ideas raised through the platform were delivered, leading to material business value for the bank and its customers.

Technology. The bank launched the Unleashing Innovation platform by using existing enterprise collaboration tools such as Microsoft SharePoint and Yammer. That way, the bank could colocate its digital platform with its other enterprise social tools. This connection between the digital and social tools has since helped scale some of the bank's other internal collaboration initiatives. For example, employees are encouraged to submit new ideas that either enhance customers' experience with the bank or improve efficiency in internal operations. Ideas are uploaded by employees and voted on by a group of peers. Since launching Unleashing Innovation, the bank has seen a significant increase in engagement with ideas and innovation across its entire organization.

In 2017, the bank opened up its Unleashing Innovation platform externally, to customers, for the first time, by inviting members of its loyalty network to post their ideas on how Commonwealth Bank could better engage with them as customers. Members of the public then voted on these ideas, and in this case, the platform received over forty-five hundred votes. The bank also saw hundreds of comments posted on these suggestions from customers who either up-voted or down-voted them. Because of this initiative, the bank has identified over fifty ideas to be tested in its branches across Australia and New Zealand.

Follow-up and execution. The Unleashing Innovation platform community is available to employees 24-7. Employees can access online surveys about their thoughts on the bank's current status and any opportunities they see for change. This survey then automatically populates to all the employees within the respondents' network. The bank offers follow-up to employee feedback via live workshops four or five times a year for its staff.

The bank also continues to invite its customers in by allowing them to post their ideas on how the bank can improve its customer experience. These suggestions are then reviewed by employees, who either up-vote or down-vote the idea and comment on whether these ideas should move to the next stage. Every idea has an equal chance of being adopted into the bank's products or strategies because every employee can vote on each idea and provide feedback on whether it should be taken further.

Leadership

The next element in our COLOR method, leadership, is paramount for scaling open talent. Just as leaders need to set the tone for the initial adoption of platforms, they also need to drive any scaling effort. Passion is contagious; if you as a leader are passionate about open talent, your people will be too. Model curiosity and open-mindedness. Most important of all, take responsibility for both your successes and your failures. There can be no change without learning, and no learning without failure.

Open talent requires transformational leadership rather than transactional leadership. While transactional leaders limit choices, transformational leaders develop fresh approaches to long-standing problems, surfacing new options and making corrections continually and in real time. Leaders who share power with employees rather than holding it over them influence people more deeply. A good leader should learn from others in the organization and around the world. They should be willing to try something unusual and take advice from peers, colleagues, and even competitors where appropriate. And because everything is changing so rapidly around the globe, a networked leader should keep up with the latest technologies and trends and embrace the mindset of a student-leader.

Consider the example of James "Hondo" Geurts, who served as an executive for the US Special Operations Command (SOCOM)'s $8 billion acquisitions organization for more than seventy thousand civil servants and operatives. Despite the fixed resources and dollar constraints of his deeply bureaucratic governmental organization, Geurts was always on the lookout for fresh new ideas to inject into his projects, which often concerned soldier safety.[2]

In the spring of 2015, Geurts found one of his best ideas: the renovation of a 10,000-square-foot abandoned telephone book factory in Tampa, Florida, into an innovation engine to bridge ideas, talent, and entrepreneurship. With limited funds ($2 million), Geurts and his team launched SOFWERX—an open architecture for tech acquisitions and rapid prototyping for entrepreneurs in partnership with a nonprofit.

For SOFWERX, the objectives were not solely around software capabilities to build networks; the real power came from tying together themes around soldier safety. Traditionally, SOCOM's missions carried an aura of secretive strategy with highly specialized experts. With the new platform's mission to improve soldier safety, Geurts needed to reframe the problem and find collaborators. He also knew that to accomplish its goals, SOCOM needed to make the problem apparent to anyone using the platform, which eliminated the big contractors that were lacking innovative solutions. Almost overnight, SOCOM—one of the world's most secretive organizations—became the most open.

Geurts's most pressing concern was to accelerate SOCOM's software and data analytics capabilities. Using SOFWERX's architecture, his team conducted maker fairs and collaborative events that set the stage for virtual problem-solving challenges. In another project, Hack the Pentagon, the government legally authorized hackers to detect threats inside the Department of Defense network infrastructure for cash payments. Of the 250 submitted reports, 138 were credible and addressed by the government. Later, Geurts and his team scaled SOFWERX by inviting more and more users into its virtual network of hackers and members of the maker community who provided valuable intel on cybersecurity vulnerabilities.

The excitement over SOFWERX was largely the reason for Geurts's promotion to assistant secretary of the navy for research, development, and acquisition, where he was asked to scale SOFWERX-type activities across the Department of Defense.

Among the leadership lessons we learned from Geurts:

- **Think about how to bring outsiders in.** Though SOCOM is supposed to be more agile in acquisitions than the rest of the department, the command was still not fast enough to address soldier safety issues and credible threats. By thinking outside the box, Geurts brought onboard small nontraditional companies to put together ideas that the larger contractors could never come up with or that would take too long. He encouraged micro-entrepreneurship through open means as a way to flip the system on its head.

- **Leverage what's already happening as a way to attract and create a network.** Open talent leverages how individuals find problems, not just assigning a challenge to a single outsourcing company. Traditional actors are good at spotting the well-known, but some situations call instead for the fastest approaches. SOFWERX was interested in a speed report about what was credible without the need for a full assessment. Eventually, open talent contributions came at no cost, with some contributors offering guidance and help to create new opportunities. A similar phenomenon occurs with open-source software and contributors to open code.

We've also seen how developing and scaling open talent must sometimes come from the outside in, from a leader, or from a customer of a COE. The outside-in approach is especially appropriate if an internal leader is struggling to get traction. For example, in 2017 we met Mina Bastawros, vice president of creative and digital marketing at Airbus, when he became interested in open talent and crowdsourcing. We connected him with Steve Rader at NASA, and Bastawros used NASA's

CoECI as an inspiration for building a COE at Airbus. After his efforts gained some momentum, Bastawros became frustrated by the bureaucracy. When he tried to spin the division out, Airbus wouldn't let him. So, he took another job at Airbus in strategy and started doing the open talent work as a side gig for other companies. The Airbus open talent efforts were still bumping along with the team Bastawros had put in place but with little traction. Then, Bastawros was offered the job of leader of all of digital marketing for Airbus. He accepted—but only if he could use open talent, crowdsourcing, and freelancers to build his team. Today, he's the biggest user of the COE he established years ago, and he spends 90 percent of his budget with open talent.

We love this perspective—that sometimes the best way to solve the adoption problem is to move from being a change agent building a capability to a leader or an internal customer who is *using* that capability. Now, other Airbus divisions are gaining momentum using open talent, having seen Bastawros as the pioneering customer.

Operations

The next part of the COLOR method for scaling networked organizations is your operations. The exponential growth of remote work has shown the power of new digital operating systems like Slack, Trello, Miro, Figma, and Zoom. By 2020, most employers had already switched to cloud-based storage, email, word processing, and video streaming. Cloud data centers are much more efficient than their on-site counterparts because the cloud uses modular structures that can be expanded as needed for face-to-face meetings. The same kinds of tools that enabled the shift to remote work can smooth the transition to open talent—provided that they are backed up by changes in policy.

When thinking about operational changes, you'll want to take the following approaches:

- **Prioritize partnerships over structure.** Take a keen look at internal policies and processes that prioritize structure and work, and replace them with ones that encourage partnerships. For example, put a hard limit on the number of meetings that can be scheduled into your calendar—no exceptions.

- **Motivate people by giving them more influence and responsibility.** Encourage your team to take an open, merit-based approach to giving and receiving feedback. For example, invite all staff on the path toward promotion or leadership roles (including nonleadership or nonmanagement positions) to give and receive feedback from their peers or customers using formal 360-degree feedback processes.

- **Reward innovation and excellence.** Consider different ways to encourage your people to come up with and execute new ideas. For example, create a community of practice in your organization where employees from different areas can share their expertise and best practices using a tool like Slack or Yammer.

- **Focus on individuals and interactions.** Introduce systems that facilitate interactions between the extended workforce. For example, invest in and promote a learning culture that creates opportunities for people to share their expertise with others who don't have the same skill sets.

- **Create organizational operational standards.** Use processes and guidelines that are easily accessible to external collaborators and freelancers. Replace proprietary software with open-source, nonexclusive tools and templates. Accessible tools and processes will reduce the learning curve for external crowd participants.

Relationships

Finally, the last part of the COLOR model is a focus on relationships, one of the keys to success when scaling your open talent efforts. Leaders should focus especially on the tension that might exist between people who work inside the company full-time and those contributing from the outside. Historically, leaders used this tension in a positive way to recruit and retain talent. In the new world of talent, the insider-club mentality works against you. You need to build strong relationships that allow you to exchange information, knowledge, advice, and influence from both inside and outside the company. That brings us back to honing your basic communication tools and remembering the power of courtesy, reciprocity, and a culture of inclusiveness and mutual respect.

Many models can help us think about the relationships in communities and companies and how these relationships might inform and scale a networked strategy and prompt real innovation. One such model is the ecological concept of *ecotone*. An ecotone is an area where two distinctive ecosystems—such as a forest and a wetland—meet, creating an ecosystem that is neither wholly one ecosystem nor the other but has all the attributes of both. Ecotones are found at the fringes of natural systems and organizations alike. The greater the overlap, the deeper the dialogue and the better the opportunity to create deeper relationships. Explore this overlap, understand it, and communicate your insights widely.

. . .

All five elements of the COLOR spectrum require a basis of trust between leaders and the rank and file. Trust is not something we can take for granted. You can only build and sustain it by keeping your promises and commitments. The goal is to be in sync with the talent you work with and give them the process and tools to be in sync with each other. When they are, your group enjoys network effects and synchronicities.

Next, we look at the case of UST and how it scaled into a networked organization.

Case Study: UST's Efforts to Scale Open Talent

While some open talent efforts like Deloitte Pixel and those we've seen at NASA take years to develop, others can accelerate rather quickly. The example of UST highlights a post-pandemic effort to gather large amounts of talent at scale. Based in California, UST provides services in cloud computing, digital transformation, development operations, cybersecurity, and innovation. It has thirty-five thousand full-time employees and suffers from the same shortages of technology talent as everyone else in its space.

In late 2021, when Manu Gopinath, the company's chief operating officer and chief people officer, surveyed the landscape, he became very nervous. Before the pandemic, the talent shortage had been an issue but was mostly manageable. In some ways, it even helped UST, which was often hired by companies that needed to fill gaps in their own capabilities. But now UST was losing people to the Great Resignation; the loss was threatening to slow UST's revenue growth and possibly derail its planned growth in 2023.

Gopinath tapped Vinod Kartha, the aforementioned vice president of strategic initiatives, to explore open talent. Kartha connected with Barry Matthews, CEO of Open Assembly, to create a strategic plan.

Kartha quickly dove into learning mode as he formed a COE and began an assessment. UST had recently signed an enterprise agreement with Upwork to help it find freelancers to create marketing collateral. Kartha quickly expanded the relationship to encompass open talent and began to think about pilots.

"When companies like Salesforce, Facebook, and Twitter announce that everybody working for them can now work from home, you think, 'How do we compete with that?'" Kartha recalled. "So we thought, instead of trying to do something incremental, why not do something disruptive?" As Kartha put it, he didn't see any other options, and the change was just a question of when, not why. "I started feeling the pulse of the organization," he said. "Everybody I talked to said yes. There was not a single person who said no. The only question left was, How do we make it happen? So I dug in."[3]

Although UST was open to change, Kartha understood that its clients might not be. He decided to study and experiment with any sticking points. Kartha discovered that the most important issue to solve was cybersecurity. Any breach of a client's security would be catastrophic. For this reason, rather than allowing freelancers into their systems, most companies ship laptops to them because it's the only way to secure the data. The alternative solution Kartha came up with was a virtual desktop infrastructure (VDI). With a VDI, remote employees and freelancers can use their own devices to obtain access to a company's system. Solving this security issue created a lot of momentum for UST.

Kartha described how conversations go today: "Clients always ask, 'How do you handle privacy and security? What about vendor verification? What about interviews?' We have answers for most of them, which puts us in a very, very good place."

It's one thing to build and scale an open talent ecosystem and toolset within your own organization, but the benefits grow exponentially if you can share what you're learning and building with your whole ecosystem, including your clients and your suppliers. Open talent is not the be-all and end-all; it is certainly not about replacing your full-time talent. UST calls it a plus-one option that has both upsides and downsides. On the upside, there are saved costs, as open talent hires for tasks, not roles. Not only do you save on fees, which are considerably less than the 20 to 35 percent that traditional recruiting organizations charge, but the workers are only paid for the tasks that they do.

"Everybody realizes that when I hire somebody like an architect to do the work, they're not busy for the full six months or for that year," Kartha said. "The actual work takes two months. The rest of the time is meetings and all the other stuff."

UST is now starting to say no to clients. It wants to create a scarcity mindset, similar to the luxury industry model. "I want to only produce a hundred Gucci bags," Kartha said. "I don't want this to be a solution for everyone, because I wouldn't be able to support it. Our goal is to learn. My ultimate vision is to create an open talent ecosystem. I don't care if it's internal full-time, contractor, or freelance talent."

Transforming the ecosystem starts with fortifying the operational elements for UST's open talent practice and giving them the ability to have apple-to-apple comparisons with current talent options, including hiring someone full-time.

Kartha shared a story about getting a data science project done internally versus using open talent: "Traditionally what you do is build the API. Then you hire a data scientist to do the algorithm. It's all sequenced, and it takes three people and a few weeks to do. Instead, we put the project on Upwork." Kartha uploaded the dataset and the goals, and a freelancer took two days and $150 to solve it. "You don't need to reinvent the wheel," Kartha added. "And the accuracy was there, 92 percent." This data science project would have been a six-month effort. Instead, Kartha's team got it done in two weeks.

"That's the only way I can help to make open talent scale," said Kartha. He presents the clients with each of the talent choices one by one to show them the actual differences. "None of our clients will ever say that they're only going to work with open talent," he said. "It's always going to be a combination—internal hires, external hires, freelance, contractors, etc. It's about giving our clients a choice. For [our client] Anthem, the most important thing is to solve for their retiring workforce in the next five years. How do you retain the knowledge? How do you transfer it? That's their primary challenge. For Visa, on the other hand, the problem is that they need tech talent to fill over thirteen hundred open positions. Currently, the only option they see is to go and hire full-time talent or get contractors. But the rates are too high and the talent is not available. It's an impossible problem for them."

But UST is also scaling its internal network. One project is the company's HR management software platform, which is built on Fusion software. There's a huge shortage of Fusion talent looking for full-time work, but there are many freelancers globally who have Fusion experience, who can be found on Upwork, and who are willing to work for $15 to $35 an hour. UST's development backlog is two years old. Kartha's team compartmentalized the tasks and put them out to bid.

Using open talent not only got UST through its talent crunch but also added a multiplier to the company's valuation as it prepared to go public. Open talent changed UST from an analog consulting business to a talent network built on a platform.

. . .

The scale phase is crucial to the organization's full adoption of open talent practices. You must continually assess, learn, and experiment—all while building on the COE's core foundation to impact the entire organization.

With the right person at the helm, your company can commit to investing even more into open talent models that will be fully integrated throughout its entire culture and systems. But to do so effectively, leaders must move quickly. In the next chapter, we will explore how to speed up the integration of open talent. Although we have already established the cultural and operational framework, leaders must exercise an abundant mindset and shift to intertwine tasks, talent, and technology.

KEY IDEAS

Scaling will be the most difficult part of your journey in leveraging open talent. You need to review what has worked strategically for the assess, learn, experiment, and build and replicate phases of the journey across parts of your organization. A strong COE can help continually build on the culture and the operations of what has worked. It can also maintain the base of the open talent already in place in your organization while exploring new pathways to scale ETC, open innovation capabilities, and ITM more efficiently and effectively.

Scaling open talent at Deloitte and NASA. Both NASA and Deloitte have demonstrated success, with each organization taking less time to get to where it needed to be.

Scaling with the COLOR spectrum. The COLOR spectrum (communications, organizational structure, leadership, operations, and relationships) is a good guide to ensure that everything runs smoothly. Tell the story, make it human, and bring people along with you. It can feel like a marathon more than a sprint, but passion and conviction are contagious. But at the same time, be pragmatic and clear about the results and the steps needed to achieve them. Make an exciting new idea feel tangible and not remain in the clouds. Remember that your audience and every conversation will almost always start on the defense.

Case study: UST's efforts to scale open talent. There's no need to reinvent the wheel. Clients want choices, so be sure to communicate that there's a list of options.

Chapter 9

Accelerate the Adoption
of Open Talent

On May 29, 1953, Edmond Hillary and Tenzing Norgay became the first two people to reach the summit of Mount Everest. Getting to the top of the world was a triumph that had been decades in the making. Previous expeditions had tried new techniques and slowly gained altitude, only to fail at the end. Hillary and Norgay used a siege strategy, deploying 362 porters, 20 Sherpa guides, and five tons of baggage. After hiking for sixteen days to reach the foot of the mountain, they established a base camp. Over the next two and a half months, they made several trips up and down the mountain to ferry oxygen and other gear up the slope, fix ropes, and establish camps, making certain that when the window of opportunity opened in late May, they would be ready for the push to the summit.

Now, consider the modern alpine climbing approach. A climber, usually alone or with a single partner, puts everything on their back for one push. In 2017, Kilian Jornet, a Spanish climber, set a new record, summiting Everest and returning to his base camp in just twenty-six hours, using no oxygen or fixed ropes. Less than a week later, he did it again.

Hillary's, Norgay's, and Jornet's breakthroughs are all connected, since without those earlier efforts, Jornet would not have known what was even possible. But the biggest shift was not in physical capabilities or even equipment—although both played a role—but mindset. Jornet redesigned what it means to climb Everest. This might have seemed like an overnight shift, but Jornet had been preparing for Everest his whole life. First, he grew up in the mountains, at two thousand meters above sea level, at a cross-country ski resort in the Pyrenees, where his father was a hut keeper and mountain guide. He started climbing at the age of three, ascending to the highest peak in the Pyrenees when he was five. At fifteen, he became a junior member of the Spanish national ski mountaineering team. And at twenty, he became the world champion mountain runner for the next three years.

Along the way, Jornet had been trained to think differently about mountains. Rather than climb them, he embraced what they were—natural formations to freely explore rather than to conquer. (Organizations hoping to return to owning talent might take Jornet's experience as an object lesson.) Then, before he even attempted Everest, he started by climbing smaller mountains, practicing and perfecting his no-oxygen and no-ropes technique. This is how Jornet gradually proved his methods until he was ready for Everest, the biggest climb of his life. He did this by focusing on the tasks he needed to accomplish rather than the talent he needed to have.

This chapter examines specific things leaders can do to continually change their own minds. It looks at how leaders can refocus to make key culture shifts, and it explores the impact of AI on talent.

Pushing the Boundaries of an Abundant Mindset

Chapter 2 discussed in detail the culture around a growth, or an abundant, mindset. For leaders, having an abundant mindset means that they recognize that chaos and organizational discomfort can be precursors of innovation. Leaders with scarcity mindsets, in contrast, believe that intelligence and creativity are innate and fixed. They preserve their identities as smart people by avoiding risks, and therefore failure, at all costs. But avoiding failure is not the same thing as pursuing success. People who resist change are complacent about their deficiencies; they rationalize or deny their failures instead of learning from them.

People with abundant mindsets believe that their talent, creativity, and knowledge can be developed through education, training, coaching, community, and, most importantly, the learning that comes from constant experimentation and exposure to different viewpoints. Leaders and organizations with closed mindsets see everyone outside the organization as either a threat or inferior and therefore unworthy of attention. If you have an abundant mindset, you benefit from the network effects that come with adding more participants. You believe that your resources are dynamic and that you can build relationships with outsiders that benefit both sides. Such a mindset creates a flywheel effect in which learning and performance build on one another in a virtuous cycle. As Satya Nadella, Microsoft's CEO, says, "The learn-it-all does better than the know-it-all."[1] Leaders who embrace an abundant mindset bring to their organizations the following qualities:

- **They aren't afraid to fail.** Deploying open talent techniques is often a seesaw of trial and error. When a promising idea doesn't work as expected, abundant-minded leaders have the resilience and confidence to tweak it and try again. When, after enough tries, a good idea turns out to be not as good as it first appeared to be, they have the fortitude to cut their losses, even if doing so seems to be an admission of failure.

- **They know they need to develop or get left behind.** These leaders are proactive when it comes to development. They don't just maintain their systems; they work constantly to add new and better functionalities to them, and they make certain that every member of their teams is empowered to do the same. To that end, they hold hackathons, encourage experimentation, and put value (or potential value) above process. They are willing to ask why something is the way it is, and they never say no reflexively.

- **They know how to adapt.** To meet the organization's vision and goals, abundant-minded leaders constantly improve existing processes and systems and adopt new ones that will help them get there.

- **They are always learning.** These leaders keep up with the latest technologies and trends and assiduously share what they have learned. As student-leaders, they act as role models, inspiring their people, peers, and competitors to do the same.

- **They are open talent super users.** Growth-minded, abundant-minded leaders don't just help their organization succeed with open talent; they also use it themselves.

Shifting Your Focus from Talent to Task

To build growth-oriented, networked organizations, leaders today need to embrace another big change—just as Jornet did: a shift in focus from talent to tasks. As described in the introduction, SEI's Ryan Hicke was so caught up in bringing people back to the office and the problem of staffing projects that had lain dormant during the early months of Covid-19, he and the company completely lost sight of the bigger picture: the tasks themselves. Unfortunately, he wasn't the only one. The talent crisis of the current era has left many leaders scrambling to solve dire staffing issues while deadlines are missed and clients complain.

But there's something you can do as a leader. Make a list of the most common work tasks, and then figure out which jobs need to be done right now and which ones need internal talent to work on them for a while. Task-based work doesn't always involve a full-time employee, so you don't need to scramble to hire everyone before you start doing the work.

For example, let's say a CEO decides to pursue an AI strategy. In the traditional mindset, the executive asks the chief of HR to find and recruit a technology leader with a deep knowledge of AI. In today's labor market, that process could take up to six months. Once the process is in place, the company will need another six months to assemble the right team. After that, it could take another six months to develop the strategy. Unfortunately, the world is moving much faster than that. By the time the AI strategy is developed, the technology might have changed enough to render it obsolete.

Now let's think about an alternative mindset, one based on the task of building an AI strategy. Focusing on that task, the CEO asks the head of strategy to bring together the best AI experts in the industry and to think of accessing the right talent instead of trying to own it. The chief strategy officer logs on to a platform like Gerson Lehrman Group (GLG) or Business Talent Group and invites five top AI thinkers to participate in a virtual workshop the next week. When the meeting is over, the leadership team has a high-level strategy mapped out. To develop it in detail, the team break it down into twenty-five tasks, perhaps even using generative AI. The strategy head goes back out to the platform and finds the best people to work on each task and gives them a deadline of a week. In three weeks and for the price of a few dozen per diems, the CEO has a detailed strategy that has been designed and vetted by the best people in the world, and the company can start implementing it.

But that isn't how we do things, traditional managers might say. Their doubts are not completely unfounded, because unless it is accompanied by a change in mindset and culture, an open talent strategy can create an existential crisis of confidence. Managers think, If everything can be taskified, where is the freedom for talent to add their own unique value?

When we hear this argument, we tell managers about Dick Fosbury and his unconventional approach to high jumping. As a high school student in the late 1960s, Fosbury was obsessed with the high jump. The problem was that he was not particularly good at it. None of the commonly accepted techniques—the straddle, the Western roll, the Eastern cut-off, or the scissors jump, all of which involved sailing over the bar face-down—allowed him to get any higher than five feet. His inadequacy with these traditional methods meant that he couldn't qualify for the varsity team. So Fosbury started thinking about the task differently. He thought about various ways to jump. What if he flipped himself over the bar with his face up, landing on his back in the foam pit? The first time he tried it, it was an ignominious failure that didn't exactly fill him with confidence. But he kept at it, trying again and again until it clicked.

By his junior year, he had cleared 6 feet 3 inches, and as a senior, he cleared 6 feet, 5.5 inches. A local sportswriter said that he looked like "a fish flopping in a boat," and the name "the Fosbury Flop" stuck. As a sophomore at Oregon State University, Fosbury cleared 6 feet 10 inches, breaking the school's record, and in 1968, he qualified for the Olympics. He not only took home a gold medal but also set a world's record, clearing 7 feet, 4.5 inches. Although the record didn't stand for very long, Fosbury is considered one of the most influential athletes in the history of track and field because once his competitors adopted his technique, the records began to tumble.[2]

Something seldom talked about is the fact that Fosbury's mindset shift around the task he hoped to accomplish was driven by a change in equipment. He thought differently about what he had access to. Fosbury's high school was an early adopter of foam landing pads instead of the traditional sawdust pit. Could you imagine doing a backflip into a pit of sawdust? It sounds painful, and it was, as Fosbury learned when he competed at a high school that hadn't made the switch yet and compressed several of his vertebrae.

The analogies that leaders can apply to the open talent marketplace are clear. With the change in the cultural conditions around talent, leaders need to rethink (as Fosbury did) the way they approach the talent bar. New technologies allow for things to be done differently. The value becomes more tactical and much faster.

The mindset shift is all about trying a lot of things fast. Breaking things. Failing fast. But putting failure at the center of a company's strategy is an incredibly scary shift for most folks inside incumbent organizations that are trained not to fail. As a leader, you can remind your staff that using outside talent to get tasks done does not inherently devalue employees. In many ways, it encourages them to develop new skills, such as managing task-based workers.

In the beginning, your company needs just a few rogue leaders asking *why not?* Quickly, new possibilities open up to them. Just as the track and field establishment initially disdained the Fosbury flop (Valeriy Brumel, a former world record holder, called it "an aberration"), scarcity-minded leaders and business establishments might look at turning to open talent as wrong, even unethical in the context of "taking advantage of" talent. Some think that there is too much exploitation and not enough regulation. But many people pursuing digital jobs in the open talent market do so not only to make ends meet but also because they no longer want to be tied to a single employer. Talent wants to work in a new way. Leaders either must shift their mindset or risk ending up in the dustbin of history. But when the abundant-minded leaders keep succeeding, the tools they use become widely adopted and the whole marketplace is transformed.

Becoming a leader of a networked organization requires a similar shift in mindset. You have the inevitable mountains in front of you, yet the same old tools won't get the job done. Over the past several decades, firm after firm got left behind because their leaders were unable to adapt to a changing world. IBM could not see or understand Microsoft's emergent strategy, and once Microsoft became established, it could not comprehend Google's. Tesla and Uber redefined the automotive industry before GM, Ford, and Toyota even noticed that the ground was shifting under their feet.

The future belongs to those who know how to seize the advantage. As we upgrade our hardware, software, operating models, and business models to make ourselves more competitive and up to date, we as leaders must also upgrade our mindsets. Think of leadership as a gardener preparing the soil. Though it's tempting to step right in and start planting, any good gardener will tell you that a successful crop starts with ensuring that the soil has the right consistency and nutrients to support growth. It's no different in organizations. To change their cultures, strategic models, and work processes, leaders first need to till the ground of their own minds to make growth possible.

Reframing Your Questions

At its core, leadership for a networked organization has ways of translating fundamentally lasting principles to many verticals. Through open talent, firms find solutions to difficult problems by using search functions outside their general boundaries. By examining and analyzing a problem, leaders find a much deeper connection between the root causes and potential solutions. In open talent, the focus is less about "Will it be solved?" but is more about "Is this the right issue to tackle?"

Most leaders today know they have a talent problem, but they don't recognize how much of it is of their own making. They need to question their assumptions; more importantly, they need to ask themselves the *right* questions. In the words of an unnamed Yale professor (whose words are often erroneously ascribed to Einstein), "If I had only one hour to solve a problem, I would spend up to two-thirds of that hour in attempting to define what the problem is."[3] Managers these days feel so much pressure to deliver results that they settle for stopgaps that allow them to keep doing the things that aren't getting results. Running around in circles is terrible for firms and the careers of the people that run them. Yet that behavior is precisely what gets rewarded the most.

To compete in the age of open talent, organizations and business leaders need to rethink the business catchphrase "Don't bring me problems; bring me solutions." This problem-solving ideology is so deeply rooted that businesses use it as the basis for hiring, compensation, promotions, and task assignments. However, in the current business climate, where solutions are ubiquitous, business leaders must spend more time and attention drafting the right questions. Leaders should ask what they can solve, given the access to task-based workers or worldwide experts available through platforms.

Consider how Balaji Bondili did just that. Bondili, the Deloitte management consultant we cited in previous chapters, couldn't find enough of the talent he needed to tackle client consulting projects. That's when he broke down the work into tasks and used platforms like Topcoder to hire freelancers to complete them—an experience that helped him rethink what he believed was possible regarding hiring and working with talent. Then, in 2014, Bondili established a division inside the company, called Deloitte Pixel, dedicated to redesigning clunky old hiring processes and using open talent methods, including crowdsourcing challenges.

All was going well until around 2018, when Bondili got enough momentum that Deloitte Pixel started to threaten the old way of resourcing strategy projects. A senior executive even stated that he wouldn't let the division survive; it was too much of a threat to the way Deloitte did business and its mindset and culture. More to the point, Deloitte Pixel was a threat to how the partners were compensated.

A bit of background is in order. Deloitte had created a seamless system of hiring young, talented strategists, maximizing their hours and the staff size to get the clients' work done. This system aligned the work with Deloitte's revenues and the partners' bonuses. Part of what made this system work so well is that Deloitte, like other consulting companies, charged five times its staff's salaries. In other words, the job of Deloitte partners was to sell their internal team members' hours to clients. The more hours they could sell, the more money Deloitte would make and the bigger the partners' bonuses would be.

In the analog world of Deloitte and other similar firms at the time, this approach made sense, especially from the partners' point of view. Deloitte Pixel's digital hiring solution threatened the partners' livelihoods because it could accomplish strategy work with equal results, four to five times faster and with eight to ten times the cost savings. The trouble was that the analog world was quickly becoming obsolete in almost every other category of work, and Bondili had seen the writing on the wall. Platforms like Amazon, for example, had already taken huge chunks out of the retail world of corner shops and malls. He realized that the same thing would happen in talent, because digital platforms were already making finding and matching talent a much cheaper and faster choice for clients to get work done.

Still, the question remained: given the partner pushback, would Deloitte shutter a potentially transformative strategy like Deloitte Pixel? Not if Bondili and few of Deloitte's more progressive-minded partners had anything to say about it: they saw the threat that came from *not* pursuing the opportunity that the new division presented. Although they understood why some partners didn't like change, they were certain those same partners would like irrelevance even less. Bondili aligned with these senior partners to ensure that he'd get top-level buy-in and loop them in for the right messaging both internally and with clients.

To prove their point, the Deloitte Pixel team started looking around the organization for somewhere that talent was particularly hard to find—but wasn't blanketed in the heavy bureaucracy that hampered the hiring of strategy consultants. The answer? Deloitte's data analytics and data science capabilities, a centralized function that served as the consulting agency's hub for putting in client requests. Managers in those areas were having a terrible time hiring to staff projects. And even when they found the right people, it would take months to get them onboarded and work-ready for projects that should have been done yesterday. Meanwhile, Deloitte's competitors and tech industry giants were rapidly attracting and onboarding new talent who didn't want to work at a traditional consulting firm like Deloitte. Facebook and Google were scooping up the best data scientists right and left.

As we discussed earlier, Bondili had heard about a new platform where some of the best such talent had been flocking to lately: Experfy. When Bondili's team made an investment in the company to have exclusive rights to the platform, the team gained access to the data scientists they needed for projects within days. Internally, it was a massive success. All of a sudden, partners who were waiting four or five months to hire a data scientist could do it in four or five days. This transformation helped the firm start charging clients again and helped the partners start making bonuses. What seemed like a threat was now a proven tool that increased revenue and profitability.

Deloitte Pixel was saved, at least for the moment. Bondili knew the solution he was undertaking was risky, to say the least. There would be dragons to slay along the way, including his own numerous doubts. He'd have to assuage those before convincing the organization at large. The biggest questions? Why would anonymous people know more than we do? What would our clients think of this talent arrangement? How do we know that open talent can even work at scale? He already understood the answer to the first question. The folks at Experfy and his first hires had provided the proof: when you pose a problem to a much larger set of minds than what's in your own limited office, the long tail of extreme values delivers a far better solution than does the state of the art.

The second question, as it turns out, wasn't such a leap for Deloitte's clients. More than 30 percent were already experimenting with talent platforms. Instead of seeing these clients' forays into platforms as a threat, Bondili saw them as an opportunity for partnering with clients to embrace open talent solutions on a bigger scale.

Along the way to answer the third question, about scale, Bondili needed to convince himself and the remaining doubters at Deloitte with a series of quick wins. To provide proof of his concept, he created a process to rerun a handful of Deloitte's past consulting projects, but this time using open talent solutions, thus paying freelancers to solve the same problems that had already been solved internally. Then he compared the results, which proved that open talent yielded better and more cost-efficient outcomes in a shorter project timeline. By rerunning old projects, the rest of Deloitte felt less threatened; Bondili worked behind the scenes so that his project wasn't taking away from the new work the consulting teams were sourcing.

These projects gave his approach credibility and established a set of solid metrics and benchmarks he could point to in the future. After a couple of years, Bondili had accumulated enough evidence to counter any doubters: Deloitte could use open talent to help its clients—and it could help its clients use open talent. Win-win.

Understanding the Rapid Changes in AI

The conundrum of AI begins with its abilities, often attributed to the availability of data. The latest advances are in natural language processing (NLP) and have boosted generative AI's prowess. However, in a series of interviews with technical experts, Jin discovered that generative AI's limitations in accessing deeper data can lead to inaccurate decisions, thus highlighting the indispensability of human intuition.

We must acknowledge both the promises and the pitfalls of increased reliance on technology. Despite the potential and excitement, the final decisions often still fall on human shoulders. Real-world work scenarios emphasize the connection between AI's data-driven insights and human judgment, an interaction that leads to a more accurate and reliable outcome.

Given this mutual reliance between AI and humans, the evolving workforce now places a premium on open talent workers. These professionals bring with them a wealth of deeper knowledge and contextual intelligence, both of which pave the way for new roles like prompt engineering (see chapter 1)—a testament to the dynamic nature of this relationship.[4] As AI and human collaboration deepens, companies are recognizing the need for skill-based assessment. Organizations must determine how to evaluate and train talent, all while handling the complexities of proprietary information and data security.

In tandem with this new work landscape, generative AI technology is making waves, enabling open talent workers to enhance their skills, streamline their workflows, and produce better results. Workers in the open talent economy juggle multiple projects and clients, necessitating a high degree of adaptability and efficiency. This is where generative AI comes into the picture, providing dynamic solutions to enhance open talent's capabilities and workflows.

Generative AI-driven tools are revolutionizing the way open talent operates across a variety of domains. By leveraging advanced models such as NLP, computer vision, neural style transfer, and generative adversarial networks, talent can unlock tremendous potential in content creation, customer engagement, and marketing.[5]

For example, generative AI enables content creators to produce text, images, and videos that are more engaging and tailored to specific audiences.[6] One notable example of generative AI in open talent is the use of generative adversarial networks in creating realistic, customized images for digital marketing campaigns. Freelance graphic designers can leverage this technology to generate high-quality visual content, saving time and resources while delivering impressive results.

Despite the numerous benefits brought by generative AI, concerns persist. One such concern is the potential reliance on AI as a manager or an executor rather than a support companion or an aid. Such overreliance may impede critical human intervention in certain situations. To mitigate these concerns, companies must establish comprehensive guidelines and protocols that encourage the responsible use of AI, fostering a collaborative environment where both humans and AI systems work in tandem. These guidelines would ensure that generative AI aids and enhances open talent workers' performance but that a manager of open talent resources would continually monitor to evaluate the work and intervene when issues arise. Domain knowledge and tacit knowledge may still be embedded in the organization.

This discussion ultimately goes back to the premise of reframing questions. Prompt engineering has become a new task that's important not only to open talent workers but also to people inside organizations as they attempt to develop skills around how they ask questions.

KEY IDEAS

We're living in the age of abundant talent. But before companies can fully tap into it, their leaders must create a dynamic culture that thinks critically about tasks rather than talent. Embracing that change will accelerate the breaking down of silos and the move toward agile strategies for getting work done efficiently and effectively.

Pushing the boundaries of an abundant mindset. Reframing mindsets starts with leadership that wants to learn and can think in terms of growth and abundance, experimentation and education. A scarcity mindset believes that talent is innate and that people already know all they need to know. Most organizations are comfortable with predictability and will perceive external talent as a threat. Getting out of our own way, swallowing our pride, and removing a sense of status will be the difference between capitalizing on disruption and succumbing to it. But the real work is building a coalition of willing people. Chaos and discomfort in the organization are inevitable, and teams might naturally feel devalued by the idea of seeking talent externally through networks. That's when leaders must inspire their teams and cultures toward a mindset that understands the value of organizations built on open talent. Today, agile leadership means having a workforce ready to move quickly both with what they do and with whom they do it.

Shifting your focus from talent to task. Reflecting on the idea that talent is not owned by a single organization, how can you think more concretely about the tasks your teams perform rather than just the people who do it? This type of thinking leads to the light and fast strategy discussed in this chapter. Leadership must find new ways to stimulate decentralized and dispersed work.

Reframing your questions. Many entrepreneurs have already reframed their focus and recognize that talent is abundant. With the development of labor platforms, entrepreneurs can build small companies by using open talent principles in the digital space. Enterprise leaders need to imagine how the talent solution world goes beyond what exists in the organization today, much as Balaji Bondili did with Deloitte Pixel.

Understanding the rapid changes in AI. While advanced capabilities such as NLP have made it easier for organizations to use AI, its limitation in accessing deeper data highlights the need for human intuition. The changing nature of work emphasizes the dynamic interaction between AI and humans, placing a premium on open talent workers who bring with them deeper knowledge and contextual intelligence. Generative AI-driven tools are revolutionizing gig workers' capabilities and workflow, enabling task automation for content creation, customer engagement, and marketing tasks. Despite the benefits of generative AI, organizations must establish protocols that ensure responsible usage and continual monitoring to evaluate the process and intervene if problems arise.

Conclusion

A New Era of Talent and Organizations

As we conclude *Open Talent*, think of this book as the beginning, not the end. The future is now, and the story is only beginning to be told. For years, the ideas in this book had been percolating in the minds of many of us. But it took the catalyst of the pandemic to change the direction of the market so that an open talent economy suddenly went from a once-innovative oddity in the talent business to the digital transformation for talent writ large.

Today at Open Assembly, we regularly have conversations about open talent solutions that would have felt impossible a couple of years ago. For example, we consult with people in a dozen countries that recognize that their citizens can now participate in the global work economy. Those countries are building policies to welcome the digital transformation of work. We also work with large staffing companies that in the past had viewed platform-based open talent as an experiment. Now they're active participants who see that solving their talent crisis means leaning into this new world of talent and work. Other conversations are with organizations like UST and Airbus, which are using open talent as a value multiplier. UST in particular has demonstrated its cutting-edge mentality, moving from an analog managed services organization with thirty-two thousand employees to a digital organization that can access a global ecosystem of talent.

Two pillars to successful open talent integration in any organization are the creation of a center of excellence (COE) to manage, transform, and maintain the transition and effective scaling (the biggest sticking point for companies). Unfortunately, we've found that some organizations experimenting with open talent are not yet serious about scaling and lack the initiative to leap into a real effort. They're looking for immediate results, rather than the long-term gain that comes with persistence.

We have spent many hours with many companies, listening to stories about the pain of experimenting and building. So often, the testimonies were around the hardship and failures that occurred just when the organization was on the verge of transformation. Those stories affected our thinking in this book. We know that open talent solutions work and that, in time, people and organizations will come to see that. But we admit that sometimes we too feel the friction. For example, in writing this book, we often went back and forth on strategy and what types of tools work best. With that, let's take a look at what you can expect with the rise of AI and its application for scaling open talent.

How the Rise of AI Works with Platforms

The demand for technology-enabled platforms will be the next step in transforming the open talent industry. We can be confident that assumptions running companies in the past no longer apply. Despite the many successful open talent strategy implementations discussed in this book, the acceleration of digital talent moves in parallel with the speed of technology.

Organizations are increasingly using AI to capture data on customers and employees.[1] AI uses various data science techniques to parse out large amounts of information and predict how matches can be made. The advantage of new and emerging platforms is that this

AI-first strategy allows them to capture customer needs with information on potential workers. An AI solution might suggest, for example, that a particular project is not limited to just how this one person might be a good fit; it will also signal how others throughout various platforms can contribute.

Most current open talent platforms operate with matching algorithms that are limited to user ratings and search terms. As a project owner, you need to post a project that gets amplified on the platform to draw new talent, who then see the project and decide whether to bid or participate. The project owner doesn't have much to rely on, except past ratings and the bidder's user profile with self-disclosed skills.

But AI-powered platforms will now be able to collect more information about the supply of this new talent. One keen development is the rise of testing and evaluation. The workers come to a platform to validate their own skills, not just through past history on the platform but through a series of assessments and gamified interactions that they take in real time. The rating they receive is then transferable from platform to platform. To some degree, platforms such as LinkedIn have already experimented with this. However, these older platforms lack the granularity and scale needed to continue to learn about the talent they draw. The future is about precision. You need to match the required skill with the best people with those skills. AI gets us there faster.

Jin's company, Altruistic, has built technology around the mapping of talent and skills, starting with data professionals and prompt engineers. Jin and his cofounders, Rob Maguire and Steven Randazzo, have developed an AI-based platform for skills matching that uses machine-learning algorithms to analyze vast amounts of data and extract valuable insights about individual employees and their skills, interests, and career aspirations. By doing so, the platform enables organizations to create comprehensive talent profiles that can be used to match the right people to the right jobs, identify skills gaps and training needs, and optimize workforce prediction and development strategies.

However, there is a risk that HR departments may lack the necessary expertise in this area. This risk is particularly great for organizations that are digitally transforming but that have little experience dealing with hiring data professionals and AI-based talent. These entities are at the greatest risk of making hiring mistakes and being left behind in today's competitive environment.

Is Generative AI the Modern Lance?

The word *freelance* first appeared in Sir Walter Scott's *Ivanhoe*, written in the early 1800s. He describes how a medieval lord hired an army of "Free Lances." These mercenaries would fight for the highest bidder, presumably using their lances.[2] Could it be that these knights of the modern world will master new lances, from open talent platforms to generative AI, bringing organizations the skills and expertise they need to be successful?

In the winter of 2022, OpenAI launched ChatGPT, a generative AI tool that feels as if it might signify the beginning of a new era. Several other generative AIs followed in early spring 2023. Although the tool is still nascent, many in the world of work are bracing for the dramatic effects that generative AI might have on how companies get work done. But we are also curious about what it will mean for freelancers and open talent, since it seems that AI can do most of the tasks that, for example, a mid-level copywriter or software developer can do.

In fact, at Upwork, the top ten skills in demand since those AI programs emerged show a significant overlap with jobs that generative AI would affect. Balaji Bondili, who has now moved beyond the open talent project of Deloitte Pixel, today runs Deloitte's contingent-work efforts, with a budget of $650 million. As the person in charge of Deloitte's AI strategy, he wants to see a combination of both human and AI input into work, creating a kind of super worker. He says, "As a buyer, I would want comfort that my freelance team member has utilized all available AI abilities when providing deliverables. But right now, access to humans and access to AI is siloed and opaque."[3] We are already seeing this super worker emerge with systems like GitHub's Copilot (which gives software engineers access to a generative AI system to analyze and complete the code they are writing).

The world is moving fast, and we're certain that open talent and freelancers can learn and adapt faster than enterprises do. As technology becomes faster and cheaper, companies are always the slowest to react to these changes because they have processes, customers, products, and a cash flow to protect.

There's no doubt that more work-disrupting technologies will be created in the future. We're confident that open talent will be quicker to adapt to these changes and that the real effect will be on organizations that can no longer keep up. They will be forced to work with open talent that is continually learning instead of relying on internal employees who need to be trained. For better or worse, the world is becoming decentralized at a faster pace. The world has not yet figured out how to manage these decentralized principles, but the combination of generative AI and open talent is spurring leaders and managers to think about how these principles will work.

The Potential Impact of AI and Skills Development on Open Talent Workers

The launch of ChatGPT has sparked discussions on the potential for AI to replace human workers on a large scale. Although the implementation of generative AI technology does require the development of proprietary machine-learning systems and the acquisition of talent, once companies learn how to leverage this technology, we can expect significant restructuring that may result in job cuts in various industries.

While concerns about the impact on the workforce are valid, we must also recognize that these advancements can yield more-efficient processes and improved productivity. As noted earlier in the book, programmers will benefit from the decreased need to write code from scratch, while creatives will have less pressure to constantly come up with new ideas. These advancements in AI technology have the potential to significantly increase productivity.

Knowledge-based workers who have traditionally relied on their ability to quickly integrate information and make decisions may see their job security threatened. Consequently, leaders must approach AI implementation with a balanced and ethical perspective. Many generative AI tools are designed not to display accurate knowledge but to generate content according to the likelihood of certain words or phrases. As a result, users of generative AI must conduct audits to ensure accuracy and correctness when they are using these tools. We need to recognize that AI models can still make mistakes in logical reasoning and make mistakes that a human wouldn't. Simply put, not all things can be replaced by AI—something that Jin has discussed extensively with the thought leaders at the newly minted Digital, Data, and Design Institute at Harvard. To that end, we are starting to see a call for policy and legislative action to help governments navigate how generative AI tools are used in certain countries. Sam Altman, the CEO of ChatGPT, has tried to get nations to work collaboratively and reduce risks.[4]

Among the advantages of AI is its ability to transform processes and practices. And this unique ability explains precisely why we have been advocating for task-based structures over talent-based ones in certain roles and why agility matters in applying open talent. Internal-facing AI applications can automate numerous routine tasks, allowing knowledge workers to concentrate on value-adding activities where human expertise is indispensable, such as interpreting context and boosting innovation. AI's capacity to free up knowledge workers for more-valuable tasks can be a great benefit in internal talent marketplaces (ITMs).

The development of text analysis and natural language processing (NLP) tools will also play a significant role. Over the past few years, NLP has made a massive jump as the go-to technique to turn audible words (e.g., Zoom call meetings) into reliable transcription. Cutting-edge technology will enable faster synthesis of text-driven ideas both internally and externally. Imagine not having to scroll through every review or consumer idea from a focus group to pinpoint problems and find commodities. Companies are using NLP to analyze results from hackathons and employee engagement tools. You can turn your ITM into so much value. You are constantly generating insights on what motivates your employees and, at the same time, are learning about the common problems the organization faces operationally. Technology can help resolve these issues. With the buzz in human-centric design, employees have become part of the open talent movement. Rather than organizing communities around products, you can better understand what communities are saying by using NLP to understand social media posts. This capability can help you get more than a pulse on what's happening in the industry.

For external talent clouds (ETCs) and open innovation capabilities, the skills to test, edit, innovate, or otherwise improve on AI outputs are likely to become more valuable. Skills development in general has also been thrown into the mix, with open talent workers exploring skills beyond generative AI. Jack Hughes, former chair of Topcoder and current CEO of Skills.com, spoke with us about these changes:

> The networked organization will change all types of work. Our current methods of skill development and application are too slow for how fast the world is changing. A more fluid workforce environment presents real opportunity to drive real earnings growth and puts financial security in reach of people who would not have had access in the past. But people can only take advantage of these opportunities if they have the right information to guide them and the proper training to take advantage of these opportunities. I think we are looking at a world where training, skill development, and opportunity matching will be always on for a large portion of the workforce.[5]

The pivot is in developing skills through digital means.

Practice, Policy, and Perception: Finding a Balance

You probably won't win all your battles, but you should recognize the trade-offs that you and your organization will have to make on practice, policy, and perception. As a starting place, take a good hard look at where you stand along the journey in terms of these three issues. Namely, you can begin practicing the open talent ideas we've explored in this book, even if these ideas aren't completely aligned with either the policies or the perceptions that your organization has traditionally embraced. For example, NASA continued to march forward with open talent solutions even though its senior leadership was unconvinced for many years that these solutions were not only viable but also necessary to future-proofing R&D.

Moreover, even when your CEO is an enthusiastic supporter of open talent solutions, that doesn't mean that everyone will be convinced. But mindsets and perceptions can be changed when a policy change from the C-suite is followed up with formal training in open talent practices. Start by thinking about which policies need tweaking and which ones can stay as they are. And look closely at whether the use of ETCs, open innovation contests, or ITMs will be most closely aligned with what's happening in the company at various points. Uncertainties around bottlenecks to policy and internally navigating funding and HR protocols will always be barriers, no matter how great your results look. Remember that policy will follow the action, and unspoken assumptions are likely to shape unofficial policies.

During the recent ten-year anniversary of NASA's center of excellence (CoECI), Lynn Buquo, the outgoing manager, reflected on something Karim used to say: that his ambition was to make open talent boring and ordinary, meaning that all organizations had fully embraced the change. She remarked, "It certainly is not boring by any means but certainly has become more ordinary."[6] CoECI can stand on its own two feet without having to justify its existence. People throughout the organization are catching on, and they see how the center continues to push the boundaries.

Jin caught up with Buquo about a week after that anniversary and shared with her something he'd never thought about before: a real turning point was when CoECI started to use the government credit card for micropurchases. Why was it a turning point? Using a government card was a way to ensure a positive perception of the center's work. It proved that the organization was operating transparently, just as the rest of NASA had to do. So even though CoECI did things by the book from the beginning, the credit card transactions provided an open record that the center was not a rebel that broke the rules for the sake of getting things done. It valued policy and worked in plain sight.

Too often, managers give up when it comes to open talent solutions because it's too hard to change policies around hiring, for example. But with perseverance, you start to see opportunities.

At CoECI, the shift to complete transparency was a fundamental change, showing the center was willing to keep exploring within the boundaries of what the larger organization and, to some degree, the policy allowed. It's a good example of how the true power of organizational transformation comes from within. When that happens, you know the change can withstand the test of time.

Creating the kind of positive perception that CoECI built will be critical to any company's success, especially when it comes to scaling into a networked organization. That's because you're trying to do something that seems nearly impossible: transforming a onetime use of open talent into a systemic process in your organization.

One of the biggest overarching concerns for the open talent economy is the slow movement of governmental agencies and large enterprises around the world to shift their mindsets to this new way of working. Part of the problem is that many such organizations are staffed by people who will lose positions and control in this new world of work. Nevertheless, change will happen, whether we're ready for it or not. It's a matter of *when*, not *if.* As we often hear in the technology space, it's easy to understand where things will be in ten years but difficult to know what will happen in the next few months.

As stated in the preface, the war for talent is over. Talent won. Not everyone in your organization will believe this, however. So the message you need to circulate is, "We need a better talent strategy. The conversation needs to change." Then, everything you do needs to be about how you keep advancing. Try to find the conversation drivers in the C-suite to make the process easier at every turn. Equally important, look for the kind of public affirmation that will come from clients and other users of open talent; their opinions will highlight results and celebrate achievements.

A Platform of Platforms

We are now getting to the point where platforms can be aggregated. So many have different standards and modes of operation. Their business models all differ. Like-minded talent platforms are starting to join ranks to think and strategize about the future. This aggregation led to the genesis of the *platform of platforms*—an affiliate and aggregation compositor that not only describes what platforms do but also will begin to assess how they acquire and certify talent.

The idea of open platforms working together is not a new one. Ideation platforms have often worked with coding platforms and marketing amplifiers to find the right technical crowd for complex problems. To that end, Jin and LISH created the first platform aggregator (open to the public) on its website in 2017 as a means to clarify what each platform specializes in. Although this was a strictly academic exercise, organizations have now turned to Open Assembly to build fully networked platforms that track data on solved problems, users, and company engagements over time. This effort provides an opportunity for platforms to compete together while making things simple for the demand side by creating common language and common processes. Think of it as a Kayak of open talent platforms, where some platforms might not contribute but most will probably play along.

There is also a need for clarity around how work is assessed and how workers actually validate their skills aside from ratings. To further this idea, platforms will also allow migration of profiles and worker credentials from one platform to another. Badges and status signaling are essential; they can exist on single platforms or carry more of a universal weight. Open Assembly and Harvard have put considerable thought into how workers carry their credentials from platform to platform. Recognition features (e.g., a universal badging system) are feasible and encouraged.

Perhaps some people think that competition between the platforms will destroy the idea of the platform of platforms, but the open talent ecosystem functions much like European soccer. You can have teams play in their respective leagues (e.g., clubs in the UK's Premier League) and join together in different countries for different purposes (e.g., the Champions League of the Union of European Football Associations, which features all of Europe's best leagues and top teams). The open talent ecosystem is pliable and accommodating enough for individual platforms to survive with joint credentialing.

The End of the Beginning

Our efforts over the last two decades have convinced us that the future of work will change in specific ways. The focus will shift from acquiring talent to defining tasks within work to be done—and then accessing a network of global workers (or AI or both) to complete those tasks. This change in focus has gone full circle. When open talent started, crowdsourcing was the most important component because organizations bought outcomes. They pursued outcomes because it was impossible to verify the location and identity of the freelancers working on the solution. As these problems were overcome, hiring for roles allowed open talent to fit into the old talent paradigm. Now, with a combination of talent and AI, we're reentering an era where organizations again acquire outcomes. It's back to the future. Every organization will move from trying to own and manage a workforce to instead accessing the talents of a global ecosystem of workers by building and connecting to platforms that will remove the friction from the process of getting work done.

While this is the end of the book, it feels like the beginning of the journey. By writing about the vast knowledge accumulated from our community of passionate open talent advocates and entrepreneurs, we've tried to create a framework that might enable all of us to work from a common language and a common process.

This is the start. We look forward to the journey ahead.

Notes

Preface

1. Jeff Howe, "The Rise of Crowdsourcing," *Wired*, June 1, 2006.

2. Cliff Kuang, "Crispin Porter + Bogusky's Crowdsourcing Experiment Backfires," *Fast Company*, August 28, 2009, https://www.fastcompany.com/1341425/crispin-porter-boguskys-crowdsourcing-experiment-backfires.

3. Maureen Morrison, "A Tale of Two Crispins: Why There Won't Be Another Agency of the Decade," *Ad Age*, February 4, 2014, https://adage.com/article/agency-news/tale-2-crispins-agency-decade/291465.

4. Stuart Elliot, "Dish Network Looking to the Crowd," *New York Times*, April 14, 2010, https://archive.nytimes.com/mediadecoder.blogs.nytimes.com/2010/04/14/marketer-says-dish-out-the-ad-and-marketing-ideas/

Introduction

1. "2021 Work Trend Index: Annual Report," Microsoft, March 22, 2021, https://ms-worklab.azureedge.net/files/reports/hybridWork/pdf/2021_Microsoft_WTI_Report_March.pdf.

2. Alyssa Fowers and Eli Rosenberg, "The Geography of the Great Resignation: First-Time Data Shows Where Americans Are Quitting the Most," *Washington Post*, October 22, 2021, https://www.washingtonpost.com/business/2021/10/22/states-labor-quitting-turnvoer-jolts/.

3. Matthew Mottola and Matthew Douglas Coatney, *The Human Cloud: How Today's Changemakers Use Artificial Intelligence and the Freelance Economy to Transform Work* (New York: HarperCollins, 2021).

4. Brad Smith, "Microsoft Launches Initiative to Help 25 Million People Worldwide Acquire the Digital Skills Needed in a Covid-19 Economy," *Official Microsoft Blog*, Microsoft, June 30, 2020, https://blogs.microsoft.com/blog/2020/06/30/microsoft-launches-initiative-to-help-25-million-people-worldwide-acquire-the-digital-skills-needed-in-a-covid-19-economy/.

5. Michael Franzino, Alan Guarino, Yannick Binvel, and Jean-Marc Laouchez, "The 8.5 Trillion Talent Shortage," Korn Ferry, accessed May 9, 2023, https://www.kornferry.com/insights/this-week-in-leadership/talent-crunch-future-of-work.

6. This research was uncovered in Jin H. Paik, "Architecting the Art and Practice of Open Talent at NASA: Implications for Perception, Policy, and Practice" (PhD

diss., New York University Steinhardt School of Culture, Education, and Human Development, 2023).

7. Kiran Aditham, "V&S Sends Unsolicited Brief to Harley," *AgencySpy*, September 3, 2010, https://www.adweek.com/agencyspy/vs-sends-unsolicited-brief-to-harley/8349/.

8. Jack Hughes, interview with Jin H. Paik, April 2023.

9. Simply Wall St, "Upwork Full Year 2022 Earnings: EPS Beats Expectations," *Yahoo! News*, February 18, 2023, https://news.yahoo.com/upwork-full-2022-earnings-eps-121317998.html.

10. Erin Skarda, "Technology? What's That?," *Time*, October 21, 2011, https://content.time.com/time/specials/packages/article/0,28804,2097462_2097456_2097467,00.html.

11. Zoe Szajnfarber, Taylan G. Topcu, and Hila Lifshitz-Assaf, "Towards a Solver-Aware Systems Architecting Framework: Leveraging Experts, Specialists, and the Crowd to Design Innovative Complex Systems," *Design Science* 8 (March 11, 2022): e10, doi:10.1017/dsj.2022.7.

12. Klaus Schwab, *The Fourth Industrial Revolution* (New York: Crown Business, 2016).

Chapter 1

1. "Impact of the Coronavirus Pandemic on the Global Economy," Statista, January 17, 2023, https://www.statista.com/topics/6139/covid-19-impact-on-the-global-economy/#topicOverview.

2. David Schatsky, Craig Muraskin, and Rameeta Chauhan, "Democratizing Data Science to Bridge the Talent Gap," *Deloitte Insights*, December 13, 2018, https://www2.deloitte.com/us/en/insights/focus/signals-for-strategists/democratization-of-data-science-talent-gap.html.

3. Joseph Fuller, Manjari Raman, Allison Bailey, and Nithya Vaduganathan, "Rethinking the On-Demand Workforce," *Harvard Business Review*, December 2020, https://hbr.org/2020/11/rethinking-the-on-demand-workforce.

4. Michael Franzino, Alan Guarino, Yannick Binvel, and Jean-Marc Laouchez, "The 8.5 Trillion Talent Shortage," Korn Ferry, accessed May 9, 2023, https://www.kornferry.com/insights/this-week-in-leadership/talent-crunch-future-of-work.

5. Brad Smith, "Microsoft Launches Initiative to Help 25 Million People Worldwide Acquire the Digital Skills Needed in a Covid-19 Economy," *Official Microsoft Blog*, Microsoft, June 30, 2020, https://blogs.microsoft.com/blog/2020/06/30/microsoft-launches-initiative-to-help-25-million-people-worldwide-acquire-the-digital-skills-needed-in-a-covid-19-economy/.

6. Adi Ignatius, "Tsedal Neeley on Why We Need to Think of the Office as a Tool, with Very Specific Uses," hbr.org, January 14, 2022, https://hbr.org/2022/01/tsedal-neeley-on-why-we-need-to-think-of-the-office-as-a-tool-with-very-specific-uses.

7. Tyler Halloran, "A Brief History of the Corporate Form and Why It Matters," *Fordham Journal of Corporate and Financial Law*, November 18, 2018, https://news.law.fordham.edu/jcfl/2018/11/18/a-brief-history-of-the-corporate-form-and-why-it-matters/.

8. Rob Maguire, interview with Jin H. Paik, April 2023.

Chapter 2

1. "Manifesto for Agile Software Development," accessed July 26, 2023, https://agilemanifesto.org.

2. Rebecca M. Henderson and Kim B. Clark, "Architectural Innovation: The Reconfiguration of Existing Product Technologies and the Failure of Established Firms," *Administrative Science Quarterly* 35, no. 1 (March 1990); Clayton Christensen, *The Innovator's Dilemma: When New Technologies Cause Great Firms to Fail* (Boston: Harvard Business School Press, 1997).

3. Karim R. Lakhani and Jill A. Panetta, "The Principles of Distributed Innovation," *Innovations: Technology, Governance, Globalization* 2, no. 3 (summer 2007), https://direct.mit.edu/itgg/article/2/3/97/9500/The-Principles-of -Distributed-Innovation.

4. Rich Karlgaard, "How Fast Can You Learn?," *Forbes*, November 8, 2007, www .forbes.com/forbes/2007/1126/031.html. Emphasis in original.

5. Topcoder Admin, "Harvard and the Broad Institute Deliver Precision Medicine Advancement through Crowdsourcing," Topcoder, June 11, 2016, https://www .topcoder.com/blog/harvard-and-the-broad-institute-deliver-precision-medicine -advancement-through-crowdsourcing/.

6. Steve Rader, interview with Jin H. Paik, May 2022.

7. Tim Proehm, interview with John Winsor, September 21, 2022.

8. Kirstin Hammerberg, interview with John Winsor, November 4, 2022.

Chapter 3

1. Sam Orrin, interview with John Winsor, October 4, 2022.

2. Dan Beck, interview with John Winsor, October 21, 2022.

3. "Volta Bureau," National Park Service, accessed May 11, 2023, https://www .nps.gov/places/volta-bureau.htm.

4. Hila Lifshitz-Assaf, Michael L. Tushman, and Karim R. Lakhani, "A Study of NASA Scientists Shows How to Overcome Barriers to Open Innovation," hbr.org, May 29, 2018, https://hbr.org/2018/05/a-study-of-nasa-scientists-shows-how-to -overcome-barriers-to-open-innovation.

5. Lynn Buquo, interview with Jin H. Paik, May 2023.

6. National Aeronautics and Space Administration, "2021 Administrator's Agency Honor Awards: Unfold the Universe," NASA, accessed May 11, 2023, https://searchpub .nssc.nasa.gov/servlet/sm.web.Fetch/2021_Administrator_s_Agency_Honor_Awards _Ceremony_Program.pdf?rhid=1000&did=6688430&type=released&FixForIE=2021 _Administrator_s_Agency_Honor_Awards_Ceremony_Program.pdf.

Chapter 4

1. The initial model—learn, pilot, scale, and sustain—was developed at LISH with Elizabeth Richard, Jeffrey R. Davis, Jin Paik, and Karim R. Lakhani, "Sustaining Open Innovation through a 'Center of Excellence,'" *Strategy and Leadership* 47, no. 3 (2019), doi: 10.1108/SL-02-2019-0031.

2. The figures and commentary in this paragraph are from John Winsor's interviews with organizational leaders.

3. Fred C. Kelly, "Miracle at Kitty Hawk: Unpublished Letters of the Wright Brothers (Part 1)," *Atlantic*, May 1950, https://www.theatlantic.com/magazine/archive/1950/05/miracle-at-kitty-hawk-unpublished-letters-of-the-wright-brothers-part-i/306537/.

4. James Bessen, "History Backs Up Tesla's Patent Sharing," hbr.org, June 13, 2014, https://hbr.org/2014/06/history-backs-up-teslas-patent-sharing.

5. Michael I. Norton, Daniel Mochon, and Dan Ariely, "The IKEA Effect: When Labor Leads to Love," *Journal of Consumer Psychology* 22, no. 3 (July 2012): 453–460.

6. Thatcher Cardon, quoted in Elizabeth Howell, "How to Poop in Space: NASA Unveils Winners of Space Poop Challenge," Space.com, February 15, 2017, www.space.com/35714-nasa-space-poop-challenge-winner-unveiled.html.

7. Dyan Finkhousen, interview with John Winsor, December 18, 2021.

8. Jana Gallus, Olivia S. Jung, and Karim R. Lakhani, "Recognition Incentives for Internal Crowdsourcing: A Field Experiment at NASA," working paper 20-059, Harvard Business School, Boston, May 22, 2020, https://www.hbs.edu/ris/Publication%20Files/20-059_c9a52274-ce8b-441e-9f8a-21231c66e642.pdf.

9. Rachel Layne, "When Experts Play It Too Safe: Innovation Lessons from a NASA Experiment," *Working Knowledge, Business Research for Business Leaders*, Harvard Business School, September 12, 2022, https://hbswk.hbs.edu/item/when-experts-play-it-too-safe-innovation-lessons-from-a-nasa-experiment.

Chapter 5

1. Freelancer.com, "Company Overview," accessed May 14, 2023, https://www.freelancer.com/about.

2. Harisha Grama, "IBM Cloud and Freelancer Combine Forces to Help Companies Close the Cloud Skills Gap," IBM, May 20, 2021, https://www.ibm.com/cloud/blog/announcements/ibm-cloud-and-freelancer-combine-forces-to-help-companies-close-the-cloud-skills-gap; Christopher Stanton, Karim R. Lakhani, Jennifer L. Hoffman, Jin Hyun Paik, and Nina Cohodes, "Freelancer, Ltd.," case 820-075 (Boston: Harvard Business School, January 2020).

3. Stanton et al., "Freelancer, Ltd."

4. Liane Scult, interview with John Winsor, June 4, 2021.

5. Laura Jordan, "Microsoft's Contingent Worker's Lawsuit," OLR Research Report 99-R-0775, Connecticut General Assembly, August 12, 1999, https://www.cga.ct.gov/PS99/rpt/olr/htm/99-R-0775.htm.

Chapter 6

1. Albert Yu-Min Lin, Andrew Huynh, Gert Lanckriet, and Luke Barrington, "Crowdsourcing the Unknown: The Satellite Search for Genghis Khan," *PLOS ONE* 9, no. 12 (December 30, 2014), https://doi.org/10.1371/journal.pone.0114046.

2. "'Boaty McBoatface' Tops Public Vote as Name of Polar Ship," BBC News, April 17, 2016, https://www.bbc.com/news/uk-england-36064659.

3. Raymond H. Mak et al., "Use of Crowd Innovation to Develop an Artificial Intelligence–Based Solution for Radiation Therapy Targeting," *JAMA Oncology* 5, no. 5 (2019), https://jamanetwork.com/journals/jamaoncology/fullarticle/2730638.

4. Reinhilde Veugelers and Bruno Cassiman, "Make and Buy in Innovation Strategies: Evidence from Belgian Manufacturing Firms," *Research Policy* 28, no. 1 (1999), https://www.sciencedirect.com/science/article/abs/pii/S0048733398001061.

5. Jin H. Paik et al., "Innovation Contests for High-Tech Procurement," *Research Technology Management* 63, no. 2 (2020), https://doi.org/10.1080/08956308.2020.1707007.

6. Steve Rader, interview with Jin H. Paik, March 2022.

7. Jason Crusan, interview with Jin H. Paik, March 2022.

8. Lynn Buquo, interview with Jin H. Paik, May 2022.

Chapter 7

1. Alan Jope, quoted in Aman Kidwai, "Inside Unilever's Program That Allows Employees to Try Out New Jobs and Gig Working Opportunities at the Company," *Business Insider*, May 5, 2021, www.businessinsider.com/unilever-program-allowing -employees-try-out-new-jobs-gig-working-2021-5.

2. Aman Kidwai, "Inside Unilever's Program."

3. Nicole Schreiber-Shearer, "What Is a Talent Marketplace?" Gloat, January 24, 2022, https://gloat.com/blog/the-talent-marketplace-explained/.

4. Sanjay Sharma, interview with John Winsor, June 12, 2022.

5. Barry Matthews, interview with John Winsor, January 16, 2023.

6. Jesse Arundell, interview with Jin H. Paik, May 2019.

7. Eva Guinan, Kevin J. Boudreau, and Karim R. Lakhani, "Experiments in Open Innovations at Harvard Medical School," *MIT Sloan Management Review*, March 19, 2013, https://sloanreview.mit.edu/article/experiments-in-open-innovation -at-harvard-medical-school/.

Chapter 8

1. Laura Furstenthal, Alex Morris, and Erik Roth, "Fear Factor: Overcoming Human Barriers to Innovation," McKinsey & Company, June 3, 2022, https://www .mckinsey.com/capabilities/strategy-and-corporate-finance/our-insights/fear-factor -overcoming-human-barriers-to-innovation.

2. Herman Leonard, Mitchell Weiss, Jin Hyun Paik, and Kerry Herman, "SOFWERX: Innovation at U.S. Special Operations Command," case 819-004 (Boston: Harvard Business School, 2018).

3. Vinod Kartha, interview with John Winsor, August 2, 2022.

Chapter 9

1. Wall Street Journal Digital Network, "Satya Nadella: 'The Learn-It-All Does Better Than the Know-It-All,'" *WSJ Video*, January 23, 2019, https://www.wsj.com /video/satya-nadella-the-learn-it-all-does-better-than-the-know-it-all/D8BC205C -D7F5-423E-8A41-0E921E86597C.html.

2. Sean McAlister, "Dick Fosbury, the Fosbury Flop and Four Other Techniques That Revolutionised Sport," Olympics.com, updated June 27, 2023, https://olympics .com/en/news/dick-fosbury-fosbury-flop-game-changing-sport-techniques.

3. William H. Markle, "The Manufacturing Manager's Skills," in *The Manufacturing Man and His Job*, ed. Robert E. Finley and Henry R. Ziobro (New York: American Management Association, 1966), 18.

4. Nik Popli, "The AI Job That Pays Up to $355k—and You Don't Need a Computer Engineering Background," *Time*, April 14, 2023, https://time.com/6272103 /ai-prompt-engineer-job/.

5. Megan Graham, "Five Things Marketers Should Know about Generative AI in Advertising," *Wall Street Journal*, March 16, 2023, https://www.wsj.com/articles/five-things-marketers-should-know-about-generative-ai-in-advertising-5381c1d0.

6. McKinsey & Company, "What Is Generative AI?," McKinsey & Company, January 19, 2023, https://www.mckinsey.com/featured-insights/mckinsey-explainers/what-is-generative-ai.

Conclusion

1. Steven Randazzo, Jin H. Paik, and Yael Grushka-Cockayne, "Commonwealth Bank: Amplifying Customer Centricity with AI," *Management and Business Review*, Special Issue: AI for Customer Engagement 3, no. 1 (winter 2023).

2. Merriam-Webster, "The Surprising History of 'Freelance,'" *Word History*, Merriam-Webster, accessed June 20, 2023, www.merriam-webster.com/words-at-play/freelance-origin-meaning.

3. Balaji Bondili, interview with John Winsor, April 8, 2022.

4. Thomas Germain, "Sam Altman Is 'Optimistic' He Can Get the AI Laws He Wants," *Gizmodo*, June 12, 2023, https://gizmodo.com/chatgpt-login-plus-openai-sam-altman-ai-laws-tokyo-1850529436.

5. Jack Hughes, interview with Jin H. Paik, April 2023.

6. Lynn Buquo, interview with Jin H. Paik, May 2022.

Index

Acknowledgments

FROM JOHN WINSOR: There's so much to be grateful for as I've pursued building businesses and studying open talent over the last twenty-five years. My passion for open talent came not when I was an academic or even when I was an innovation strategist, but when I recognized it as a survival imperative.

My partnership with Alex Bogusky at Crispin Porter + Bogusky galvanized my passion for the pursuit of open talent, which led me to the launch of Victors & Spoils with Claudia Batten and Evan Fry. Soon the charisma and vision of David Jones, now CEO of the Brandtech Group, helped me take my vision for open talent global.

Karim Lakhani, Mike Tushman, and Bharat Anand, from Harvard Business School, not only helped me start thinking about open talent more strategically but also encouraged me to create models that people could adopt. When Karim gave me the opportunity to hang my hat at the Laboratory for Innovation Science at Harvard (LISH), I met Jin Paik, and we began planting the seeds for this book.

But the real inspiration and ideas for this book came in 2018, when Karim and Jin hosted the first Crowd Academy at Harvard. There Balaji Bondili, Steve Rader, Dyan Finkhousen, and Mike Morris started having weekly conversations that turned into our Open Assembly community. That community has now grown to over four thousand people. This book would not have been possible without the inspiration of the leaders of the open talent community, including Brandon Dwight, John Healy, Barry Matthews, Bryn Barlow, Vinod Kartha, Jeff Schwartz, Jon Younger, Simon Hill, Mina Bastawros, Paul Hlivko,

Ryan Hicke, Sanjay Sharma, Jesse Arundell, Hayden Brown, Matt Barrie, Jerry Wind, Chris Stanton, San Rahi, Jeff Davis, Dean Bosche, Catherine McGowin, Prakash Gupta, Dave Messinger, Mark Hannant, Ashley Ryall, Bryan Pena, Ritika Arya, Carin-Isabel Knoop, Adam Sandlin, Rich Copsey, Paul Estes, Steve Hatfield, Tim Sanders, and countless others I've had the pleasure of interacting with.

Thank you to each and every person in our community for helping Jin and me get this book out to the world.

FROM JIN H. PAIK: I want to extend my heartfelt gratitude to Karim Lakhani for his guidance. Thanks for challenging me to see the impact of the open talent world and for providing pathways to present a collective voice on these topics. Special thanks to my team at the Laboratory for Innovation Science at Harvard: Andrea Blasco, Nina Cohodes, Timothy DeStefano, Eva Guinan, Hila Lifshitz-Assaf, Jacqueline Ng Lane, Mike Menietti, Steven Randazzo, and Rinat Sergeev for their support, encouragement, and help in unpacking research into pragmatic insights over the past decade. I am also grateful to my colleagues at NASA: Lynn Buquo, Jason Crusan, Jeff Davis, Steve Rader, Elizabeth Richard, and the entire Center of Excellence for Collaborative Innovation (CoECI) team. Noel Anderson, Caroline Hanan, Ben Maddox, Robert Maguire, and Lucy McCauley thank you for your expertise, advice, and support, which have been instrumental.

On a personal note, I could not have done this without my wife, Amber. Thank you for your unwavering support of everything I do and for holding down the fort. To my children, Elle, Amelia, Ainsleigh, and Asher, thank you for always brightening my days and those long nights when daddy had to write. And more importantly, for being the best kids on earth. I am eternally grateful to my mother, Jung Yun Kim, for her countless sacrifices, for giving up her life so I could have an education, and to my stepfather, Jo Bok Hei, for taking care of her. 엄마 정말 고맙고 사랑합니다. I want to thank the Lord God for His grace in my life and for blessing me with opportunities I never thought possible.

About the Authors

JOHN WINSOR is a globally renowned thought leader, recognized for his trailblazing work in marketing, open talent, collaboration, co-creation, and crowdsourcing. At the crossroads of innovation, disruption, and storytelling, Winsor's multifaceted insights have been shared through his writings, speeches, and groundbreaking companies.

As the founder and chairman of the digital gateway to freelance talent, Open Assembly, Winsor has led the global open talent movement to help organizations transform their talent practices. His visionary leadership extends to his role as the executive-in-residence at Harvard Business School's Laboratory for Innovation Science at Harvard (LISH), where he continually fosters groundbreaking innovation.

At the core of Winsor's work is the four thousand member Open Assembly Community, with its mission to transform work for a billion people by 2025.

Before his journey in the open talent domain, Winsor was Chief Innovation Officer at global communications group Havas and founder and CEO of Victors & Spoils, one of the world's first advertising agencies built around crowdsourcing principles. He also served as VP/Executive Director of Strategy and Innovation at Crispin Porter + Bogusky and CEO of Radar Communications. He began building transformative business models in the magazine publishing arena, particularly with *Women's Sports & Fitness*, which he rejuvenated, launching profitable titles and events such as The Gravity Games before selling to Condé Nast in 1998.

He has authored multiple influential books, such as *Baked In: The Power of Aligning Marketing and Product Innovation, Spark: Be More Innovative through Co-Creation,* and *Beyond the Brand.*

A sought-after speaker and prolific writer and podcaster, Winsor shares his innovative paradigms through his popular blog at johnwinsor.com. Outside the realm of business, he is a husband and father as well as an avid surfer, climber, and cyclist, constantly seeking new adventures worldwide.

JIN H. PAIK has worked at the intersection of digital transformation, artificial intelligence, and the future of work over the past fifteen years, both in academia and industry. He is a cofounder and managing partner at Altruistic, an AI consultancy that builds disruptive technology, and a principal visiting research scientist at Harvard Business School. Previously, he was the Head of Labs at the Digital, Data, and Design Institute at Harvard, developing the institute's strategic vision and directing research programs. Paik was the founding general manager and senior researcher at the Laboratory for Innovation Science at Harvard (LISH), where he oversaw the development of open innovation and data science projects with NASA, Harvard Medical School, Broad Institute, and other companies and was responsible for the execution of more than eight hundred innovation projects. He has taught both in-person and online seminars and courses at Harvard.

He holds a bachelor's degree from the University of Michigan, a master's degree from Harvard, and was awarded his doctorate from New York University, investigating innovation and leadership in organizations.

Born in South Korea and raised in the New York metropolitan area, Paik lives in southwest Florida with his wife and four children. He is passionate about living life, loving God, and serving the local community.